CORVAIR
PERFORMANCE PORTFOLIO
—— 1959-1969 ——

Compiled by R M Clarke

ISBN 1 85520 4509

 BROOKLANDS BOOKS LTD.
P.O. BOX 146, COBHAM,
SURREY, KT11 1LG. UK

Printed in Hong Kong

Brooklands Books

MOTORING

BROOKLANDS ROAD TEST SERIES

Abarth Gold Portfolio 1950-1971
AC Ace & Aceca 1953-1983
Alfa Romeo Giulietta Gold Portfolio 1954-1965
Alfa Romeo Giulia Coupés 1963-1976
Alfa Romeo Giulia Coupés Gold Port. 1963-1976
Alfa Romeo Spider 1966-1990
Alfa Romeo Spider Gold Portfolio 1966-1991
Alfa Romeo Alfasud 1972-1984
Alfa Romeo Alfetta Gold Portfolio 1972-1987
Alfa Romeo Alfetta GTV6 1980-1986
Allard Gold Portfolio 1937-1959
Alvis Gold Portfolio 1919-1967
AMX & Javelin Muscle Portfolio 1968-1974
Armstrong Siddeley Gold Portfolio 1945-1960
Aston Martin Gold Portfolio 1948-1971
Aston Martin Gold Portfolio 1972-1985
Aston Martin Gold Portfolio 1985-1995
Audi Quattro Gold Portfolio 1980-1991
Austin A30 & A35 1951-1962
Austin Healey 100 & 100/6 Gold Portfolio 1952-1959
Austin Healey 3000 Gold Portfolio 1959-1967
Austin Healey Sprite Gold Portfolio 1958-1971
BMW 6 & 8 Cyl. Cars 1935-1960 Limited Edition
BMW 1600 Collection No.1 1966-1981
BMW 2002 Gold Portfolio 1968-1976
BMW 6 Cylinder Coupés & Saloons Gold P. 1969-1976
BMW 316, 318, 320 (4 cyl.) Gold Port. 1975-1990
BMW 320, 323, 325 (6 cyl.) Gold Port. 1977-1990
BMW M Series Gold Portfolio 1976-1997
BMW 5 Series Gold Portfolio 1981-1987
BMW 6 Series Gold Portfolio 1976-1989
Bricklin Gold Portfolio 1974-1975
Bristol Cars Gold Portfolio 1946-1992
Buick Automobiles 1947-1960
Buick Muscle Cars 1965-1970
Cadillac Allanté 1986-1993
Cadillac Automobiles 1949-1959
Cadillac Automobiles 1960-1969
Checker Limited Edition
Chevrolet 1955-1957
Impala & SS Muscle Portfolio 1958-1972
Corvair Performance Portfolio 1959-1969
El Camino & SS Muscle Portfolio 1959-1987
Chevy II & Nova SS Muscle Portfolio 1962-1974
Chevelle & SS Muscle Portfolio 1964-1972
Caprice 1965-1976 Limited Edition
Chevrolet Muscle Cars 1966-1971
Chevy Blazer 1969-1981
Camaro Muscle Portfolio 1967-1973
Chevrolet Camaro & Z-28 1973-1981
High Performance Camaros 1982-1988
Chevrolet Corvette Gold Portfolio 1953-1962
Chevrolet Corvette Sting Ray Gold Port. 1963-1967
Chevrolet Corvette Gold Portfolio 1968-1977
High Performance Corvettes 1983-1989
Chrysler 300 Gold Portfolio 1955-1970
Imperial 1955-1970 Limited Edition
Valiant 1960-1962
Citroen Traction Avant Gold Portfolio 1934-1957
Citroen 2CV Gold Portfolio 1948-1989
Citroen DS & ID 1955-1975
Citroen DS & ID Gold Portfolio 1955-1975
Citroen SM 1970-1975
Cobras & Replicas 1962-1983
Shelby Cobra Gold Portfolio 1962-1969
Cobras & Cobra Replicas Gold Portfolio 1962-1989
Crosley & Crosley Specials Limited Edition
Cunningham Automobiles 1951-1955
Daimler SP250 Sports & V-8 250 Saloon Gold P. 1959-1969
Datsun Roadsters 1962-1971
Datsun 240Z & 260Z Gold Portfolio 1970-1978
Datsun 280Z & ZX 1975-1983
DeLorean Gold Portfolio 1977-1995
De Soto Limited Edition 1952-1960
Charger Muscle Portfolio 1966-1974
Dodge Muscle Cars 1967-1970
Dodge Viper on the Road
ERA Gold Portfolio 1934-1994
Excalibur Collection No.1 1952-1981
Facel Vega 1954-1964
Ferrari 1947-1957 Limited Edition
Ferrari 1958-1963 Limited Edition
Ferrari Dino 1965-1974
Ferrari Dino 308 & Mondial Gold Portfolio 1974-1985
Ferrari 328 348 Mondial Gold Portfolio 1986-1994
Fiat 500 Gold Portfolio 1936-1972
Fiat 600 & 850 Gold Portfolio 1955-1972
Fiat Pininfarina 124 & 2000 Spider 1968-1985
Fiat X1/9 Gold Portfolio1973-1989
Fiat Abarth Performance Portfolio 1972-1987
Ford Consul, Zephyr, Zodiac Mk. I & II 1950-1962
Ford Zephyr, Zodiac, Executive Mk. III & IV 1962-1971
Ford Cortina 1600E & GT 1967-1970
High Performance Capris Gold Portfolio 1969-1987
Capri Muscle Portfolio 1974-1987
High Performance Fiestas 1979-1991
High Performance Escorts Mk. I 1968-1974
High Performance Escorts Mk. II 1975-1980
High Performance Escorts 1980-1985
High Performance Escorts 1985-1990
High Perf. Sierras & Merkurs Gold Portfolio 1983-1990
Ford Automobiles 1949-1959
Ford Fairlane 1955-1970
Ford Ranchero 1957-1979
Edsel 1957-1960 Limited Edition
Ford Thunderbird 1955-1957
Ford Thunderbird 1958-1963
Ford GT40 Gold Portfolio 1964-1987
Ford Bronco 1966-1977
Ford Bronco 1978-1988
Goggomobil Limited Edition
Holden 1948-1962
Honda CRX 1983-1987
Hudson 1946-1957 Limited Edition
International Scout Gold Portfolio 1961-1980
Isetta Gold Portfolio 1953-1964
ISO & Bizzarrini Gold Portfolio 1962-1974
Jaguar and SS Gold Portfolio 1931-1951
Jaguar C-Type & D-Type Gold Portfolio 1951-1960
Jaguar XK120, 140, 150 Gold Portfolio 1948-1960
Jaguar Mk. VII, VIII, IX, X, 420 Gold Port. 1950-1970
Jaguar Mk. 1 & Mk. 2 Gold Portfolio 1959-1969
Jaguar E-Type Gold Portfolio 1961-1971
Jaguar E-Type V-12 1971-1975
Jaguar S-Type & 420 Limited Edition
Jaguar XJ12, XJ5.3, V12 Gold Portfolio 1972-1990
Jaguar XJ6 Series I & II Gold Portfolio 1968-1979
Jaguar XJ6 Series III Perf. Portfolio 1979-1986
Jaguar XJ6 Gold Portfolio 1986-1994
Jaguar XJS Gold Portfolio 1975-1988
Jaguar XJS Gold Portfolio 1988-1995
Jaguar XK8 Limited Edition
Jeep CJ5 & CJ6 1960-1976
Jeep CJ5 & CJ7 1976-1986
Jensen Interceptor Gold Portfolio 1966-1986
Jensen Healey 1972-1976
Kaiser - Frazer 1946-1955 Limited Edition
Lagonda Gold Portfolio 1919-1964
Lancia Aurelia & Flaminia Gold Portfolio 1950-1970
Lancia Fulvia Gold Portfolio 1963-1976
Lancia Beta Gold Portfolio 1972-1984
Lancia Delta Gold Portfolio 1979-1994
Lancia Stratos 1972-1985
Land Rover Series I 1948-1958
Land Rover Series II & IIa 1958-1971
Land Rover 90 110 Defender Gold Portfolio 1983-1994
Land Rover Discovery 1989-1994
Land Rover Story Part One 1948-1971
Lincoln Gold Portfolio 1949-1960
Lincoln Continental 1961-1969
Lincoln Continental 1969-1976
Lotus Sports Racers Gold Portfolio 1953-1965
Lotus Seven Gold Portfolio 1957-1973
Lotus Caterham Seven Gold Portfolio 1974-1995
Lotus Elan Gold Portfolio 1962-1974
Lotus Elan Collection No. 2 1963-1972
Lotus Elan & SE 1989-1992
Lotus Europa Gold Portfolio 1966-1975
Lotus Elite & Eclat 1974-1982
Lotus Turbo Esprit 1980-1986
Marcos Coupés & Spyders Gold Portfolio 1960-1997
Maserati 1965-1970
Matra 1965-1983 Limited Edition
Mazda Miata MX-5 Performance Portfolio 1989-1996
Mazda RX-7 Gold Portfolio 1978-1991
McLaren F1 Sportscar Limited Edition
Mercedes 190 & 300 SL 1954-1963
Mercedes G-Wagen 1981-1994
Mercedes S & 600 1965-1972
Mercedes S Class 1972-1979
Mercedes 230 • 250 • 280SL Gold Portfolio 1963-1971
Mercedes SLs & SLCs Gold Portfolio 1971-1989
Mercedes SLs Performance Portfolio 1989-1994
Mercury Muscle Cars 1966-1971
Messerschmitt Gold Portfolio 1954-1964
MG Gold Portfolio 1929-1939
MG TA & TC Gold Portfolio 1936-1949
MG TD & TF Gold Portfolio 1949-1955
MGA & Twin Cam Gold Portfolio 1955-1962
MG Midget Gold Portfolio 1961-1979
MGB Roadsters 1962-1980
MGB MGC & V8 Gold Portfolio 1962-1980
MGB GT 1965-1980
MGC & MGB GT V8 Limited Edition
MG Y-Type & Magnette ZA/ZB Limited Edition
Mini Gold Portfolio 1959-1969
Mini Gold Portfolio 1969-1980
Mini Gold Portfolio 1981-1997
High Performance Minis Gold Portfolio 1960-1973
Mini Cooper Gold Portfolio 1961-1971
Mini Moke Gold Portfolio 1964-1994
Morgan Three-Wheeler Gold Portfolio 1910-1952
Morgan Plus 4 & Four 4 Gold Portfolio 1936-1967
Morgan Cars Gold Portfolio 1968-1989
Morris Minor Collection No. 1 1948-1980
Shelby Mustang Muscle Portfolio 1965-1970
High Performance Mustang IIs 1974-1978
High Performance Mustangs 1982-1988
Nash & Nash-Healey 1949-1957 Limited Edition
Nash-Austin Metropolitan Gold Portfolio 1954-1962
Oldsmobile Automobiles 1955-1963
Oldsmobile Muscle Portfolio 1964-1971
Cutlass & 4-4-2 Muscle Portfolio 1964-1974
Oldsmobile Toronado 1966-1978
Opel GT Gold Portfolio 1968-1973
Opel Manta 1970-1975 Limited Edition
Packard Gold Portfolio 1946-1958
Pantera Gold Portfolio 1970-1989
Panther Gold Portfolio 1972-1990
Barracuda Muscle Portfolio 1964-1974
Pontiac Tempest & GTO 1961-1965
GTO Muscle Portfolio 1964-1974
Firebird & Trans-Am Muscle Portfolio 1967-1972
Firebird & Trans-Am Muscle Portfolio 1973-1981
High Performance Firebirds 1982-1988
Pontiac Fiero 1984-1988
Porsche 356 Gold Portfolio 1953-1965
Porsche 912 Limited Edition
Porsche 911 1965-1969
Porsche 911 1970-1972
Porsche 911 1973-1977
Porsche 911 SC & Turbo Gold Portfolio 1978-1983
Porsche 911 Carrera & Turbo Gold Port. 1984-1989
Porsche 911 Gold Portfolio 1990-1997
Porsche 924 Gold Portfolio 1975-1988
Porsche 928 Performance Portfolio 1977-1994
Porsche 944 Gold Portfolio 1981-1991
Porsche 968 Limited Edition
Range Rover Gold Portfolio 1970-1985
Range Rover Gold Portfolio 1986-1995
Reliant Scimitar 1964-1986
Renault Alpine Gold Portfolio 1958-1994
Riley Gold Portfolio 1924-1939
R.R. Silver Cloud & Bentley 'S' Series Gold P. 1955-1965
Rolls Royce Silver Shadow Gold Portfolio 1965-1980
Rolls Royce & Bentley Gold Portfolio 1980-1989
Rolls Royce & Bentley Limited Edition 1990-1997
Rover P4 1949-1959
Rover 3 & 3.5 Litre Gold Portfolio 1958-1973
Rover 2000 & 2200 1963-1977
Rover 3500 & Vitesse 1976-1986
Saab Sonett Collection No.1 1966-1974
Saab Turbo 1976-1983
Studebaker Gold Portfolio 1947-1966
Studebaker Hawks & Larks 1956-1963
Avanti 1962-1990
Sunbeam Tiger & Alpine Gold Portfolio 1959-1967
Toyota Land Cruiser Gold Portfolio 1956-1987
Toyota Land Cruiser 1988-1997
Toyota MR2 Gold Portfolio 1984-1997
Triumph Dolomite Sprint Limited Edition
Triumph TR2 & TR3 Gold Portfolio 1952-1961
Triumph TR4, TR5, TR250 1961-1968
Triumph TR6 Gold Portfolio 1969-1976
Triumph TR7 & TR8 Gold Portfolio 1975-1982
Triumph Herald 1959-1971
Triumph Vitesse 1962-1971
Triumph Spitfire Gold Portfolio 1962-1980
Triumph 2000, 2.5, 2500 1963-1977
Triumph GT6 Gold Portfolio 1966-1974
Triumph Stag Gold Portfolio 1970-1977
TVR Gold Portfolio 1959-1986
TVR Performance Portfolio 1986-1994
VW Beetle Gold Portfolio 1935-1967
VW Beetle Gold Portfolio 1968-1991
VW Beetle Collection No.1 1970-1982
VW Karmann Ghia 1955-1982
VW Bus, Camper, Van 1954-1967
VW Bus, Camper, Van 1968-1979
VW Bus, Camper, Van 1979-1989
VW Scirocco 1974-1981
VW Golf GTI 1976-1986
Volvo PV444 & PV544 1945-1965
Volvo Amazon-120 Gold Portfolio 1956-1970
Volvo 1800 Gold Portfolio 1960-1973
Volvo 140 & 160 Series Gold Portfolio 1966-1975
Westfield Limited Edition

Forty Years of Selling Volvo

BROOKLANDS ROAD & TRACK SERIES

Road & Track on Alfa Romeo 1964-1970
Road & Track on Alfa Romeo 1971-1976
Road & Track on Alfa Romeo 1977-1989
Road & Track on Aston Martin 1962-1990
R & T on Auburn Cord and Duesenburg 1952-84
Road & Track on Audi & Auto Union 1952-1980
Road & Track on Audi & Auto Union 1980-1986
Road & Track on Austin Healey 1953-1970
Road & Track on BMW Cars 1966-1974
Road & Track on BMW Cars 1975-1978
Road & Track on BMW Cars 1979-1983
R & T on Cobra, Shelby & Ford GT40 1962-1992
Road & Track on Corvette 1953-1967
Road & Track on Corvette 1968-1982
Road & Track on Corvette 1982-1986
Road & Track on Corvette 1986-1990
Road & Track on Ferrari 1975-1981
Road & Track on Ferrari 1981-1984
Road & Track on Ferrari 1984-1988
Road & Track on Fiat Sports Cars 1968-1987
Road & Track on Jaguar 1950-1960
Road & Track on Jaguar 1961-1968
Road & Track on Jaguar 1968-1974
Road & Track on Jaguar 1974-1982
Road & Track on Jaguar 1983-1989
Road & Track on Lamborghini 1964-1985
Road & Track on Lotus 1972-1983
R & T on Mazda RX-7 & MX-5 Miata 1986-1991
Road & Track on Mercedes 1952-1962
Road & Track on Mercedes 1963-1970
Road & Track on Mercedes 1971-1979
Road & Track on Mercedes 1980-1987
Road & Track on MG Sports Cars 1949-1961
Road & Track on MG Sports Cars 1962-1980
R & T on Nissan 300-ZX & Turbo 1984-1989
Road & Track on Pontiac 1960-1983
Road & Track on Porsche 1951-1967
Road & Track on Porsche 1968-1971
Road & Track on Porsche 1972-1975
Road & Track on Porsche 1975-1978
Road & Track on Porsche 1979-1982
Road & Track on Porsche 1985-1988
R & T on Rolls Royce & Bentley 1950-1965
R & T on Rolls Royce & Bentley 1966-1984
Road & Track on Saab 1972-1992
R & T on Toyota Sports & GT Cars 1966-1984
R & T on Triumph Sports Cars 1953-1967
R & T on Triumph Sports Cars 1967-1974
R & T on Triumph Sports Cars 1974-1982
Road & Track on Volkswagen 1951-1968
Road & Track on Volkswagen 1968-1978
Road & Track on Volkswagen 1978-1985
Road & Track on Volvo 1957-1974
Road & Track on Volvo 1977-1994
R & T - Henry Manney at Large & Abroad
R & T - Peter Egan's "Side Glances"
R & T - Peter Egan "At Large"

BROOKLANDS CAR AND DRIVER SERIES

Car and Driver on BMW 1955-1977
Car and Driver on Corvette 1978-1982
Car and Driver on Corvette 1983-1988
C and D on Datsun Z 1600 & 2000 1966-1984
Car and Driver on Ferrari 1955-1962
Car and Driver on Ferrari 1963-1975
Car and Driver on Ferrari 1976-1983
Car and Driver on Mopar 1956-1967
Car and Driver on Mopar 1968-1975
Car and Driver on Mustang 1964-1972
Car and Driver on Pontiac 1961-1975
Car and Driver on Porsche 1955-1962
Car and Driver on Porsche 1963-1970
Car and Driver on Porsche 1970-1976
Car and Driver on Porsche 1977-1981
Car and Driver on Porsche 1982-1986
Car and Driver on Volvo 1955-1986

RACING

Le Mans - The Jaguar Years - 1949-1957
Le Mans - The Ferrari Years - 1958-1965
Le Mans - The Ford & Matra Years - 1966-1974
Le Mans - The Porsche Years - 1975-1982

A COMPREHENSIVE GUIDE

BMW 2002

BROOKLANDS PRACTICAL CLASSICS SERIES

PC on Austin A40 Restoration
PC on Land Rover Restoration
PC on Metalworking in Restoration
PC on Midget/Sprite Restoration
PC on MGB Restoration
PC on Sunbeam Rapier Restoration
PC on Triumph Herald/Vitesse
PC on Spitfire Restoration

BROOKLANDS HOT ROD 'MUSCLECAR & HI-PO ENGINES' SERIES

Chevy 265 & 283
Chevy 302 & 327
Chevy 348 & 409
Chevy 350 & 400
Chevy 396 & 427
Chevy 454 thru 512
Chrysler Hemi
Chrysler 273, 318, 340 & 360
Chrysler 361, 383, 400, 413, 426, 440
Ford 289, 302, Boss 302 & 351W
Ford 351C & Boss 351
Ford Big Block

BROOKLANDS RESTORATION SERIES

Auto Restoration Tips & Techniques
Basic Bodywork Tips & Techniques
BMW 2002 Restoration Guide
Classic Camaro Restoration
Chevrolet High Performance Tips & Techniques
Chevy Engine Swapping Tips & Techniques
Chevy-GMC Pickup Repair
Chrysler Engine Swapping Tips & Techniques
Engine Swapping Tips & Techniques
Ford Pickup Repair
Land Rover Restoration Tips & Techniques
MG 'T' Series Restoration Guide
MGA Restoration Guide
Mustang Restoration Tips & Techniques

MOTORCYCLING

BROOKLANDS ROAD TEST SERIES

AJS & Matchless Gold Portfolio 1945-1966
BSA Singles Gold Portfolio 1945-1963
BSA Singles Gold Portfolio 1964-1974
BSA Twins A7 & A10 Gold Portfolio 1946-1962
BSA Twins A50 & A65 Gold Portfolio 1962-1973
BMW Motorcycles Gold Portfolio 1950-1971
BMW Motorcycles Gold Portfolio 1971-1976
Ducati Gold Portfolio 1960-1974
Ducati Gold Portfolio 1974-1978
Ducati Gold Portfolio 1978-1982
Laverda Gold Portfolio 1967-1977
Moto Guzzi Gold Portfolio 1949-1973
Norton Commando Gold Portfolio 1968-1977
Triumph Bonneville Gold Portfolio 1959-1983
Vincent Gold Portfolio 1945-1980

BROOKLANDS CYCLE WORLD SERIES

Cycle World on BMW 1974-1980
Cycle World on BMW 1981-1986
Cycle World on Ducati 1982-1991
Cycle World on Harley-Davidson 1962-1968
Cycle World on Harley-Davidson 1978-1983
Cycle World on Harley-Davidson 1983-1987
Cycle World on Harley-Davidson 1987-1990
Cycle World on Harley-Davidson 1990-1992
Cycle World on Honda 1962-1967
Cycle World on Honda 1968-1971
Cycle World on Honda 1971-1974
Cycle World on Husqvarna 1966-1976
Cycle World on Husqvarna 1977-1984
Cycle World on Kawasaki 1966-1971
Cycle World on Kawasaki Off-Road Bikes 1972-1979
Cycle World on Kawasaki Street Bikes 1972-1976
Cycle World on Norton 1962-1971
Cycle World on Suzuki 1962-1970
Cycle World on Suzuki Off-Road Bikes 1971-1976
Cycle World on Suzuki Street Bikes 1971-1976
Cycle World on Triumph 1967-1972
Cycle World on Yamaha 1962-1969
Cycle World on Yamaha Off-Road Bikes 1970-1974
Cycle World on Yamaha Street Bikes 1970-1974

MILITARY

BROOKLANDS MILITARY VEHICLES SERIES

Allied Military Vehicles No.2 1941-1946
Complete WW2 Military Jeep Manual
Dodge Military Vehicles No.1 1940-1945
Hail To The Jeep
Military & Civilian Amphibians 1940-1990
Off Road Jeeps: Civilian & Military 1944-1971
US Military Vehicles 1941-1945
US Army Military Vehicles WW2-TM9-2800
VW Kubelwagen Military Portfolio 1940-1990
WW2 Jeep Military Portfolio 1941-1945

20018

CONTENTS

ACKNOWLEDGEMENTS

This new Performance Portfolio replaces our earlier Road Test book on the corvair, which is now out of print. What we have done is to select the material from that book which covered the performance models, and we have combined it with a large amount of new material which has now become available. As a result, only 26 of this book's 140 pages remain from the first book.

We are always pleased to express our thanks to the publishers who generously allow us to reproduce their material in Brooklands titles. On this occasion, we acknowledge the help and co-operation of *Automobile Topics, Auto Topics, Car and Driver, Car Life, Car South Africa, Foreign Cars Illustrated, Mechanix Illustrated, Modern Motor, Motor, Motorcade, Motor Sports Illustrated, Motor Trend, Road & Track, Road Test, Special Interest Autos, Sports Car Graphic, Sports Cars Illustrated, Sporting Motorist* and *Track and Traffic.*

R.M. Clarke

The Corvair was General Motors' entry in the compact sedan race which started in 1960, and in the beginning it looked as if it would stack up well against Chrysler's Valiant and Ford's Falcon. Where they were both ultra-conventional, ultra-cautious designs, the Chevy had borrowed a number of ideas from Volkswagen in Europe and came with a rear-mounted, air-cooled flat-six engine. Unfortunately, that engine proved to be its undoing when it turned out heavier than anticipated, and affected the handling. Ralph Nader's *Unsafe at any Speed* terminally damaged sales, and the line was allowed to die at the end of the 1960s. But none of that prevented the Corvair from spawning some interesting variants in the meantime.

The first was the Monza, which made its bow in the middle of the 1960 season as a sporty bucket-seat coupe. It had no more power than was available elsewhere in the Corvair line, but Chevy recognised its appeal and through 1962 and 1963 the Corvair Monza Spyder models could be had with high-performance editions of the air-cooled flat-six. For '64, a long-stroke motor gave better performance in the intermediates, and for '65 power peaked at 180bhp in a new sporty model called the Corsa.

Unfortunately, sales had peaked by this stage, too. GM instructed Chevy not to develop the Corvair any further, and power started dropping after '67 until the best available was a 110bhp motor. It didn't sell strongly and the Corvair died before the decade was out. Yet the Corvair continued to have an appeal for enthusiasts, and the articles reproduced in this book are a reminder of why it has endured, and of why it has outlived the terrible reputation it acquired in the mid-1960s.

James Taylor

by Karl Ludvigsen

SCI ANALYZES Ed Cole's CORVAIR

▶ It looks as if Ed Cole threw up his hands and said, "Okay, okay, I've had enough. Let's build this car that all the critics and magazines have been asking for and *then* see how they like it. We'll do everything they suggest and add a few ideas of our own." That's about what Chevrolet has accomplished with the Corvair. It is the most profoundly revolutionary car, within the framework of the U.S. automotive industry, ever offered by a major manufacturer.

It is a fact that, unlike the Corvette SS (promoted by GM Styling) the impetus for the Corvair came directly from Ed Cole, the engineering-oriented Vice President in charge of Chevrolet Division. When the first meetings were held in the Fall of 1956 it was possible to review fairly complete proposals for both the mechanical layout and styling of a "smaller car" which had already been prepared just in case by the Research components of both the Styling and Engineering departments. By Fall of 1957 these had been translated to detail drawings and to prototype engines which were put to work on the test benches and in such divers vehicles as a Porsche and a gutted Vauxhall sedan. A handful of complete prototypes were then built, along rather bulbous lines which have become familiar to readers of our contemporary, *Motor Life*. The test engineers had a real ball sending to Australia for "Holden" insignias and trim for these cars and disguising them in general. They all had fraudulent grilles in front, of course, and one car—for testing down in the Kentucky/Tennessee area . . . even had a bug screen in front of the fake grille!

There was adequate time in the Summer and Winter of 1958 to hammer the prototypes across the country from the 120 degrees of Mesa, Arizona to 30 below at Duluth, Minnesota, proving many features, but primarily the feasibility of air cooling. In the meantime the stylists had completed their revision of the lines, enabling Fisher Body to put together the final prototypes for debugging in early 1959. Only the four-door edition will be introduced for 1960, but other body styles are sure to follow if the Corvair is well received. What about a station wagon? The Chevy line of thought may be traced from a VW Kombi we saw at the proving grounds, completely outfitted with Corvair engine and suspension, used ostensibly to test the Corvair components. The possible commercial applications of the Corvair's simple and practical propulsion unit aren't likely to be overlooked.

The Corvair bears no direct relation to the somewhat similar "Cadet" project initiated by GM just after the war. Under the direction of Maurice Olley an exhaustive study was then made of all possible engine and vehicle configurations and a final proposal reached which in shape foreshadowed the 1948 Packard. The whole deal was called off probably with good reason. We hope it may be possible at some future date to publish some of the details of the Cadet study.

THE "CHEVY-VW"?

With only a slight attempt at badinage the Corvair project was frequently referred to at GM as the "Chevy-VW", an appellation which has very meaningful overtones. The completed Corvair reflects the same brand of restless, ruthless emphasis on essentials that characterized most of Dr. Porsche's work. It parallels the Volkswagen's imaginative approach to utility, but within the North American frame of reference,. and in realistic fact closely follows the VW line in its actual general layout.

For their first essay at unitized construction in this country, GM engineers have gone the whole way. That is, there was no intermediate platform or backbone frame stage (though in all fairness a current X-frame GM car derives about 70 percent of its torsional stiffness from the body) and the integrated Corvair retains only the most subtle vestiges of a frame. At the front a pair of hat-section rails curve back from the bumper mounts over the front suspension to blend with the underbody, taking on the qualities of boxed members where their open face is closed by the wheel housings. With deeply boxed side, cross and vertical members, the body proper uses few new techniques. Over the rear suspension and alongside the engine it's also reinforced by an additional pair of channel-section members extending to the back bumper.

Many happy returns to sanity are evident in the Corvair, one being the use of an old-fashioned non-wraparound windshield which makes it a lot easier to get in and out of this relatively small car. Further help comes from the doors, which are very wide and open at a generous angle. Locking is effected by the interior handle instead of the traditional GM window sill buttons. Though the door pillars aren't especially slim they're well placed, and vision all around is superb. A special effort was made to reduce costs in the instrument panel layout, but it doesn't show it. (It isn't as cheap as they had hoped, either!) Easy adaptation to right-hand-drive is facilitated by the twin-hood layout, the radio, when fitted, being slung from the center of the dash. A 100-mph speedometer is accompanied by a fuel gauge of a new, more accurate counterbalanced-pointer type. A warning light flashes on if the oil's temperature is too high or its pressure too low, while another lights up if the fan belt ceases to drive the generator or blower. Even on the deluxe 700 model (chrome window moldings, door-operated interior light) there's no horn ring on the appealingly simple steering wheel.

For a tall driver the Corvair offers plenty of head room, and the unobstructed floor leaves adequate area for big feet, but Chevy engineers didn't quite catch the secret of the VW's remarkable habitability. When only two passengers are riding in the German car — the most common situation, you'll grant — it's possible to move the front seat well to the back, almost touching the rear seat. Attempting to retain rear seat leg room under *all* circumstances, Chevy limited front seat travel just at that point where a moderately tall driver feels somewhat cramped. A running change to a longer rearward travel is respectfully but urgently suggested.

LUGGAGE LOCKERS

Similarly, if Renault's clever stowage of the spare tire had been imitated or at least paralleled the Corvair's "trunk" would not be any roomier but would have a more usable shape and would be easier on fine leathers. About 9½-cubic feet at the front are supplemented by a 4½-cubic-foot volume behind the rear seat, VW-style. A very attractive option at moderate extra cost is a rear seat that folds forward, station-wagon-style, to form a flat platform from the front seat to the firewall on which most anything can be heaped. The conversion can be made quickly and easily.

Some trunk space is stolen by the optional gas-fueled heater developed by Harrison Division of GM to lick the twin heating problems of a car that is both rear-engined and air cooled. A 2700 rpm centrifugal blower supplies air to the seven-inch cylindrical stainless-steel burner, which receives fuel at 4 to 5 psi from the engine fuel pump and is lit by a simple igniter which continues to spark constantly while the unit is in operation, as a precaution against "flame-out". Before passing to a tiny exhaust pipe under the car, the hot gases from this burner flow through a heat exchanger which warms the interior air, drawn from the cowl vent and fed to the cockpit by a two-speed centrifugal blower. A thermostatic control adjusts temperature by turning the fuel supply on and off as required.

Several precautionary controls are provided. One switch cuts off the gasoline supply if the unit temperature rises too high, while another does the same if too much fuel drains back, unburned, to the gas tank. A third switch keeps the combustion blower running half a minute after the heater is shut off, to purge all gases from the system. Chevrolet states that the maximum possible fuel consumption of the unit is about a quarter of a gallon per hour, a more normal winter figure being a tenth of a gallon per hour (or ten hours per gallon). This seems a moderate price for instant and powerful heating. Convenient to all this is the 11-gallon gas tank, nestling between the front suspension and the toeboard. It's held up against a fiber cushion by a single transverse strap and receives fuel from a filler on the leftfront fender.

BODY DETAILS

The rear "hood" (Chevy is just as confused over what to call these lids as SCI) is opened by pressing a trigger next to the license plate light. Like all the crevices at top and bottom of the engine room this trigger is rubber-sealed to ensure that the air flow goes just as the engineers planned, a detail that was found essential to quick hot starting. Cooling air enters through rear deck louvers equipped with pans to catch and drain away rain water. Aerodynamic tests made recently, well after the styling was finalized, indicated that by lucky chance there was a high-pressure area just over the intake louvers!

Ned Nickels and the special studio set up for Corvair body design deserve all possible credit for a shape which has proved aerodynamically sound and which also, less definably, reflects the functional and useful character of the Corvair without actually flaunting these facets of the car. Its lines are trim and meaningful and its ornamentation more restrained than on most European cars. Assembled completely by Fisher, the body is united on the line with suspension and engine in very quick time, the chassis assemblies rising to meet the descending body shell.

Bolted directly to the body, a massive boxed crossmember carries all the front suspension parts and permits initial wheel alignment even before the subassembly is joined to the car. Stamped upper wishbones are inclined rearward to combat nose-dive on braking, while the lower wishbones are divided into two parts, as has been done by Chrysler for some time: a stamped hat-section arm carries the lower of the two ball joints as well as the bottom ends of the coil spring and concentric shock absorber, and is braced by a rod which trails rearward at about 45 degrees. Caster can be set by varying the screw adjustment at the rubber-cushioned chassis end of this rod, which would shift the position of the lower ball joint in relation to the upper one. Rubber is used liberally to damp out sound transmission to the unitized body, there even being a rubber shim between the top of each coil spring and its retaining cup. Although an anti-roll bar was fitted on many of the prototypes and in fact appears in some of the early publicity photos, it is not being used on at least the first cars to roll off the Willow Run line.

A neatly detailed three-piece track-rod steering linkage is actuated by a recirculating ball gear encased in an aluminum housing. The ratio of the gearbox is 18 to 1 and that of the whole system 23.5 to 1, values midway between those of the Corvette and the standard Chevrolet. Even adding the fact that only 38 percent of the Corvair's weight is on the front wheels, bald figures like these cannot convey an inkling of the excellence of this car's steering. It is so light that at parking speeds it feels power-assisted; it is so precise as to be absolutely without play, and it is fast enough to allow complete control over every situation. In speed and smoothness and in that delightful ability to "wish" a car around a bend, even an early-type Porsche would have to give points to the Corvair. Judged by itself, the steering system is among the finest I have ever had the pleasure to handle. It's even unusually easy to direct in reverse.

New answers to the braking question are also provided by the Corvair's rearward weight bias. Forward transfer of weight on braking brings the weight distribution close to 50/50, so 9-inch brake drums with equal-sized linings 1¾ inch wide are fitted all around, for a total area of 120.8 square inches. To guarantee that the back wheels lock up first on a panic stop the front/rear braking ratio is

an initially surprising 46/54, obtained by fitting the compound servo mechanisms with ⅞-inch cylinders in front and 15/16-inch in the rear. A one-inch master cylinder with integral reservoir is hung from the dash structure and filled from the luggage compartment. Again these details only hint at the unusually even, stable way the Corvair comes to a halt. It crouches flat and close to the ground with maximum braking traction even on gravel surfaces. Heat loads are equally doled out among the drums but their size is small, leading to the tentative conclusion that fade resistance will not be exceptional.

A determined amount of misalignment is allowed at the Corvair's rear hubs, requiring a brake adjustment there five notches looser than at the front. Also on board is a novel hand brake found on the big Chevys as well. Its returning ratchet action allows the brake to be applied firmly in one long pull or several short ones, the release lever popping out to indicate that the brake is applied. A specially powerful hand brake was in order for the Corvair from the beginning since no "park" position was designed into the automatic transmission. 13-inch wheels were chosen because they and their tires tend to be inexpensive; a 5½-inch rim gives good sidewall support. It was hoped that the low profile of the new-type 6.50x13 tires would be a boon to the handling of the rear-engined Corvair when carrying, to quote Chevy, "normal inflation in the rear tires and a reduced pressure in the front tires". This works out to 15 psi front and 26 rear when cold, or 18/30 psi at operating temperature, a radical differential however you look at it. Whether or not you're sympathetic to the cause of the Corvair you must admit that the need for such a difference reflects poorly on the basic chassis design. Quite apart from this, it's unlikely that most Corvair owners will ever maintain the pressures recommended.

Mercedes' solution for the front end of the 180 series is recalled by the logical, neat rear suspension and powerplant package of the Corvair, the mounting of which serves to insulate the main body shell from engine and rear wheel oscillations. The semi-trailing swing arms of the independent rear suspension are rubber-bushed to forged pivot shafts, which in turn are bolted to a wide box-section crossmember. The latter develops at its extremities into abutments and housings for the shock absorbers and coil springs. Four rubber mounts join this crossmember to the body. Wheel hubs are hidden within the deep, fully-boxed ends of the rugged swing arms. The coil springs are compressed pans spread within the crotch of the swing arms.

A departure from pure swing axle geometry is made here, as in so many other cases (VW, Fiat 600 and 500, early Lancia Aurelia) to lessen the camber change with wheel travel and to introduce toe-in deflection as an inducement to understeer, both without going to the extreme of pure trailing arm suspension (Renault Fregate) which tends to reduce rear cornering power in roll. The pivot axis of the Corvair's swing arms is inclined at about 40 degrees to the longitudinal centerline, which means that the layout tends more toward the swing axle side of things. The spring rates at the wheels are 86-pounds-per-inch in front and 192 at the back, the actual rate of the rear coil being a hefty 550-pounds-per-inch, over twice that of the rear coils of the big Chevy sedan which actually has a smaller rear wheel design load.

Let us be honest, as usual: The Corvair is fundamentally a profound oversteerer. With 62-percent of its weight on the back wheels it could only be otherwise if very ingenious suspension techniques had been called into play. This was not the case. As cornering forces on the Corvair chassis increase there is an initial very mild understeer tendency, probably attributable to the rear suspension geometry, but then, well within the average driver's range of slip angles, oversteer sets in in a gradual way that is easily countered by the excellent steering — whose very lightness, of course, is in part a function of the oversteer. *text continued on page 12*

1. The problem of adequately heating an air-cooled car is solved by this gasoline heater installed in luggage compartment.
2. The car is easily converted to right-hand drive due to the symmetrical dashboard.
3. Bob Clift, Chevrolet engine development engineer, peers into odd-shaped "trunk". Spare tire would have been better placed under floor as on Dauphine.
4. To make up for lack of front luggage space, the area behind the rear seat is quite large. With seat folded, more can be carried.

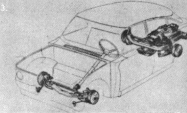

1. Prototype Corvair body in assembly stage.
2. Drawing shows general layout of body-frame unit construction.
3. An early preliminary drawing of the placement of the drive unit and front end components.
4. Engine and rear suspension assembly.
5. The left front suspension unit as viewed from the rear.
6. Right rear suspension. Axle shaft passes through rear edge of sheet steel wishbone.

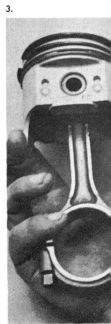

1. Cutaway drawing of Corvair engine as seen from the rear.
2. Corvair crank has four meaty main bearings and is very light even when compared with some foreign six-cylinder cranks.
3. Corvair piston and connecting rod.
4. Top view shows relationship of engine, transmission, and rear suspension.
5. Partly assembled engine on the line at Tonawanda, N. Y. engine plant.
6. The complete engine unit as it leaves the plant. Cooling fan bearing protrudes from top of engine, fan itself is belt-driven.

4.

5.

6.

4.

5.

6.

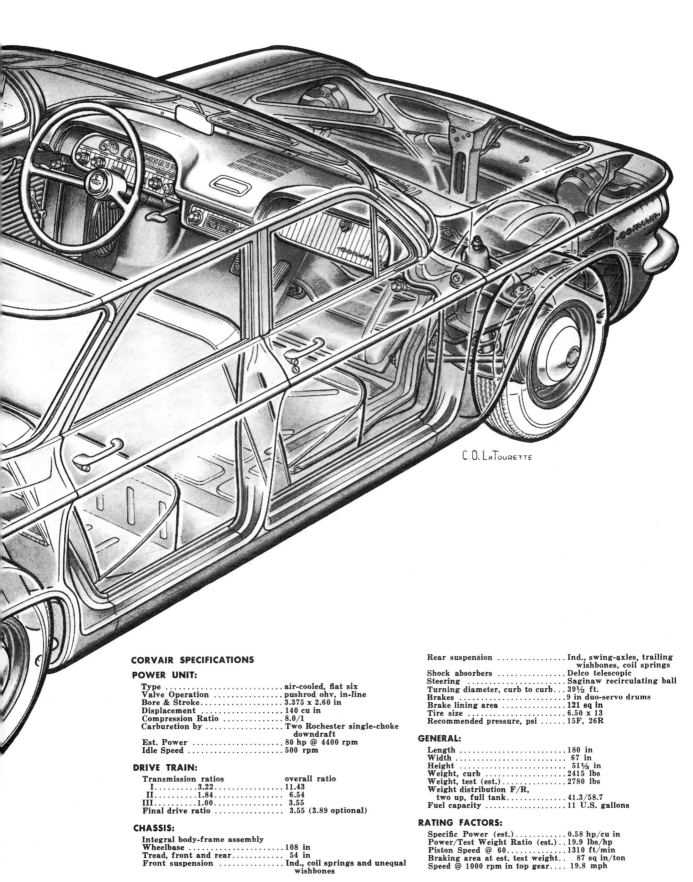

C.O. LaTourette

CORVAIR SPECIFICATIONS

POWER UNIT:

Type	air-cooled, flat six
Valve Operation	pushrod ohv, in-line
Bore & Stroke	3.375 x 2.60 in
Displacement	140 cu in
Compression Ratio	8.0/1
Carburetion by	Two Rochester single-choke downdraft
Est. Power	80 hp @ 4400 rpm
Idle Speed	500 rpm

DRIVE TRAIN:

Transmission ratios		overall ratio
I	3.22	11.43
II	1.84	6.54
III	1.00	3.55
Final drive ratio		3.55 (3.89 optional)

CHASSIS:

Integral body-frame assembly

Wheelbase	108 in
Tread, front and rear	54 in
Front suspension	Ind., coil springs and unequal wishbones

GENERAL:

Rear suspension	Ind., swing-axles, trailing wishbones, coil springs
Shock absorbers	Delco telescopic
Steering	Saginaw recirculating ball
Turning diameter, curb to curb	39½ ft.
Brakes	9 in duo-servo drums
Brake lining area	121 sq in
Tire size	6.50 x 13
Recommended pressure, psi	15F, 26R

GENERAL:

Length	180 in
Width	67 in
Height	51⅓ in
Weight, curb	2415 lbs
Weight, test (est.)	2780 lbs
Weight distribution F/R, two up, full tank	41.3/58.7
Fuel capacity	11 U.S. gallons

RATING FACTORS:

Specific Power (est.)	0.58 hp/cu in
Power/Test Weight Ratio (est.)	19.9 lbs/hp
Piston Speed @ 60	1310 ft/min
Braking area at est. test weight	87 sq in/ton
Speed @ 1000 rpm in top gear	19.8 mph

Having heard that Uncle Tom himself had declared that he "tried but just couldn't lose the Corvair", I asked Chevy's affable engine development engineer Bob Clift to keep a path clear to the basement while we tried some very fast turns. By making extremely deep corrections it was possible to hold the car on a line but, as in any automobile ever built, there was a point beyond which it wasn't prudent to proceed. For a moderately skilled driver the Corvair is a genuine ball to drive, it being possible to hustle hard into tight corners and bring the tail around with just a twitch of the wheel, counter-steering until the slide stops and the time for acceleration arrives. This is not, of course, everybody's way of driving.

Chevy spokesmen have said that they didn't feel a front anti-roll bar was needed because the car's center of gravity was so low that it doesn't roll much. This is true enough, from that standpoint, but such bars are also powerful tools for adjusting handling, and one of the first things that should be done to this car is to replace that anti-roll bar. Since this would only actually counterbalance the difficulties that exist at the rear, however, thorough redesign should commence at that end. With the conventional design methods used, the high spring rates needed to support the rear end weight have resulted in unduly high roll stiffness at the rear, a sure harbinger of oversteer. A solution like that on the Mercedes-Benz 300SL Roadster is called for, having a single central coil or a pivoted transverse leaf spring to support loads without affecting roll. For all its novelty the Corvair is surprisingly naive in this major respect.

The pivot axis of the rear swing arms was aimed right through the inner Hooke-type universal joints, allowing the slim axle shafts to swing in the plane of the arm and making outboard U-joints unnecessary. Minor length changes and servicing ease are catered to by short splines at the inner ends, while small misalignments at the hub end of the axle are accepted by the double-row "spherangular" roller bearings used at the hubs.

The engine/transmission assembly, of conventional rear-engine type in sequence and placement, is suspended at three points: two between the front of the transmission and the rear suspension crossmember, and one between the rear of the engine and the car body. The whole group is very easily removed for service in the familiar VW manner. It's not official, but one rough weight quoted for the whole power package, transmission not specified, was 340 pounds.

Ed Cole's decision to put the Corvair's engine in the trunk was in part predicated on his engineers' feeling that they knew enough about the use of light alloys in engine design to lick that tail-heavy problem. Apart from the validity of this, the flat-six engine does make generous use of high-duty aluminum alloys (high silicon percentage) formed in the only economical way, die casting. Throughout the engine no thread inserts are used, Heli-Coils or the like used only to salvage stripped threads, as a service operation.

Shoebox-shaped in general outline, with a total of four webbed bulkheads for main bearing support, the crankcase is split vertically down its middle. Eight through-bolts clamp it together around the crankshaft. The main bearings, like those for the rods, are basically a steel-backed copper-nickel mix coated with a thin lead babbitt overlay. Obviously overdimensioned to accept future stroke increases and given very generous sections and radii, this crankcase is a hefty item that will be reassuring to owners and promising to modifiers.

Realizing that in an aluminum engine proportionally more strength must be supplied by the crankshaft, Chevy engineers came up with a very sturdy forged steel crank with reasonably heavy cheeks but without counterweighting, by virtue of the good inherent balance of the opposed six. The No. 1 or rearward main bearings takes thrust loadings and is therefore .828 inch wide, the rest having a width of .772-inch and all four being 2.098-inches in diameter. The rod journals measure 1.80-inches in diameter and about .65-inch in width.

Scaling just 4.72-inches between centers, the connecting rods have a modest H-section shank which is, however, smoothly radiused into the big end. No circlips retain the .80-inch wrist pin, which is pressed into place in the small end of the rod. Of appealing slipper-type design, the pistons have a flat crown (for an 8 to 1 c.r.) and are lightly tin-plated. Two iron compression rings are backed up by a one-piece chrome-plated oil ring.

To get the Corvair into early production it was decided to release it with cast iron cylinders instead of the aluminum parts that may be introduced at a later date. Of course the goal is an aluminum alloy cylinder that is sufficiently wear-resistant to live without any special wall platings, as has already been done experimentally on the accessory engine of the Firebird III. On early prototypes of the Corvair engine the finning over the length of each cylinder was uniformly deep, but this apparently *overcooled* the lower portion of each cylinder, probably causing excessive wall friction, for the production cylinders have full-depth finning over their upper halves only.

These cylinders are very deeply spigoted into both the crankcase and the cylinder heads. The latter are identical left and right, a break for makers of special heads. Prototype powerplants used sand-cast heads with complex finning arrangements running in several planes, but the redesign for die-casting dictated a simpler alignment in a single plane. Also tried but found unnecessary was the sawing apart of the three combustion chambers in each head right to but not including the floor of the valve gear chamber.

Ed Cole's Corvair

COMBUSTION CHAMBER

Viewed in profile the chamber looks like a pure wedge-type, with inclined valves, but its roof is actually slightly crowned because of a small but definite angle between the intake and exhaust valves. This angle is in turn dependent on the valve gear arrangements. Following the VW tradition of mild tuning in relation to displacement, the valves are very small: 1.340-inch intake and 1.240-inch exhaust. They seat on inserts of cast nickel steel for the intake and cast chromium steel for the exhaust, and they're placed well to the sides of the combustion chamber to allow a bridge between the valves so broad that it can be supplied with its own direct finning and cooling air passage. Head finning above the chamber proper is concentrated almost exclusively around the exhaust valves and their guides.

Single valve springs, identical for all valves, close them while the familiar Chevy stamped rocker gear handles the opening. Of 1.57:1 ratio, the light rockers are pivoted from extensions of the nuts that hold the head down against the lower row of studs. Four long studs are spaced around each cylinder, those at the bottom of the engine being slightly closer together to allow them to help out with the rockers (top and bottom spacing was identical on the prototype engines). Tubular steel push rods function as on the V8's to carry oil to the rocker gear, and are surrounded by O-ring-sealed tubular housings which return oil to the crankcase.

All problems of changing clearance with expansion are sidestepped here by the use of hydraulic lifters as standard. Placed directly below the crank, the cast iron camshaft runs directly in the aluminum crankcase at four journals. The lifter bores are horizontal and very close together for each cylinder, to allow room for all the cams that had to be accommodated. Though all the intake cams are separately formed, it was found possible to save machining time by using only three very broad exhaust lobes which actuate two lifters each.

Valve timing is as follows:

	Intake	Exhaust
Opens	15° BTDC	59° BBDC
Closes	37° ABDC	13° ATDC
Duration	232°	252°
Overlap		28°
Lift	0.360 in.	0.360 in.

LUBRICATION AND COOLING

A helical steel gear at the *flywheel* end of the crankshaft, just outboard of the No. 4 main, drives the camshaft through a cast aluminum gear. At the other end of the engine is a deep aluminum casting which adds rigidity to the crankcase. It carries the aft engine mount and crankshaft oil seal and houses the gear-type oil pump. This latter is driven by the bottom extension of the distributor drive shaft, which angles across the back of the engine and is driven by the crankshaft through a spiral gear set. Maximum oil pressure of 35 psi is reached at 2000 rpm and is limited to that figure by a spring-loaded relief valve.

After oil leaves the pump it passes through a full-flow oil filter, which will be bypassed only if the pressure drop through it exceeds 10 psi. If its temperature is higher than 160° F., it then flows through an oil cooler nestling at the left rear corner of the engine, relatively far from the cooling blower. Somewhat pessimistically some prototype engines had two long oil coolers placed along both sides of the blower. Two main oil galleries serve the lifters as well as the cam and crank bearings, the lubricant finally returning to the shallow pressed-steel four-quart oil pan.

Both centrifugal force and engine vacuum advance the Delco-Remy distributor, which fires 14-mm AC plugs of type 44-FF. At first glance the plugs look hard to reach but they're actually close to the generous openings in the cooling shroud, and should be more serviceable than those of most U.S. V-8's. The upper cooling shroud could be a very simple stamping because the ingenious fan arrangement worked out by Chevy engineers did away with the need for diffuser vanes. Placed horizontally on a ball-bearing mount atop the engine, the centrifugal blower is 11-inches in diameter and has 24 vanes. Spinning at 1.58 times engine speed it can deliver 1800 cubic feet per minute at 4000 crankshaft rpm, while taking up a minimum of space. Temperature is regulated by a ring within the blower intake which is raised and lowered at the command of a thermostatic bellows.

How to drive this flat-placed fan might, of course, have blocked progress without a little "imaginering" on the part of the G.M. research crew. An ordinary notched fan belt does the job by allowing itself to be bent over two transfer pulleys high at the back of the engine. The left-hand pulley is called upon to drive the generator at a rapid 2.3 times engine speed while the right-hand one is an adjustable ball-bearing-mounted idler. Between these pulleys protrudes the oil filler and the fuel pump, which is driven directly by a push rod and a conical cam on the crankshaft. Since it oscillates twice as fast as an ordinary fuel pump its stroke is proportionately shorter.

MANIFOLDING, IN AND OUT

Twin Rochester carburetors are featured on the Corvair engine, designed especially for this job. They're single-throat units, with a cluster of four radial tubes replacing the usual secondary or booster venturi within the main venturi. Chevy reports that this is "more effective with the relatively slow gas velocities developed with the dual carburetors and small displacement engine." They mount atop manifolds which were split on experimental engines but which are now cast integrally with the cylinder heads.

One of the mechanical disadvantages of a twin-carb layout on an opposed engine is minimized on the Corvair by placing the automatic choke at the air entry to the single air cleaner which feeds both carbs through rubber hoses, buttressed against collapse by coiled wire inserts. The cleaner itself is novel too, having a spongy polyurethane element soaked with oil.

As cast in the head the exhaust ports are very short. They're extended downward away from the finned region by short steel pipes which are pressed into the ports to stay. Cast iron manifolds are clamped up against these stub pipes by three clamps each, and exhaust forward into pipes which curve around to the cylindrical reverse-flow muffler hung along the right side of the engine. A lot of muffling had to be and in fact was accomplished in a restricted space.

No horsepower figures have been announced as this is being written, but they're likely to be in the region of 85 bhp at 4600 rpm, naturally using regular gas. The emphasis is definitely on smooth running and reliability, enhanced by starkly rugged design and the extremely short stroke. As the engine is mounted it's sealed off from the Corvair interior both by the insulated firewall and by the shrouding of the air-cooling system, with the result that virtually all noise is left behind. The much-maligned "air-cooled sound" is evident only when decelerating from high engine speeds at closed throttle. The air cooling wasn't finalized until a lot of dyno time had been logged with a standard 1600 Porsche engine, so that's likely to be in good order.

As might be expected Zora Arkus-Duntov already has a special camshaft and modified cylinder heads ready for the Corvair, but it's unlikely that they'll be utilized until the model has proven itself commercially. Corvette-type versions of the car are an even longer way off.

AUTOMATIC TRANSMISSION

Interestingly and logically, it was originally intended to market the Corvair with automatic transmission only. Above all the car is intended to be a practical machine for transportation, especially in crowded urban areas, which means that it should be as easy and simple to operate as possible. Automatics, especially at GM are now developed to the point where their efficiency and simplicity are at acceptable levels for vehicles designed with economy in mind. The general arrangement of the

Corvair automatic box had in fact been laid out and tested long before the Chevy program began. Why is a standard shift also available now? Partly, it must be admitted, because performance and mileage didn't come quite up to expectations with the automatic, but overwhelmingly because Ford and Chrysler decided to get

13

Continued on page 17

CORVAIR

Away with the myths, up with an important and very sound new car

PRODUCTION of Chevrolet's new compact car began in July, and early in August Road & Track was invited to see and drive the new baby. Armed with stop watches and our trusty Tapley meter, we drove out from Detroit to the famous GM proving grounds near Milford, Mich.

The Corvair's announcement date was two months away, and security regulations in the form of passes, etc., were very strict. However, we got through with no difficulties and were cordially received at the Chevrolet Divi-

sion's experimental garage within the proving grounds.

After a slight delay, we were admitted into the main area. Here cars of all sizes and types, including several compact cars with weird fins, were sitting around. These, it seems, were the jokers, designed to mislead the competition. Finally we were led up to a neat but plain black 4-door sedan. This was a standard production Corvair with stick shift, and it was to be our test car.

The Corvair, as everyone knows by now, is an ex-

The lack of a phony grille is to GM designers' credit.

Cooling air goes in atop the deck, out under the bumper.

PHOTOS BY POOLE

Low seats, but no windshield post to dodge, and no hump.

tremely astute package: very good looking, extremely low, and one which, though compact, seats 6 adults in comfort. The car is very well planned from bumper to bumper, from the inside to the outside. It truly was designed from a clean sheet of paper to do a job and to do it efficiently and properly. Hip room, leg room, head room—all are so nearly equal to what has become standard practice in U.S. cars that all excuses for having a "big" car become silly. Shoulder room (at 53.6 in.) is somewhat less than some of the 80-in.-wide (over all) cars of 1959, if that's any drawback. The Corvair's very nearly dead-flat floor makes the large 6-seater even sillier. The central tunnel, such as it is, measures about one in. high and 4 in. wide and is quite flat on top. It is primarily for the purpose of housing the necessary control rods and goes virtually unnoticed.

A second surprise offered by the Corvair is the general tenor of its noise level. When it goes by, the sound is like that of any other conventional car; the coffee grinder effect of most air-cooled engines is missing. (*continued*)

Needed: a Dauphine-like spare tire mounting underneath.

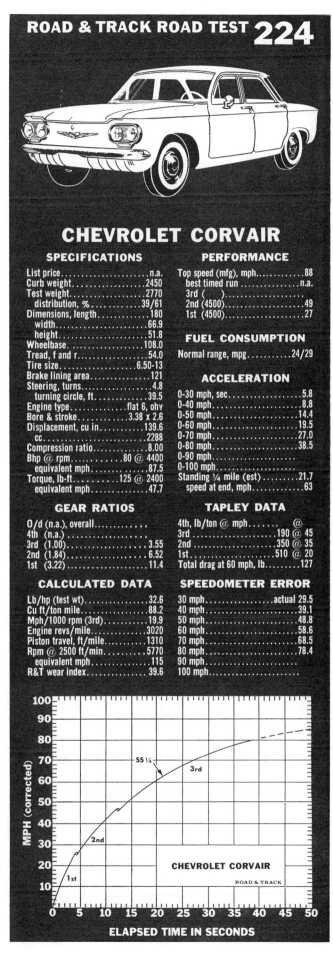

CHEVROLET CORVAIR

SPECIFICATIONS

List price	n.a.
Curb weight	2450
Test weight	2770
distribution, %	39/61
Dimensions, length	180
width	66.9
height	51.8
Wheelbase	108.0
Tread, f and r	54.0
Tire size	6.50-13
Brake lining area	121
Steering, turns	4.8
turning circle, ft	39.5
Engine type	flat 6, ohv
Bore & stroke	3.38 x 2.6
Displacement, cu in	139.6
cc	2288
Compression ratio	8.00
Bhp @ rpm	80 @ 4400
equivalent mph	87.5
Torque, lb-ft	125 @ 2400
equivalent mph	47.7

PERFORMANCE

Top speed (mfg), mph	88
best timed run	n.a.
3rd ( )	
2nd (4500)	49
1st (4500)	27

FUEL CONSUMPTION

Normal range, mpg	24/29

ACCELERATION

0-30 mph, sec	5.8
0-40 mph	8.8
0-50 mph	14.4
0-60 mph	19.5
0-70 mph	27.0
0-80 mph	38.5
0-90 mph	
0-100 mph	
Standing ¼ mile (est)	21.7
speed at end, mph	63

GEAR RATIOS

O/d (n.a.), overall	
4th (n.a.)	
3rd (1.00)	3.55
2nd (1.84)	6.52
1st (3.22)	11.4

TAPLEY DATA

4th, lb/ton @ mph	@
3rd	190 @ 45
2nd	350 @ 35
1st	510 @ 20
Total drag at 60 mph, lb	127

CALCULATED DATA

Lb/hp (test wt)	32.6
Cu ft/ton mile	88.2
Mph/1000 rpm (3rd)	19.9
Engine revs/mile	3020
Piston travel, ft/mile	1310
Rpm @ 2500 ft/min	5770
equivalent mph	115
R&T wear index	39.6

SPEEDOMETER ERROR

30 mph	actual 29.5
40 mph	39.1
50 mph	48.8
60 mph	58.6
70 mph	68.5
80 mph	78.4
90 mph	
100 mph	

(graph) CHEVROLET CORVAIR — ROAD & TRACK — MPH (corrected) vs ELAPSED TIME IN SECONDS, showing 1st, 2nd, 3rd and SS ¼ markers.

Gear noise, too, is conventional; there is none of the typical whine normally associated with rear-engined vehicles. Inside the car, the effect is quite unlike anything we have ever experienced. It almost seems that there is no engine, and the general effect is so quiet as to be almost uncanny. Obviously, Chevrolet engineers have taken full advantage of the engine location and have completely eliminated the usual air-cooled engine noise, as well as rear-engine gear whine.

The next driving impression is perhaps the most pertinent of all, considering the idle (and uninformed) gossip concerning the car's handling qualities. The steering is slower than we personally like (4.8 turns, lock to lock), but it is exceptionally light both during parking maneuvers and brisk cornering. It is not quite so light as a VW, perhaps, but nevertheless it is very satisfactory. In technical terms, and despite a rear-end weight of 60–62% of the total (dependent on load), the Corvair positively understeers under any and all conditions, up to the point of total loss of adhesion. This is accepted as the best design practice and only during the wildest possible cornering is the effect lost. Only then does the rear-end weight make itself felt, with the usual and expected result—on a total spin-out the rear end swings out into oversteer.

Several reports on the Corvair's handling qualities have incorrectly emphasized the importance of its special tires. The Corvair's tires are of an improved type to be used on all makes and types of 1960 cars. Corvair does use extra-wide-base rims (5.5 in.), and varying front and rear pressures are specified according to the load carried. The rated load capacity of a *standard* 6.50-13 tire is 835 lb when inflated at 24 psi. Since load capacity varies almost directly with pressure, the Corvair's specification of only 15 psi at the front is not under-inflation: the two tires at 15 psi are designed to carry only 62.5% of their rated load or 521 lb each. This is very close to their actual loading as tested.

All the gossip about this car's dangerous handling characteristics can be dismissed. Summarized, this is how it handles:
1) It definitely understeers at all times.
2) The understeer is less than usual and the car is much easier to "hold" in a high-speed bend.
3) The light understeer does not change with loading. It's the same whether the driver is alone or has 5 others with him.
4) On total spin-out (or loss of all adhesion) the Corvair's tail goes out and through the fence first. (A nose-heavy car will generally go through the fence nose-first.)

As for performance, we were frankly a little disappointed. For example, four trials from a standstill to 60 mph (corrected, by GM fifth-wheel-type electric speedometer) gave only 19.5 sec. We expected better acceleration times, and in this connection we can only say that the car falls well below the norm of ability when compared to others of similar power to weight ratio. This deficiency seems to be due primarily to the engine's inability to rev, with the specification of only a 3-speed gearbox as a secondary factor. The first 0–60 mph run took 22.5 sec and even in four subsequent tests (which averaged 19.5 sec) the engine seemed to fall off very rapidly at speeds of 25 in first gear and 45 mph in 2nd. Obviously economy and durability have taken precedence over high engine speeds, and it is a fact that at least one 1.6-liter imported sedan will trim the Corvair.

However, none of the imports can even come close to the Corvair's amazingly low wear factor of under 40 (engine rpm x piston travel per mile, divided by 100,000). In this connection we might also note that the usual conversion for computing safe cruising speed (2500 fpm piston speed) gives a theoretical 115 mph for the Corvair. Of course it won't go that fast even down the side of a mountain, but at least this means an absolutely unburstable powerplant. Top speed was given to us as an honest 88 mph; we believe it accurate. There was also no opportunity to check fuel consumption, but no driver need expect less than 25 mpg and careful, steady driving should give 30 mpg or even better.

Although the car looks extraordinarily small from outside, it is very easy to enter at both front and rear. Once inside, the space quickly dispels any early impression of a miniature car. The front seat, for example, has a hip room dimension of 57.8 in. An offset gear lever curves upward from the floor and is easy to operate, though a little restricted, with three adults in the front seat. The optional 2-speed automatic transmission avoids this difficulty but we didn't even try one. All controls are well placed, and certainly this is one of the easiest cars to literally jump into and take off. The clutch and brakes are light in action, and the brakes appear to be almost fade-proof because of ample provision for air circulation (9-in. drums, 13-in. wheels) and because braking effect is almost equally divided front to rear. The shift lever provides a feel that can best be described as similar to a Volkswagen. There's a little play, but gear engagement is quick and positive. Our car had a tendency to stumble a *(continued on page 17)*

Stubby at the rear as well as the front, the Corvair has a light roof structure. Bumper bracket is for mounting 5th wheel.

little just after a standing start, but the fault was our own—it needs revs a little higher than expected to avoid this when trying hard for best possible acceleration.

In connection with the brakes the Corvair's weight distribution works to excellent advantage, because rapid deceleration puts more weight on the front wheels. The net result is that total braking effort is very close to 50/50, front to rear.

A pistol grip handbrake of conventional type is used, but the release mechanism is of an entirely new kind which we think extremely clever and worthwhile. When the handbrake is applied, a dash knob pops out a distance of about 2 in. This gives visual indication that the brakes are applied. The knob is not pushed in to release the brakes, as you might expect. Instead the knob must first be pulled before it will release. This action was chosen to avoid accidentally releasing the brakes.

A technical description of the Corvair appears on earlier pages of this issue, but it is interesting to note that this is the first modern American car to offer these features:

1) Independent rear suspension
2) Transaxle
3) Aluminum engine
4) Air cooling (engine)
5) Rear mounting (engine)

The latter two items cause a problem which was not overlooked—the difficulty of getting sufficient heat into the car's interior. On the Corvair we find a specially designed heater located inside the forward luggage compartment. This burns gasoline and provides heat and/or defrosting almost instantly in any weather. Fuel consumption at maximum heat is about ¼ gal./hr, but on a normal winter day the rate is seldom higher than 1/10 gal./hr.

Another problem with rear-mounted engines is finding enough luggage space. The forward compartment has a volume of 9.8 cu ft, not including the spare wheel and tire. A well behind the rear seat back adds 4.5 cu ft, giving a total of 14.3. In addition, an optional folding rear seat is available. This provides 10.4 cu ft, including the well, inside the vehicle for a total capacity of 20.2 cu ft.

Other accessories are available including the usual de luxe trim items, seat covers and belts, radio and automatic transmission. But there's nothing else— no power brakes, power steering, power seats. This is wonderful and, for a low-priced car at least, a return to sanity. In fact, the Corvair is a sane, sensible, well designed car of a type we've been asking for for 10 years. Now that it's here, we think even Chevrolet will be pleasantly surprised by the demand for it—and be working overtime to supply cars.

Continued from page 13

into the act too, forcing GM to engage in radical cost-cutting to meet this unexpected competition.

Driven by the crankshaft through a flexible plate is the three-element torque converter of ten-inch diameter giving a torque multiplication at stall of 2.6 to 1. Its input and output shafts are right on line with the hypoid pinion of the final drive, which is straddle-mounted above the differential; the drive goes forward from the engine and converter *through* the hollow or "quill" pinion shaft into the planetary gearing within its aluminum case. A compound planetary gear set is controlled by clutches and bands to supply a 1.82 to 1 reduction for low range and reverse, and eventually sends the drive back-forward to the final drive pinion. It was found possible to make use of such parts as the front and rear oil pumps, governor and planetary gearing from the Chevy Powerglide and Turboglide boxes. Weight of the automatic installation is only 53 pounds more than that of the standard gearbox.

The same cast iron final drive casing and differential gearing is used for both gearboxes, and also houses the speedometer drive gearing which is machined on the pinion shaft. Traction is so outstandingly good (I couldn't drive an Impala over a soapy inclined plate that the Corvair didn't even know was there) that no limited-slip differential option is even contemplated. Final drive ratio is a standard 3.55 to 1, with 3.89 an option if the standard gearbox is used.

With the three-speed syncromesh box, a 9⅛-inch clutch is used, along standard Chevrolet lines except that no cushioning springs are fitted to the hub of the driven disc. Chevy engineers have designed the heavy-rimmed flywheel in such a way that it "damps out vibrations and radial deflections before they are transmitted to the drive line". So fundamental an approach is essential in this close-coupled system, which has no long propeller shaft to soak up random jolts.

SYNCHROMESH ON TWO

Gearing and synchro from the standard Chevy transmission are used in a very clever way for the Corvair box, housed in an aluminum case which keeps the unit's weight down to about 30 pounds. The

gearbox is placed forward of the final drive, and the internal gearing is placed just as it would be if the engine were in *front*; that is, the countershaft drive gear set and direct-drive clutch are in the front, and the second gear set with its clutch at the back, next to the hollow shaft driving the hypoid pinion. The drive from the

clutch reaches the front of the transmission via a long, slim shaft that extends all the way through the pinion shaft and through a hollow mainshaft. Besides allowing the use of many available parts, this layout has the advantage, claimable by no other rear-engined car, of a direct, locked-up top gear.

To exploit the utilitarian aspects of the Corvair the countershaft drive gear ratio was changed, unfortunately to lower the second and first gear ratios as compared with the standard Chevy box. This is unfortunate from the over-the-road performance angle, since as geared the Corvair is hard pressed to do 50 in second — a ratio in which a car of its power and weight should be able to do some serious passing work. Using the handy floor shift lever with only moderate vigor a 0-60 time of 17.5 seconds was obtained, with two aboard. This relates as expected to a time of 18.4 seconds for an automatic-equipped car, which makes the shift from low to high at about 45 mph and can be kicked down to low at any speed under 40. The automatic's dashboard control lever is accessible and easy to operate.

WAS TUCKER RIGHT?

Before this cycle in the development of the American car is complete, somebody is bound to protest either in print or in private that GM has stolen poor Preston Tucker blind. It's true that the general layout of the Corvair resembles the one that Mr. Tucker chose for his batch of 26 Franklin-powered, Cord-geared "production cars", but Tucker didn't even have the good sense to leave the Franklins air-cooled. There is probably more engineering in the rear swing arm of the Corvair than there was in the entire Tucker car (with apologies to the few good men whose names were intertwined with that promotion). Enough of that line of thought.

Like rated power, price is also up in the air as this is written, but it's well known that the Big Three are aiming at "sticker prices" of under $2000 for their smaller cars, which infers a base price on the order of $1750. If they can do this, it will be a real accomplishment and a credit to Detroit's production know-how. It will also strike right at the heart of the imported car market in the U.S., which is, after all, what Detroit is counting on. If this mammoth gamble is to pay off, it *must* cut into the buyer pool created by the imports; it cannot draw deeply from the manufacturers' existing lines. More than ever, the future for the imported car will be the very specialized vehicle.

Does SCI like the Corvair? Yes, with the important reservations quoted above. It is a veritable technical orgy, and a promising basis for a long and useful development life. But most of all it personifies what we feel is important in the field of automotive safety: its fine steering and stable braking restore to the driver of an American car the kind of honest and precise control over his vehicle that he has had to do without for some three fast-moving decades. It has live nerves and quick reflexes that are worth more than all the seat belts and crash pads in the world. In the bargain, it's sparkling fun to drive. —kl

ROAD TEST OF THE CORVAIR 'MONZA'

By Floyd Clymer

MY TEST of the new luxurious Monza Club Coupe, recently announced by Corvair, was from New York City to Los Angeles, a distance of 3,620 miles, which included a lot of off-road testing in the desert and mountain driving on the back roads of the Colorado Rockies. It is the longest road test I have ever done in the many years I have been testing cars.

I first tested the Corvair shortly after its introduction, and there is certainly a tremendous difference and much improvement in models now being produced. The Chevrolet Division of General Motors, through its General Manager, Engineer Ed Cole, certainly deserves a lot of credit for their foresight and determination to get away from a conventionally designed U.S. car. It is no secret that the first Corvairs had troubles and this must be expected of anything so radically new as the design Corvair pioneered. The first models had belt troubles, mileage troubles, carburetor icing troubles, and rear end bearing troubles. These problems, however, have all been licked and General Motors certainly did a fine job of rectifying the "bugs" that so often crop up in any new model.

After leaving New York City our first stop was at the national capital in Washington, D.C. By this time I was thoroughly convinced that the Corvair has superior handling qualities and roadability over any U.S. car, whether it be compact or conventional size. I compare its roadability to the best of the German sports car—the Porsche. Its ability to take the bumps at high speeds, as well as its maneuverability around curves, either sharp or gradual, is almost uncanny. The rear axles are sprung independently, which contributes greatly to Corvair's roadability.

Everyone has heard a lot of "hog wash" about the rear engine car being difficult to handle. It is true that most rear engine cars, due to the lightness of the front end, do have a tendency to oversteer. Corvair, however, seems to have overcome this problem. Under all driving conditions, few drivers would find any difficulty or difference in its handling because of the rear end location of the engine. Under normal conditions the driver has nothing but a feeling of safety and

The start was from the Park Sheraton Hotel in busy New York City.

The Monza in Washington, D. C.—the White House in the background.

Along the route there were many signs telling of Civil War history.

Civil War country in West Virginia.

18

The excellent Pennsylvania Turnpike.

Through the rolling hill and mountain country of West Virginia.

complete control of the car. The only time anyone might get into difficulty with a rear engine car is on gravel roads or ice or snow when he tries to drive too fast. The rear end of a rear engine car will break away faster on a sharp curve if taken at too fast a speed than a front engine car. On the other hand, the rear engine car has many highly desirable features. Due to the weight of the engine over the rear wheels, the car definitely has better traction and can go through snow or mud with less difficulty than a front engine car.

Another thing I found on Corvair is that a high average speed can be maintained across country without 90 or 100 mph maximum top speed. For many miles across the Midwest, where speed limits are 65 and 70 mph I averaged a mile a minute for long distances. In conventional cars, to maintain a 60 mph average, I have found 75 to 80 mph speeds must be maintained where possible.

The 6-cylinder, opposed, air-cooled engine has a displacement of 140 cu. in., with an 8.0:1 compression ratio, and a bore of 3.375" and a stroke of 2.60". The wheelbase is 108", with a height of 53.13", width of 66.9", and a total length of 180"—making it a fantastic car to handle in heavy traffic, to park in tight places, or small garages, or for backing out of narrow driveways.

The gasoline economy was quite good—in fact, much better than on the first Corvair I tested, shortly after they

were introduced. The 11-gallon tank capacity is ample and it was a pleasure to receive gas bills of from $2.10 to $3.20 for filling the tank and covering about the same distances as the larger and conventional car requiring from $3.75 to $6.00 for refueling. Regular gas is entirely satisfactory and this, of course, is another saving that a Corvair owner gets over the cost of operating a high compression engine conventional model.

The maximum top speed was 88-90 mph by speedometer, which checked out about 3% fast. On the Kansas Turnpike, where the speed limit is 80 mph, we averaged 72 mph between Kansas City and Wichita, Kansas.

Another thing I found about Corvair is that it handles exceptionally well on wet roads. For about half of the distance across the United States we drove in rain, and for many miles in almost a downpour around Washington, D.C. and across Missouri and Kansas. Also, I did considerable testing on back roads in the Colorado Rockies at altitudes above 11,000 feet. The car performed well even here. I also did a lot of testing on the winding back roads of the Mojave Desert, many of which were nothing more than trails, where the Corvair's traction in sand was excellent. I am sure that I got through some deep sand that I could not have made with a front engine car.

Coming across the Mojave Desert around Needles, the temperature was 112°. If anybody tells you that air cooling

Continued on next page

In scenic Virginia.

Corvair handled well through rain and over wet roads in Maryland.

At the summit of 9382 ft. La Veta Pass in Colorado.

Mule Shoe Lodge at the foot of La Veta Pass in Colorado.

doesn't work, they don't know what they are talking about, because it does. At no time did the car overheat. It should never overheat, of course, providing the fan belt, which operates the blower, is properly adjusted and functioning. Although Chevrolet cured their fan belt difficulties with deeper-grooved pulleys, the Corvair owner should carry an extra fan belt as a matter of precaution, just the same as a VW or Porsche owner does. Why?—if the blower ever stops operating you are "dead as a duck" in about three minutes after it happens.

The test car had automatic transmission, with a convenient shift lever located under the cowl operated by the right thumb and forefinger. The transmission is a 2-speed unit of torque converter type. At first I felt that Corvair should have a 3-speed automatic, but after driving the car I am convinced that it does not need it. A conventional 3-speed stick shift transmission is available; and also a power pack unit with a special 4-speed transmission is now available for the sports car enthusiast who loves to shift gears and wants a little more than ordinary zip.

Carrying the luggage under the front hood is quite a novelty, and the car handles even better with some weight under the hood than it does empty. The fold-down rear seat, which I was sure I wouldn't like, turned out to be a very pleasant surprise. A tremendous amount of luggage can be carried on this rear platform, and it is especially handy for luggage that one wants to load and remove quickly.

The engine starts quickly. The radio is about average, no better or no worse than many others, and there is quite a large glove compartment. The instrument panel is well located. The side rear view mirror is highly desirable. Doors open and close with a good solid feeling, and 3½ turns of the crank opens and closes the window. The hand brake emergency lever, which was changed from the first models, now operates quickly and efficiently. The handle should be about 2 inches further back, however, as it requires a long reach, especially for a short-armed person, to get hold of it. The brake pedal and throttle are well located in relation to each other—however, the brake pedal should be at least 2 or 3 inches wider.

Drivers of automatic transmission cars, in the future, are going to learn to brake with their left foot—one can certainly coordinate throttle and brake operation much better and with faster operation if the left foot is used for braking and the right foot for throttle only. I have been braking with my left foot ever since I started driving automobiles.

If there is any one feature that I am certainly enthused about in Corvair, it is the excellent quality of the front seats. Never have I driven in a car, regardless of price, with seats as comfortable for long distance driving. The springing is excellent, both in the seat and in the back, which is slightly wider on each of the edges than it is in the center. We covered 960 miles in one day during the test and that's a lot of miles in any car, whether it be compact or conventional

Over rough, rocky back roads in Colorado Corvair's excellent suspension system smoothed out the bumps.

The inspection station at the Arizona State line.

Colorful rock formations in New Mexico.

Seldom did Corvair need oil; and usually $2.50 to $3.00 filled the gas tank.

—and, due to the excellent seat, I was no more tired than driving 700 miles in a conventional type car.

Another nice feature of the rear engine location is the fact that there is no hump and no tunnel in the floor. It is flat, and positioned about four inches below the bottom of the door frame.

Anyone interested in a different kind of car should have a ride of at least 100 miles in a Corvair Monza. It will change their conception of motoring, for this is a fun-to-drive car. Try one some time and I think you will agree. ★

ECONOMY TEST — CORVAIR "MONZA"

New York City to Washington, D.C.
(heavy traffic) ....23.8 mpg
Washington, D.C. to Cincinnati, O.
(heavy rains most of way)....................22.6 mpg
Cincinnati to Kansas City, Mo.
(moderate traffic) ....24.9 mpg
Kansas City to Wichita Kan. (averaged 72
mph on 80 mph limit Turnpikes)........18.12 mpg.
Wichita to Pueblo, Colo. (rains and high
cross winds) ....21.7 mpg
Pueblo to Gallup, N.M. (over Rocky Mountains, last part long straight stretches......23.7 mpg
Gallup to Needles, Calif. (moderate traffic—
112° heat around Needles)...................23.5 mpg
Needles to Los Angeles (moderate traffic,
freeways from Barstow to L.A.)..............25.1 mpg
At steady 30 mph...................................31 mpg
Regular gas of several brands used on
coast-to-coast test

CORVAIR GENERAL SPECIFICATIONS

Wheelbase		108.0
Tread	Front	54.0
	Rear	54.0
Maximum	Length	180.0
Overall	Width	66.9
Dimensions	Height	51.3
Transmission	Manual	3-speed
	Automatic	Optional
Axle ratio	Manual	3.55:1 Standard; 3.89:1 Optional
	Automatic	3.55:1
Tire size		6.50 x 13-4 Ply
	Type, no. cyl., valve arr.	Horizontal opposed, 6 Cyl. OHV
	Fuel system (Carb. or ing.)	Carburetor
Engine	Bore and stroke	3.375 x 2.60
	Piston displ., cu. in.	140.0
	Std. compression ratio	8 to 1
	Max. bhp at engine rpm	80 hp at 4400 rpm

Entering California as seen through windshield.

Clymer comes out of a sandy river bed onto the main highway near Salton Sea. He reported the weight of the engine in the rear was a definite advantage.

CORVAIR AUTOMATIC TRANSMISSION

Eureka! An automatic that outperforms the stick shift

SINCE OUR ORIGINAL report on the Corvair, we have had the opportunity to drive both a stick shift and an automatic for a total of nearly 1000 miles. In November we said the Corvair was ". . . a very sound new car . . . sane, sensible, well designed. . ." Experience has brought no reason to change or revise this statement, though one or two minor faults have appeared.

For this test, we wanted an automatic transmission car so that we could show our readers, once again, how automatic transmissions never perform as well as good old fashioned stick shifts. Unfortunately, it didn't work out that way: the Powerglide car definitely outperforms the stick-shift, and not by a mere fractional-second margin. This is the first time we have ever found, or even heard of, such a situation. The following comparison shows the picture:

	AUTOMATIC	STICK-SHIFT
0-30	5.1	5.8
0-40	8.2	8.8
0-50	12.5	14.4
0-60	17.5	19.5
0-70	25.0	27.0
0-80	36.5	38.5

The actual car used, by the way, belongs to Bill Corey of our Tune-Up Clinic department and it had 1800 miles on the odometer. It was tuned to factory specifications on his chassis dynamometer in Pasadena and was absolutely stock, except for the dampers (about which more later).

What happened—why does the Powerglide perform so well? At first we were completely nonplused. We re-checked the speedometer calibrations but nothing was wrong there. (Note that the speedometer was slow by a small margin, which is very unusual.) Only after we had made the checks with the Tapley meter did we begin to understand.

Powerglide consists of a torque converter, a low gear and high. The Tapley pull reading in high gear is exactly 18% better in lb/ton than the stick-shift car with identical axle ratio. The stick-shift car is all unwound at only 50 mph in 2nd gear and the automatic shifts to high at about the same point. This is rather unusual because most automatics shift at a lower rpm than that which will give peak performance. Also, Powerglide includes a torque converter with a multiplication factor of 2.1 at stall. Therefore, the car benefits at take-off by having a higher numerical ratio. As speed goes up, the converter gradually ceases to multiply and the gear ratio (1.82) becomes virtually identical with the standard transmission's 1.84:1. When the Powerglide shifts into high, it is not the true direct drive we find in the stick shift. The converter gives, in comparison, an extra boost at the start, and another boost from 50 mph upward to the point where it finally becomes a fluid coupling and the drive is virtually direct.

This accounts for the extra performance. However, it also points up the fact that the Corvair badly needs another gear in the stick-shift model. Shifting from 2nd to high brings a very sad drop, and a 3rd gear between the present 2nd and high would transform the stick-shift

A compact transmission for a compact car. The Power-glide unit rides ahead of the differential.

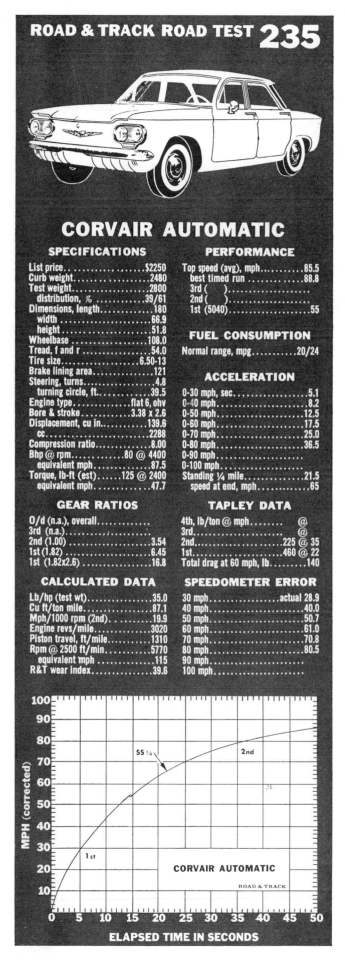

CORVAIR AUTOMATIC

SPECIFICATIONS		PERFORMANCE	
List price	$2250	Top speed (avg), mph	85.5
Curb weight	2480	best timed run	88.8
Test weight	2800	3rd ( )	
distribution, %	39/61	2nd ( )	
Dimensions, length	180	1st (5040)	55
width	66.9		
height	51.8	**FUEL CONSUMPTION**	
Wheelbase	108.0	Normal range, mpg	20/24
Tread, f and r	54.0		
Tire size	6.50-13		
Brake lining area	121	**ACCELERATION**	
Steering, turns	4.8	0-30 mph, sec	5.1
turning circle, ft	39.5	0-40 mph	8.2
Engine type	flat 6, ohv	0-50 mph	12.5
Bore & stroke	3.38 x 2.6	0-60 mph	17.5
Displacement, cu in	139.6	0-70 mph	25.0
cc	2288	0-80 mph	36.5
Compression ratio	8.00	0-90 mph	
Bhp @ rpm	80 @ 4400	0-100 mph	
equivalent mph	87.5	Standing ¼ mile	21.5
Torque, lb-ft (est)	125 @ 2400	speed at end, mph	65
equivalent mph	47.7		

GEAR RATIOS		TAPLEY DATA	
O/d (n.a.), overall		4th, lb/ton @ mph	@
3rd (n.a.)		3rd	@
2nd (1.00)	3.54	2nd	225 @ 35
1st (1.82)	6.45	1st	460 @ 22
1st (1.82x2.6)	16.8	Total drag at 60 mph, lb	140

CALCULATED DATA		SPEEDOMETER ERROR	
Lb/hp (test wt)	35.0	30 mph	actual 28.9
Cu ft/ton mile	87.1	40 mph	40.0
Mph/1000 rpm (2nd)	19.9	50 mph	50.7
Engine revs/mile	3020	60 mph	61.0
Piston travel, ft/mile	1310	70 mph	70.8
Rpm @ 2500 ft/min	5770	80 mph	80.5
equivalent mph	115	90 mph	
R&T wear index	39.6	100 mph	

[Graph: MPH (corrected) vs ELAPSED TIME IN SECONDS, showing acceleration curve for CORVAIR AUTOMATIC with 1st, 2nd gear and SS ¼ marked. ROAD & TRACK.]

car completely. Stirling Moss, during a recent visit in Los Angeles, was loaned a stick-shift Corvair and his remark pretty well sums up the situation: "First and 2nd gears feel like first and 2nd in a 5-speed box, 3rd (in the Corvair) feels like 5th!" Incidentally, during the performance checks, we tried holding the Powerglide in low range and over-revving the engine to about 5000 rpm or more before shifting to drive. Acceleration times did not improve one iota.

The timed top-speed runs were made with and against a fairly brisk wind, as can be noted by the difference between our mean or average speed and the best run. Thus, our mean speed of 85.5 mph could probably be improved upon under more favorable circumstances.

Fuel consumption seems to be the most frequent complaint among Corvair owners. Corey, who drives hard, reports a consistent 20/22 mpg and this agrees with some owners' reports, as well as our own testing. Chevrolet has really never advertised any definite figure, in case readers haven't noticed. Their ads say "25 to 40% better," not 25 to 40 mpg. However, we think most owners would not be complaining about 20/22 mpg if it were not for the fact that the fuel tank holds only 11 gal. We got 230 miles on one tank (10.4 gal. to refill, equivalent to 22.1 mpg), but the strain of watching the needle ride below E for 30 miles is unbearable and several people have mentioned to us that refueling every 200 miles is an all-fired nuisance. It certainly is. A larger tank is badly needed. There are many spots in the far West where filling stations are more than 200 miles apart.

Summarizing, the Corvair with automatic transmission will outperform the stick shift, primarily because the former allows quite high engine revolutions and the latter has a wide gap between 2nd and high with no torque converter to fill in. The biggest owner gripe is a 200-mile tank capacity and the best liked feature is undoubtedly the delightful ease of steering and handling. The suspension seems too soft under some conditions and Corey is experimenting with Koni dampers. We thought the improvement well worthwhile, but felt that the settings were not quite perfect (Konis are adjustable, and this test car seemed too stiff in front). Since Chevrolet will soon have a Corvair *sport* coupe and (reportedly) a high-performance kit, we hope they will also add a 4-speed transmission option. If they do offer 4-speeds, maybe we will let them call it a *sports* coupe.

Clean, uncluttered lines distinguish the Chevrolet Corvair. The windscreen wipers clear a large area of glass to give excellent outward visibility in rainy weather.

The luggage compartment of the Corvair is immediately above the Chevrolet "nameplate" located between the twin headlight installations.

The Corvair 700 de luxe Sedan

WHEN we took over the Corvair de luxe Sedan which forms the subject of this road test, a local Chevrolet representative remarked that the car was the finest thing ever to have been put out by General Motors. Because G.M. have been making cars rather longer than we have been testing them, we are unable to confirm or reject this view. We can, however, say that the Corvair is decidedly the most interesting of the G.M. line to have come our way.

To say at the outset that the Corvair's design marks a radical departure from established American practice is probably something of the understatement of the month. The car is fitted with an air-cooled engine at the rear with six horizontally-opposed pistons — the motor itself being built in unit with the transmission. Aluminium has been extensively used in the manufacture of this unit in the interests of saving weight. Suspension of the car is independent on all four wheels — the first time that this has been done in an American car in volume production — with swinging axles at the rear. Being the G.M. contender in the compact stakes, it is not surprising to find that by comparison with the Chevrolet Impala, for instance, the Corvair is shorter in length by at least two and a half feet. Or, to put it in another way, the car is a scant 20 inches longer than that other air-cooled, all-independent, horizontally-opposed phenomenon, the Volkswagen. In addition, although the Corvair's roof-line is below average shoulder height, the dimensions of the car are such as to seat six adults in comfort although, as we found, rear headroom for tall men is somewhat restricted.

Having mentioned the VW, it is not inapposite to point out certain design differences which exist between the two makes. On the VW, suspension is by torsion bar, on the Corvair, by coil. In the former, the fuel tank is located in the front luggage compartment above the front suspension assembly whereas in the latter, the tank is carried behind this assembly and under the rear section of the luggage compartment. Other obvious differences include, of course, the Corvair's 2,300 c.c. engine capacity and six cylinders, compared with the VW's 1,192 c.c. and four cylinders, the Corvair's horizontally mounted cooling fan compared with that which operates vertically in the VW, the Corvair's three-speed gearbox instead of the VW's four-speed unit, and the American car's greater carrying capacity, speed and so on. The cars are similar in design in that both have luggage compartments behind the rear seat and, as we have already stated, stowage space under the "bonnet". In the case of the Corvair, however, the available space

The interior of the Corvair, with the rear seat folded flat to increase the luggage stowing space. With this seat in its normal position, luggage is carried in a well between its back and the bulkhead which separates the motor from the passenger compartment.

can be considerably extended by folding down the squab of the back seat. With this seat so folded, the car is capable of carrying a great amount of luggage and for this reason, if for no other, it should prove to be popular with commercial travellers.

Folding down the rear seat squab can only be done with both rear doors open, by the way. As for the front luggage compartment: it did appear to us that the "well" is capable of holding a substantial quantity of baggage although suitcases, etc., are liable to some damage in that they have to rest against the spare wheel rim. (A set of six fitted suitcases for the Corvair sells for £17 10s. in fibre, £22 10s. in de luxe fibre, and £37 6s. in Vynide.)

Having referred to the VW, we must state that the major difference between these basically similar cars is the almost complete absence of interior noise in the Corvair — whether idling or at speed. While we have never been bothered by the allegedly high noise level in a VW, we did — possibly subconsciously — expect something of the familiar "flat-four" or, more accurately,

"flat-six" beat from behind the rear seat when we drove the Corvair for the first time. In practice, all that is heard when the car is at rest is a satisfying rumble and, at speed, what noises there are are confined to those engendered by wind or road surfaces, themselves never disturbing. The engine, in short, was no noisier than a conventional front-mounted six-cylinder water-cooled unit.

Contributing to a high standard of comfort is the interior finish — seats upholstered in genuine leather being complemented by a carpeted floor throughout the car. The starred *motif* of the plastic roof covering was not, we admit, entirely to our liking; the untrimmed edges of the carpet also striking something of a jarring note to the critical eye. But, all things considered, the Corvair's interior is furnished in good taste. There is one ashtray for the front seat passengers and two for those at the rear; arm rests are provided all round. No door pockets are provided to supplement the space

(continued overleaf)

Fleet looks are seen to advantage in the Corvair's side-view.

The flat-six motor of the Corvair — the three cylinders on each side being cooled by a belt-driven centrifugal fan. Air passes from the single filter to the two down-draught carburettors. Accessibility is excellent.

provided by the cubby-hole. A centrally located courtesy light burns when the front doors are opened.

The exterior finish in G.M.'s "Magic Mirror" acrylic lacquer ably complements the interior. Perhaps a small improvement could be made by a neater method of installing the leads which pass through the front luggage compartment to the headlights.

Instruments are confined to a fuel gauge, a speedometer, odometer calibrated in tenths, windscreen wiper, lights and ignition switches and a cigarette lighter. Two engine warning lights on the dashboard indicate, in the case of the one marked "Press. Temp", low oil pressure or excessive temperature of the engine oil and for that marked "Gen. Fan." generator not charging or fan not operating. (The driver's handbook provides implicit instructions to stop the car immediately if either of these lights glows!)

The windscreen washer unit (a standard fitting) is operated by pressing a button in the centre of the wiper control. This action also switches on the wiper motor and automatically allows a measured quantity of washing fluid to be squirted on to the windscreen. The wiper motor has, however, to be switched off manually. On the test car, it was found that the cigarette lighter had to be held in position before it heated up.

Other controls include self-cancelling direction indicators, a floor-mounted gear-lever, parking brake and the usual clutch, brake and accelerator pedals on the floor, all of which, together with the dip switch, being sensibly and conveniently placed. Reversing lights — a most useful feature — are a standard fitting.

(Now that more and more cars are being fitted with interior heaters, it is surprising to note that this feature is not available for Corvairs in this country. Although we did not drive the car in excessively cold weather, it did occur to us that without the benefit of the warmth from a front-mounted engine, or a heating unit, passengers might suffer from "cold feet" during South African winters up-country.)

Once on the road, and apart from the absence of noise which we have mentioned, the Corvair impresses by reason of being an easily controlled and — for a family car — a most stable machine. The steering is

exceptionally light although 4½ turns from lock-to-lock are perhaps rather high for a vehicle which can attain speeds on the open road in the region of the 90's. Although the car is exceptionally stable in most situations likely to be encountered by the average driver, trouble is possible if swift evasive action with low-geared steering has to be taken at really high speeds. Outward visibility from the driver's seat is good and the gear-change lever easy to shift upwards from gear to gear without fear of beating synchromesh. At first this lever seems to be rather too far to the right (only left-hand drive versions of the Corvair are to be sold in South Africa) but its use becomes second nature after a very short while. Synchromesh on first gear, as on the other two, would be welcome.

Driving the Corvair fast in gusty cross-winds did cause the car to wander from the "straight and narrow" and the driver had constantly to be making corrective use of the steering wheel. Cornering did not induce any untoward rolling and there was no tyre squeal. Only when a tight traffic island was taken fast did the rear wheels lose their adhesion and patter laterally across the road.

Rigid attention must be paid to maintaining correct tyre pressures — 15 lbs. at the front and 26 at the rear when cold, or 18 and 30 respectively when hot. Taking our lead from an overseas motoring journal, we purposely over-inflated the front tyres and under-inflated the rear by two pounds : under these conditions, the car was "all over the shop" with the rear end wagging badly when cornered. With normal pressures restored, there was a marked improvement. The car, in short, because it is produced for the family motorist and not the sports-car enthusiast, must be highly commended for its stability.

Comfortable ride

The ride, as far as comfort is concerned, is excellent over all surfaces. Bumps and corrugations are most effectively smoothed out by the suspension and all that is lacking are central arm rests to steady passengers who are thrown about somewhat from side to side when sharp turns are negotiated.

By comparison with other American sedans, the Corvair probably suffers in that its performance is not as vivid as might be expected. We recall, in this regard, that pick-up in top is not startling. At the same time, we must emphasise that the Corvair is no slouch : we managed to cover our 125-mile fuel consumption test route at an average of slightly more than 52 m.p.h. In this we were aided not only by the car's ability to maintain an indicated 90 m.p.h. without effort but by its excellent road-holding over twisting and winding gravelled passes. A maximum piston speed of some 1,900 feet a minute is indicative of long engine life and, in its manner of going, the Corvair seemed happy at any cruising speed short of the all-out maximum of 90 m.p.h.

We found that the car was dust-proof and water-proof although the engine compartment did acquire a coating of dust after some 50 miles of untarred surfaces. The speedometer proved to be about 4 m.p.h. fast at speeds above 60 and the odometer out to the extent of register-

SPECIFICATION

MAKE AND MODEL: Chevrolet Corvair 700 de luxe Sedan.
ENGINE: 6-cylinder, horizontally-opposed, air-cooled, rear mounted, twin-carburettor. Compression ratio, 8 to 1.
BORE AND STROKE: 3·375 x 2·6 ins. (86 x 66 mm.).
CUBIC CAPACITY: 140 cu. ins. (2,300 c.c.).
MAXIMUM HORSE-POWER: 80 b.h.p. (gross) at 4,400 r.p.m.
MAXIMUM TORQUE: 125 lb./ft. at 2,400 r.p.m.
ROAD SPEED IN DIRECT TOP GEAR AT 1,000 R.P.M.: 19·8 m.p.h.
ROAD SPEED IN OVERDRIVE TOP GEAR AT 1,000 R.P.M.: —
PISTON SPEED AT MAXIMUM HORSE-POWER: 1,910 ft./min.
BRAKES: Duo-servo hydraulic. Total lining area: 120·8 sq. ins.
SUSPENSION: (Front) Independent coil. (Rear) Independent coil.
TRANSMISSION: Three-speed manually controlled, floor gear-lever. Synchromesh on 2nd and top gears.

GEAR RATIOS:

1st	11·4	Top	3·55
2nd	6·5	O/D Top	—
3rd	—	Reverse	12·96
O/D 3rd	—		

FINAL DRIVE RATIO: 3·55 to 1. **TYRE SIZE:** 6·50 x 13.
LENGTH: 15 ft. **WIDTH:** 5 ft. 6·9 ins. **HEIGHT:** 4 ft. 3·3 ins.
GROUND CLEARANCE (laden): 6 ins. **STEERING:** Recirculating ball type, 4½ turns lock-to-lock. Turning circle: 39 ft. 6 ins.
FUEL TANK CAPACITY: 9·18 galls. **BOOT CAPACITY:** (see text).
LICENSING WEIGHT: 2,415 lbs. **WEIGHT AS TESTED:** 2,740 lbs.
ANNUAL LICENCE: £8. **PRICE AT S.A. COAST:** £1,101.
PRICE IN JOHANNESBURG: £1,126.
INTERIOR DIMENSIONS:
Width of front seat(s): 50 ins.
Driver's seat to clutch pedal: (Max.) 19 ins., (Min.) 15 ins.
*Front seat headroom: 4½ ins.
Width of rear seat: 51½ ins.
Rear seat kneeroom: (Max.) 12 ins., (Min.) 7½ ins.
*Rear seat headroom: 3 ins.
(*Measurements taken with 6 ft. man seated, no hat).

PERFORMANCE

ACCELERATION THROUGH GEARS:

M.P.H.	Secs.	M.P.H.	Secs.	M.P.H.	Secs.
0—30	5·1	0—60	17·6	0—90	—
0—40	8·2	0—70	25·0	0—100	—
0—50	11·9	0—80	37·1		

ACCELERATION IN HIGHER RATIOS IN SECONDS:

M.P.H.	Top	O/D Top	Second
20—40	8·8	—	5·1
30—50	9·1	—	6·3
40—60	9·7	—	—
50—70	11·8	—	—
60—80	17·2	—	—
70—90	—	—	—
80—100	—	—	—

STANDING QUARTER MILE: 20·5 secs.
REASONABLE MAXIMUM SPEEDS IN GEARS:
1st 30 m.p.h.
2nd 50 m.p.h.
3rd —
MAXIMUM SPEED IN TOP: 90 m.p.h.
MAXIMUM SPEED IN O/D TOP: —
MAXIMUM PULL IN GEARS:

	Lbs./Ton	Equivalent Gradient
1st	642	1 in 3·34
2nd	440	1 in 5
3rd	—	—
O/D 3rd	—	—
Top	247	1 in 9·1
O/D Top	—	—

BRAKING: Emergency stopping distance with car in neutral at 30 m.p.h.: 0·75 g. (equivalent to 40 ft. stopping distance).
FUEL CONSUMPTION: (Over CAR's 125-mile test route) 22·3 m.p.g. at an average of 52·1 m.p.h.
TEST CONDITIONS: Overcast, roads drying after rain, slight breeze, sea-level, 93-octane fuel.

ing 133 miles after 125 had been covered. In our view, a fuel consumption of more than 22 m.p.g. at an average of more than 50 m.p.h. is most commendable and, in the hands of the average owner, will certainly be considerably bettered.

Only in one aspect — braking ability — must we seriously criticise the Corvair which we road-tested. In fairness, it must be stated that no Corvair is meant to be accelerated from rest to 60, 70 and 80, brought to a rapid halt, turned and the process repeated again and again as quickly as possible. Thus, the slewing to right and left which we encountered during the compilation of performance figures cannot be regarded as something which an average owner is likely to encounter. However, even with the brakes cool, the best retardation figure which we could gain was 0.75 g — and this after a real emergency stop with both feet hard on the brake pedal. We have read overseas reports testifying to the "stable braking" of the Corvair and thus can only assume that the brakes of the test car needed adjustment.

(Lest there be a howl of disbelief from the sceptics on the score of a maximum of 90 m.p.h., we hasten to assure our readers that the car tested was capable of a genuine maximum of 90. The speedometer, under avourable conditions, indicated 100 m.p.h. (the avourable conditions including a longish down-hill before reaching a straight of three miles). Over four runs of a stretch of national road an indicated 96 m.p.h. was attained; as an indicated 90 m.p.h. was timed by stop watch to be an actual 86, we feel justified in giving the car a maximum of 90 m.p.h.)

To conclude, we pass on a story about the Corvair taken from the publication *General Motors World*. During its development, test drivers were told not to reveal its Chevrolet origins. When asked what make it was, they countered by asking the questioner "What do you think?" and agreed with whatever he said. On one occasion, a road crew were unable to give an evasive answer. A driver pulled up beside a Corvair, grinned across and asked : "Make it yourself?"

We hasten to assure readers that there is nothing home-made about the Corvair which, as our salesman friend remarked, is probably the best thing yet put out by General Motors. ●

The spare wheel is carried in the forward luggage compartment between the front wheel arches, suitcases being placed ahead of the spare wheel.

CORVAIR 4·SPEED

A 3-speed Corvair re-tested after installation of 4-speed gearbox

IT IS WELL KNOWN THAT Chevrolet's Corvair will offer an all-synchromesh 4-speed transmission as an option for 1961. Since no 1961 models will be shown until October 3, we were fortunate in being able to "borrow" a 4-speed assembly some two months early and have it installed on our publisher's own Corvair sedan.

This car had just over 10,000 miles on the odometer and, prior to the change-over, was given a complete road test with its original 3-speed transmission. In addition, we also re-tested an automatic transmission Corvair which had 5000 miles on the odometer.

A quick summary of the huge amount of data thus accumulated shows the following:

1. The 4-speed option definitely is the best performer of the three.
2. The 3-speed car gave better performance than our original test published a year ago.
3. The automatic transmission car duplicated exactly our previously published data (R&T, February 1960).

What the data and figures do not show is the tremendous improvement in the fun aspect of the Corvair, when 4 speeds are available. The new ratios are not ideal for best-possible performance but, nevertheless, they give the car an entirely new character. This was a standard 80-bhp model and the limiting speed in each gear (see data panel) is severely inhibited by the hydraulic valve lifters. For example, it is possible to just touch an indicated 44 mph in 2nd gear (equivalent to an actual 42 mph at 5000 rpm), but when this speed is attained the engine literally quits and feels as though it is slowing down. For our test data we used shift points equivalent to 4800 rpm and the

actual speeds were 26, 40 and 66 mph, respectively, in each gear. The "new" 2nd gear is obviously too "low" (note the short spurt on the acceleration chart), but it is very useful in traffic and low enough to permit starting up without strain on the clutch or engine. Third gear is the one that is most appreciated. A standard 3-speed Corvair has a terrible gap between 2nd and 3rd, and 3rd (high) is quite inadequate at speeds below 30 mph. The new 3rd gear is perfect for town puttering or turning corners at moderate speed. And it is high enough to be extremely useful on the highway—as for example, when baulked down to 50 mph, it can be used as a passing gear to get quickly back up to 60 or even 65 mph. All the gears are extremely quiet, which is more than can be said for the 3-speed. This quietness, combined with very effective synchronizers, the extra zip and the normal silence of the flat-6 engine makes the new combination a genuine pleasure to drive.

Corvair owners who subscribe to the traditional Chevrolet vs Ford rivalry will be pleased to note that the 4-speed, 80-bhp model is at last a Falcon-eater, by a small but definite margin.

In re-evaluating the performance of the 3-speed Corvair, we found that more vigorous techniques produced better times than recorded in our first test, prior to the public announcement on the GM proving grounds. Tapley readings were also slightly better. Some reports give this model a 0-60 mph time as low as 21 sec. We got 19.5 sec originally, but repeated tests of the car shown here gave a consistent figure of 17.8 sec, time after time, and with due allowance for speedometer error. As with the 4-speed tests, we used 4800 rpm as a rev limit, equivalent to 29 mph in first, 52 mph in 2nd. Shifting technique was vigorous, but not brutal (i.e., no speed-shifts).

For comparison purposes, here is a summary of the data; times being in seconds, Tapley pull in lb/ton:

Test	4-speed	3-speed	automatic
0-30	4.3	5.2	5.1
0-40	7.0	7.8	8.2
0-50	11.2	12.3	12.5
0.60	16.4	17.8	17.5
0-70	23.5	25.0	25.0
0-80	32.0	34.0	36.5
SS1/4	20.6	21.1	21.5
Tapley			
4th	205	n.a.	n.a.
3rd	295	205	n.a.
2nd	450	350	225
1st	540	520	460

From these results and from the accompanying acceleration plots, it is easy to see that the automatic and the 3-speed are very evenly matched, while the 4-speed model walks away from them both by a good margin. Naturally, the new optional 95-bhp engine will do even better and we understand that for 1961 the axle ratio will be increased from 3.54 to 3.89 when this engine is ordered. This will give even more performance, for the 95-bhp engine has a modified valve mechanism to permit crankshaft speeds approaching 6000 rpm.

Our only real objection to the 4-speed is that though first gear is synchronized, it is so low that it is seldom used or needed. Thus, 2nd gear becomes the normal starting gear and first is an emergency low. This prostitution of a 4-speed gearbox is exactly what killed the popularity of 4-speeds forward, which showed a brief sign of resurgence in popularity in 1930 and 1931 (used by Graham-Paige, Stutz, Durant, Chrysler and Franklin).

Our greatest praise for the new box goes for the improved performance it offers, the extreme quietness of the gears, and the enhanced fun of driving the car when so equipped.

As for the car itself, sales have not been quite up to expectations, primarily because of a very vicious rumor campaign. Stories of fan belts jumping appear to be greatly exaggerated, for we have heard this tale hundreds of times, but have yet to find even one owner who actually had it happen. (We *did* find one owner who had had a broken belt.) There were troubles with carburetor icing on the early cars and this was corrected on all cars sold, at no cost to the owners. There is no doubt also that the public has been a little cautious about buying such a "radical" car in its first year, but the same was true of the Volkswagen when it was first imported. An air-cooled car makes a lot of sense in a country with such extremes of temperature as obtain in North America, particularly as the car gets older. Anyone who has tried to hold antifreeze in an older car will understand why. Likewise, car owners who have experienced the well known engine cooling difficulties encountered on mountainous roads, particularly in the Southwest part of the U.S., will appreciate the freedom from worry offered by air-cooling.

Our own Corvair, purchased in September, has given no serious problems, with the exception of an electric windshield wiper motor failure and dropping the fast idle mechanism into the cooling fan (an awful racket, but no harm done). Certain accessories (including windshield washers, arm rests, and right hand sun visor) were impossible to get until early in 1960. But other than that the car has given safe, comfortable, economical service and Corvair resale values should hold up well. The true test of this car's public acceptance will come during its 2nd and 3rd year of production—and we think the air-cooling feature alone is enough to warrant a slight extra premium in first cost.

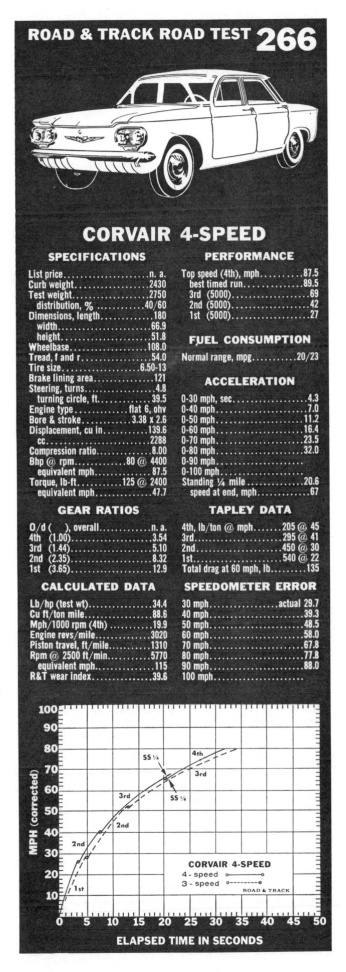

CORVAIR 4-SPEED

SPECIFICATIONS

List price	n. a.
Curb weight	2430
Test weight	2750
distribution, %	40/60
Dimensions, length	180
width	66.9
height	51.8
Wheelbase	108.0
Tread, f and r	54.0
Tire size	6.50-13
Brake lining area	121
Steering, turns	4.8
turning circle, ft	39.5
Engine type	flat 6, ohv
Bore & stroke	3.38 x 2.6
Displacement, cu in	139.6
cc	2288
Compression ratio	8.00
Bhp @ rpm	80 @ 4400
equivalent mph	87.5
Torque, lb-ft	125 @ 2400
equivalent mph	47.7

PERFORMANCE

Top speed (4th), mph	87.5
best timed run	89.5
3rd (5000)	69
2nd (5000)	42
1st (5000)	27

FUEL CONSUMPTION

Normal range, mpg	20/23

ACCELERATION

0-30 mph, sec	4.3
0-40 mph	7.0
0-50 mph	11.2
0-60 mph	16.4
0-70 mph	23.5
0-80 mph	32.0
0-90 mph	
0-100 mph	
Standing ¼ mile	20.6
speed at end, mph	67

GEAR RATIOS

O/d ( ), overall		n. a.
4th (1.00)		3.54
3rd (1.44)		5.10
2nd (2.35)		8.32
1st (3.65)		12.9

TAPLEY DATA

4th, lb/ton @ mph	205 @ 45
3rd	295 @ 41
2nd	450 @ 30
1st	540 @ 22
Total drag at 60 mph, lb	135

CALCULATED DATA

Lb/hp (test wt)	34.4
Cu ft/ton mile	88.6
Mph/1000 rpm (4th)	19.9
Engine revs/mile	3020
Piston travel, ft/mile	1310
Rpm @ 2500 ft/min	5770
equivalent mph	115
R&T wear index	39.6

SPEEDOMETER ERROR

30 mph	actual 29.7
40 mph	39.3
50 mph	48.5
60 mph	58.0
70 mph	67.8
80 mph	77.8
90 mph	88.0
100 mph	

CORVAIR 4-SPEED
4-speed
3-speed
ROAD & TRACK

MPH (corrected) vs ELAPSED TIME IN SECONDS

by JERRY TITUS

Chevrolet's otherwise admirable compact car can be treacherous in a corner.
Here, for the first time, are the real reasons—plus a number of possible solutions

WHY DOESN'T THE CORVAIR HANDLE?

THE BALLOTS are in, and the vote is virtually unanimous. Automotive experts—wtih one or two unconvincing exceptions—all agree that the Corvair is an "oversteer" vehicle. Actually, the term is extremely kind, as under certain conditions the tail end "comes out" like a shot.

Except for this one trait, the Corvair is a first-class and very likeable car. If it weren't, we'd write the whole thing off as a fumble and not bother to analyze one idiosyncracy. We still hesitate to take a manufacturer to task for the design of his product, but under the circumstances we feel that a discussion of the Corvair's handling will be of definite value to our readers. Further, in view of the prevalent rear-engine controversy, clarification of this one peculiarity should prove enlightening.

The rather weird way in which the car "wagged its tail" —as described in last issue's test—set us to thinking. The test vehicle's overall balance was otherwise fine; there was no other indication that the weight distribution between front and rear might be a problem. The tail moved outward only after a corner was entered at well above "normal" velocity.

Our suspicions were confirmed by a photo taken of a Corvair being pressed hard into a turn. The picture showed clearly that both tire roll-under and positive camber of the "outside" rear wheel were excessive. Further, the body was high above the wheel.

From this evidence we derived a rather complicated theory. The next step was to procure another test car, set out to prove or disprove the hypothesis, and if possible come up with a solution. It soon became apparent that the second car was even more of an oversteer vehicle than the first had been. On this one, the tail-wagging occurred during cornering *within* the limits of normal velocity. We began adding important facts to our data.

To insure the accuracy of our test, we selected a smooth, high-speed, high-adhesion corner, setting 55 *mph* as the velocity to be maintained through it. This proved ample to bring the tail out considerably. Our first run was made with only one person aboard, and with factory-recommended tire pressures. We had our hands full maintaining control. Instead of the tail *staying* out, as you'd normally expect, it would grab a new bite as soon as we corrected, then repeat the pattern, so that three distinct corrections were required before the turn was negotiated. This was not exactly a happy situation!

After making several of these runs to eliminate the possibility that entering the corner differently might yield better results we undertook a series of attempts to correct the problem. Before explaining the results of these, however, it would be best to clarify exactly what we had decided the problem was.

The Corvair's suspension appears—at first—to be a fully independent design. In effect, though, it's actually a swing axle. For our purposes here, the latter design has two major characteristics. First, swing axle camber *must* change with axle movement. Second, centrifugal forces acting upon the sprung mass *must* pass through the same horizontal plane as that of the inner U-joint of the half-shaft. Looking at the latter point conversely, cornering forces on the rear wheel have to exert themselves at this same pivot point. Further, with a swing axle, slight positive camber is desirable to obtain maximum tire life, and this feature Chevy has included.

None of this is detrimental in itself. The hitch lies in the *roll center,* which appears to be only slightly above the inner axle centers. As a matter of fact, almost all of the vehicle's major weight masses—engine, transmission, differential, seats and gas tank—are located about the same distance above the ground. With all this in mind, let's examine what seems to happen when the Corvair goes into a corner.

As centrifugal loading builds up, slight tire roll-under is incurred by the rear wheel on the outside of the turn. In a more conventional car, some vertical weight-loading would take place simultaneously, as the body and chassis started to lean or pivot. But this doesn't happen in the Corvair because of that low roll center—and positive wheel camber quickly induces more severe roll-under.

Up to a certain point, the latter phenomenon gives the tire a good bite, so that the car holds well at moderate velocities. As centrifugal loading increases, however, the roll-under becomes excessive and reduces the effective tire contact area until the rubber shears and the tail goes out all of a sudden.

This tail effect would eventually happen to a "normal" sedan too, but by that time the chassis would have rolled weight onto the wheel, forcing it to bite harder and make the break-away more gradual.

Why is this vertical weight-loading missing from the softly sprung and "under-shocked" Corvair? For the answer, go back to where the tire roll-under is first incurred. The resistance forces are transferred back into the chassis at hub level, through transverse arms in the same plane. As the roll-under *increases,* the distance from the axle center to the ground *decreases* and the anchor point of the arms moves *above* the hub center. The axle and the arms become, in effect, a lever which prevents chassis-roll

DURING THE FIRST SERIES OF RUNS, RECOMMENDED TIRE PRESSURES WERE USED. NOTE EXCESSIVE CAMBER, AND THE TAIL 'WAY OUT.

WITH FRONT TIRE PRESSURE RAISED TO 26 POUNDS, OVERSTEER WAS STILL CONSIDERABLE BUT MORE CONTROLLABLE THAN BEFORE.

WITH HIGHER FRONT TIRE PRESSURES AND ALMOST 200 POUNDS OF WEIGHT DIRECTLY BEHIND DRIVER, CAR HELD ITS LINE WELL.

onto the suspension. What happens instead is quite the reverse: with the weight mass concentrated on this inner pivot point, the chassis can move in only one direction—upward!

The results are far from kosher, since a rear-engined car can be practical only if the design utilizes the extra tail weight to hold the rear wheels on the ground. It must be remembered, further, that under side load the outside wheel is assuming more and more of a positive camber angle. One of the usual advantages of a swing axle is to promote *negative* camber under load and thus provide full tread contact on the outside wheel. The Corvair's geometry doesn't do this.

In trying to prove or disprove our theory and at the same time find a solution to the problem, we followed the suggestion of a Chevy engineering representative and increased the front tire pressure from the normal 15 pounds to 26 pounds. This, we were told, was supposed to improve handling, although the only way it could do so would be by increasing the slip angle of the front to compensate for the wild one in the rear. It did help a little, making the break-away less violent, but it was far from a complete answer.

After playing with the pressures of both front and rear tires, we started working on weights: adding passengers, moving them to different positions, placing a 100-pound sack of sand in the front. Some things helped a little, others didn't. One experiment, and only one, netted any real improvement—increasing the weight *in the rear!* That's right, we took a car that already has 60% of its weight in the rear, added more there, and came up with an almost 40% increase in controllability through corners. We don't blame you for asking, "How come?"

No, the weight in itself wasn't helping the cornering. But placing it over the outside rear wheel changed the angle of the "swing axle" to one that was slightly *uphill*, running from the inner pivot out to the wheel hub. Camber became just a hair negative instead of excessively positive. With this setup, lateral forces no longer "locked" the suspension, and tread contact was good. The result: a smooth, fast, and controllable cornering effect.

So, with the cause established, what can be done in the way of correction? Several things. None of them will be as effective as would the adoption of a new design similar to the low-pivot "swing axle" of the Mercedes 300SL roadster, but they'll all be a lot less expensive.

First, installing high-strength, high-adhesion tires such as Michelin X on the rear wheels would improve tread bite with no other changes. More effective, however, would be a de-cambering job. As this would lower the rear and move more weight in that direction, the front should be lowered to match. Sure, tires would wear faster but we'd rather have the improved handling. Wouldn't you?

Finally, there's another way: extend the support arms downward about an inch and a half at the point where they bolt to the frame. This could be accomplished with blocks and longer mounting bolts. Since lowering the pivots would also extend the springs, the latter would have to be shimmed almost an inch to bring the chassis back up to its original level. Such a modification would lower the pivot point without affecting the roll center, and would also produce a slight negative camber in the rear wheels.

As a sidelight, let's consider another phase of Corvair handling: in the wet. As might be imagined, the car oversteers on slick surfaces. But the effect isn't as violent as

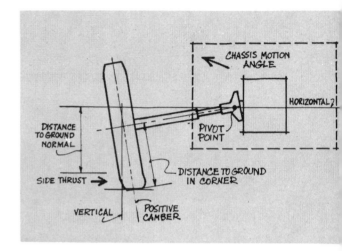

you'd expect after cornering on a dry surface. We didn't have a chance to experiment extensively under wet conditions, but a slight reduction in rear tire pressure should make the car a *good* handler in the rain. Again, Michelin X tires would do much to make the rear end stick.

To sum it up, we think the Corvair is a fine little car and wouldn't mind owning one personally, but we feel that correction of the oversteer tendency is essential if fast cornering is contemplated. It will be interesting to see what factory corrections are forthcoming. It's possible some will appear on the units entered in the compact car race at Sebring. Keep your eyes on them! ●

VISUAL PROOF THAT THE CORVAIR CAN BE A TROUBLEMAKER WHEN CORNERED AT HIGH SPEEDS EVEN ON GOOD SURFACES!

WHEN THE CORVAIR was first introduced, we tagged it as a fun-type car that was a happy wedding of the best in both the "minis" and the whales. To be sure, we griped about the handling but it was, after all, supposed to be an economy sedan so it was rather easy to rationalize that the ability to be flung around corners wasn't a design consideration. This year, however, evolution brings us the Monza — power-packed to 94 horses and sporting a four-cog transmission. In coupe form, with bucket seats, it has all the appearances of a Gran Tourismo machine. In both looks and performance, it's even more fun to drive than before, but stability and adhesion are still in the forget-it category.

We trip-tested the Monza, found it very comfortable, with adequate power for normal road usage, slightly weak in gradeability. Accurate checks on gas mileage gave us a 27.9 mpg figure that included both town and country driving (and none of it feather-footed). Susceptible to crosswinds, the car demanded an attentive hand on the light steering — its single annoying trait. Used spar-

Changed from a baby to a bear by the addition of a McCulloch blower, the trim Monza blasts down Riverside's back straight, Andy Granatelli driving.

Hot and Cold Running Monzas

ingly, the brakes worked well, weatherproofing was well above average.

Final conclusions: very pleasant and practical. To back this up, our private poll of automotive writers and experts shows that more already own (and even more *want* to own) Monzas than any make of car on the market. Sure, their gripes were identical to ours, but the overall features were still too great to resist. Consequently, there have been many varied attempts and experiments to, first, correct the miserable handling; second, get some more urge out of the powerplant. The latter we've seen accomplished. While difficult to work on, the Corvair powerplant has quite a bit of potential. Then into our test picture came a man named Granatelli. This ex-Chicago speed merchant (well-known for his successful midgets, roadsters and stock cars) now heads Paxton Products, the outfit that markets McCulloch superchargers and fabricates the kits for them. Andy's pet is the Corvair Monza and how would we like to drive one that had clocked 148 mph? Our affirmative answer was given with mixed emotions. First, though we knew McC blowers really make a difference, that kind of velocity seemed pretty unlikely. Second, if it did go that fast we wondered if we'd have the courage to

ROAD TEST / 6-61

Probably possessing the best lines out of Detroit since the '53 Stude, Chevy's Monza coupe is making inroads among many discerning sports-car admirers.

To get accurate readings on the blown Monza's velocity we borrowed Motor Life's fifth-wheel, electric speedometer.

Hot and Cold Running Monzas

drive it. After all, if it was a handful at 90 mph, what would it be at race-car velocities? Our test was delayed one day while Andy made a monumental purchase — the two Novi Indy cars! Of this he was justifiably proud and excited. He showed up at Riverside the next day, his head still buzzing with plans and ideas for these fabulous machines.

Except for a tach and a small accessory instrument panel which contained temperature and manifold pressure gauges, the super-hot Monza appeared identical to the stock one. The slight blower whistle and a modified exhaust system didn't make it *sound* stock, but certainly belied the amount of urge hiding under the rear deck. Since the tests we were going to perform would be severe, Granatelli removed the exhaust system entirely to better keep track of what was going on with each cylinder. The resultant sound was like nothing ever associated with Corvair.

The McCulloch kit is mostly bolt-on, with only a couple of holes to drill. Blower drive is direct from the crank pulley, crosses the belt into a figure-8 and twists it 180 degrees. We did some quiet head-shaking over this lash-up, but the belt stayed on during our violent tests and showed no signs of wear. The two stock carburetors and manifolds are replaced with a single, dual-throat unit that's pre-jetted and adjusted at the Paxton factory and included in the kit. A cast-aluminum box completely surrounds the carburetor and eliminates the need for pressurizing the latter. In all it seems to be a pretty fool-proof kit and one that requires minimal skill for installation.

Very little had been altered on the engine. It was disassembled and the pistons loosened an additional 0.003 inches in the bores and heavy-duty valve springs and caps installed. A Schieffer flywheel, clutch disc, and pressure plate were installed, as Andy stated, for reliability. The stock components aren't up to the extra power *and* the 7000-rpm red-line now used.

The performance was slightly sensational. We had to shut off at the end of the Riverside straight doing 129 mph, dragging 250 pounds of Granatelli and a fifth wheel along. This car has clocked over 142 mph at both Bonneville and Salton Sea, but there wasn't room enough at Riverside to get there. To aid handling, the rear of the Monza had been decambered about two degrees. This helped a lot but still was far from adequate to cope with cornering at really healthy speeds. The brakes, too, gave up the ghost after the first hard application. Our acceleration times weren't up to what had been previously garnered with this machine, so we fi-

nally tossed Andy out and installed a lighter timer, then got within three-tenths of what was claimed for it.

Nothing shook loose during our test and the pancake engine stayed healthy from beginning to end. The exhaust system was bolted back on and Andy drove away. To say we were impressed was putting it mildly. With some good roadability equipment installed, we'd like very much to take it GT racing and see how many Ferraris it would gobble. Meanwhile, this particular car is happily engaged in blowing off everything from full-sized Chevies to 300SL's on quarter-mile strips in the area. Already in the building stage is a blown-Corvair-powered sports car that will be going battle on road circuits before the season is over.

Jerry Titus

Monza's well-tailored interior is both comfortable and attractive, controls located properly. We disliked high-ratio, light steering.

McCulloch supercharger pivots on spring-loaded hinge, is driven by belt from crankshaft pulley. Troublesome, former vari-speed pulley has been changed on newest models. Drive belt twists and crosses, but stayed on during hard tests.

Stock layout of the Monza engine compartment includes dual carburetor. These are connected by a balance-tube to eliminate adjustment problems. Linkage is designed to float so heat-expansion will not change settings. Spare tire, right.

Single carburetor replaces duals in the blower installation, is placed in pressure-tight box to be entirely balanced. The blower inlet duct is attached to hood louvers, gets cool air.

TEST DATA

VEHICLE	...............Corvair	MODEL	...............Monza
PRICE (as tested)	..........$2820.	OPTIONS	...R&H, 4-Spd. Trans., engine, w/w tires, etc.

ENGINE:
Type: ....,........6-cylinder, flat-opposed, air-cooled, 4-cycle
Head: ....Removable, light alloy
Valves: ....OHV, push-rod-rocker actuated
Max. bhp ....98 @ 4600 rpms
Max. Torque ....132 lbs.-ft. @ 2300 rpms
Bore ....3.437 in. 56.32 mm.
Stroke ....2.6 in. 41.60 mm.
Displacement ....145 cu. in. 2377 cc.
Compression Ratio ....8 to 1
Induction System: ....Two Rochester Model-H single-throat carburetors, balance-tube
Exhaust System: ....four-into-two mufflers
Electrical System: ....12-volt, single Delco distributor

CLUTCH: ...Single disc, conventional pressure plate
Diameter: ....10 in.
Actuation: ....cable

DIFFERENTIAL: Transaxle, spiral-bevel
Ratio: ....3.55 to 1
Drive Axles (type): ..Open half-shafts, 2 joints

TRANSMISSION: .....Four-speed, full synchromesh
Ratios: 1st ....3.65 to 1
2nd ....2.35 to 1
3rd ....1.44 to 1
4th ....1.0 to 1

STEERING:
Turns Lock to Lock: 4.5
Turn Circle: ....39 ft.

CHASSIS:
Frame: ....Vestigal, removable units
Body: ....Welded, unit-construction
Front Suspension: ....Unequal control arms, coil springs
Rear Suspension: ....Modified Swing-axle, coil springs
Tire Size & Type: ....6.50 x 13 tubeless

WEIGHTS AND MEASURES:
Wheelbase:	................108 in.	Ground Clearance ....6.5 in.
Front Track:	..............54 in.	Curb Weight ....2520 lbs.
Rear Track:	..............54 in.	Test Weight ....2830 lbs.
Overall Height	..........51.3 in.	Crankcase ....4 qts.
Overall Width	...........66.4 in.	Cooling System ....——
Overall Length	..........180.0 in.	Gas Tank ....14 gals.

PERFORMANCE: Stock 98-hp engine
0-30	....................4.2 sec.	0-70	...............19 sec.
0-40	....................6.1 sec.	0-80	...............24 sec.
0-50	....................9.3 sec.	0-90	..............—— sec.
0-60	...................13.5 sec.	0-100	..............—— sec.

Standing ¼ mile 19.8 sec. @ 68 mph. Top Speed (av. two-way run) 90.5 mph

Speed Error	30	40	50	60	70	80	90
Actual	29	39	50	59	69	78	88

Fuel Consumption Test: .....19 mpg
Average ....24 mpg

PERFORMANCE: Supercharged Engine
0-30	....................2.8 sec.	0-70	...............11.0 sec.
0-40	....................4.5 sec.	0-80	...............13.9 sec.
0-50	....................6.1 sec.	0-90	...............16.5 sec.
0-60	....................7.8 sec.	0-100	...............21.9 sec.

Standing ¼ mile 16.5 sec. @ 90 mph. Top Speed (av. two-way run) 142 mph
Speed Ranges in gears:
1st ....0 to 22 mph   3rd ....28 to 58 mph
2nd ....12 to 40 mph   4th ....45 to top mph
Brake Test: 70.2 Average % G. over 8 stops.
Fade encountered on 5th stop.

REFERENCE FACTORS:
Bhp. per Cubic Inch 675
Lbs. per bhp 25.7
Piston Speed @ Peak rpm ....2326.6 ft./sec.

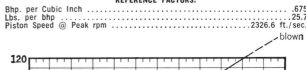

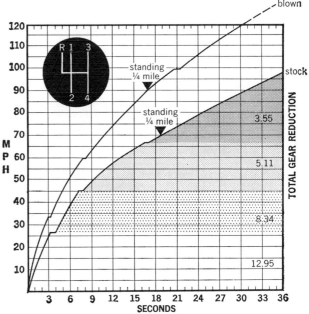

CORVAIR AMONG COCONUTS

Chev's rear-engined compact hasn't yet reached Australia, but you can buy it in New Guinea. Steve Simpson drove one in Rabaul — here's his report

SUN-STEWED, volcano-encircled Rabaul, once the leaping-off point for Japanese forces intent on invading Australia, today provides an interesting cross-section of motordom.

Only two cars—Australia's Holden (£1300) and Japan's Datsun (£795) —are merchandised here with any kind of sales organisation; yet almost every make of motor vehicle under the sun can be bought locally or imported to order.

With its huge price advantage, the beautifully finished Datsun Bluebird is making a strong bid for the best-seller position — and it's rugged enough to deal with even the most primitive Territory road.

In the higher-price brackets the various Mercedes-Benz models, with savings ranging up to £1000-odd over current Australian prices, are probably the most-sought-after conveyances among the wealthier members of Rabaul's Chinese community.

A sprinkling of Chinese, however, tend towards Detroit-style chromeware; thus one sees the occasional Ford, Chev, Buick or Pontiac shimmering its way along the road.

And then, last month, there arrived a Chevrolet Corvair direct from U.S.A.—to be quickly bought (as something most unusual) by a Chinese businessman named Bruno Chan, who hails from Kavieng.

Knowing how hard it is to latch on to a Corvair in Australia, I quickly parleyed Bruno into lending me his new buggy for a tryout before it was shipped by barge across to New Ireland.

I found the Corvair smooth, roadable, handy and forceful, with several endearing qualities all its own. And I thought it more interesting to drive than either a Ford Falcon or an EK Holden—but this would be largely a matter of personal preference.

Sleek, Low, Roomy

First thing that strikes you about the Corvair is its astonishingly low-slung appearance. And it IS low, standing only 4ft. 3¾in. off the ground—almost 5in. lower than the Falcon and a whole 8in. lower than the Holden. Bruno Chan is anything but tall at 5ft. 5in., but he invited me to drive the car under his outstretched arm, and the rooftop didn't even brush it.

Seen alongside a Holden, the Corvair looks a much smaller car—about the size of a Simca or even a Renault Dauphine. But don't let this fool you.

All its dimensions except height are almost identical to the Holden's, and it seats six adults easily.

You step down and wiggle to enter it—yet, once inside, there is an amazing amount of hip, leg and head room; more headroom, in fact, than in many full-scale Yanks.

BOOT replaces engine up front. Centrally mounted spare mars its roominess, but there's more luggage space behind the rear seat.

AIR-COOLED flat-six sits low in tail, with all accessories on top and easily accessible. Note "left-hand drive" sign near numberplate. BELOW: Corvair is 4ft. 3¾in. high, looks tiny beside a Holden.

LOW bodywork calls for low seating position; owner Bruno Chan adopts a comfortable lounging posture. Two wide benches seat six adults easily.

Upholstery, in two-tone plastic fabric, is extremely well tailored; seating is comfortable, dash layout plain but attractive: the general impression is one of neatness and simplicity. (Those who like plenty of instruments may find it TOO simple: all you get is a speedo and fuel gauge; warning lights do for the rest.)

The front "boot," while roomy enough, is marred by the fact that the spare is mounted flat on the floor right in the centre, so that luggage has to go on top of it; however, this fault is offset to some extent by a capacious luggage well inside the car, behind the rear seat — VW fashion.

The engine bay presents a strange sight: the flat-six, air-cooled 2.3-litre power unit is mounted very low and literally buried under its accessories. This arrangement may look odd, but it's eminently practical, since all "bits" are easily reached for servicing — except spark plugs, that is, which can't even be seen.

Eager Performer

Bruno's Corvair is an automatic —and, having just driven an automatic EK Holden for the first time, I was eager to compare the two transmissions.

The shift lever looks peculiar, being shaped rather like a cowl-vent handle and mounted under the dash to the driver's right (this is a left-hand-drive car). It offers two ranges—"L" for Low and "D" for Drive—plus Neutral, Park and Reverse; and the self-shifting which

WHEEL is plain, instruments reduced to minimum. Selector lever is obscured here; it's under the dash, to right of steering column.

SPECIFICATIONS

ENGINE: Horizontally-opposed 6-cylinder, o.h.v. (air-cooled); bore 85.8mm., stroke 66mm., capacity 2295c.c.; compression ratio 8 to 1; maximum b.h.p., 80 gross at 4400 r.p.m. (65 net); maximum torque 128ft./lb. gross at 2300 r.p.m. (118 net); twin carburettors; mech. fuel pump, 12v. ignition.
TRANSMISSION: G.M. Powerglide 2-speed automatic with torque-converter.
SUSPENSION: Independent all round, by coil springs and tubular shockers; swing-axles at rear.
STEERING: Recirculating - ball type; 4.8 turns lock-to-lock, 39ft. 6in. turning circle.
BRAKES: Hydraulic; lining area 120.8 sq. in.
WHEELS: Pressed-steel discs, with 6.50 by 13in. tyres.
DIMENSIONS: Wheelbase 9ft. 0in.; track (front and rear) 4ft. 6in.; length 15ft., width 5ft. 7in., height 4ft. 3¾in.; ground clearance 6½in.
KERB WEIGHT: 21cwt.
FUEL TANK: 11.7 gallons.

follows your selecting "D" is just about the smoothest in the business.

The box upshifts at about 20 m.p.h. on a normal throttle, but will hold the low cog in until 60-65 m.p.h. when you're really trying. Slippage is minimal throughout both ranges, and the change, unlike the Holden's, is both indiscernible and instantaneous.

Why didn't G.M.H. plump for this box instead of the three-range Hydra-Matic? There are two possible answers:

(a) It may not have been readily adaptable to the Holden's conventional engine layout;

(b) Three cogs may have been deemed necessary to deal with the Holden's greater weight (22¾cwt. against 21cwt.).

On the road, the flat-six engine in the Corvair's tail is unnoticeable. The car is silent, taut and well suspended at all speeds.

When idling, however, the oddly timed beat of the "pancake" sounds like a cross between a VW and a Tiger Moth — only much, much quieter.

Pep is there a-plenty: a prod of the accelerator at any speed below sixty fetches in Low range with no trace of jerk, and the revs mount rapidly, surging you forward. A trailing throttle, on the other hand, will hold the High range in mesh down to about 18 m.p.h., when the transmission slips down to Low so effortlessly that you hardly notice the change.

With such a brand-new vehicle (and on such dreadful roads) there was no opportunity to try for performance figures, but a flat-out top speed of about 85 m.p.h. is indicated, plus a Low-range peak speed of 63 m.p.h. or thereabout.

Braking is excellent, and I couldn't detect any fade after several punishing stops.

Road clearance seems adequate for all normal purposes, while the scads of power available make picking one's way over a plantation goat-track almost a pleasure. You simply sit in "D" range, idle the engine, and let the low-down torque do the rest.

(Continued on page 48)

Monza "900" two-door club coupe (upper) shows new emblems and the ornamental grille strips that simulate a front air intake.

Series "700" four-door sedan (above) illustrates restyled engine exhaust grille, brushed aluminum strip running along kick-plate.

CORVAIR

Detroit's only aircooled, rear-engined car, the Corvair, enters its third year of existence with many unseen refinements and only minor trim changes. Variations of the three series — the "500," "700" and "900" — offer a total of six models, from the basic two-door club coupe, through the four-door station wagon, to the popular two-door and four-door Monza coupe and sedan.

Corvair's appearance is changed only slightly by the addition of an ornamental grille at the front with new emblems and trim, and a restyling of the engine exhaust grille beneath the rear bumper. The kick-plate along the lower body edge is now covered with a ribbed strip of bright metal that is both functional and ornamental.

The name Lakewood has been discontinued in reference to the station wagon, this model being absorbed into the "700" series.

Engines include two versions of the six-cylinder-opposed aircooled powerplant, which by the very nature of its design employs multiple carburetion and interconnecting ballast tube. Basic engine is 145 cubic inches in displacement with 8.0:1 compression ratio and a horsepower rating of 80. When ordered with Powerglide automatic transmission, the engine supplied has a 9.0:1 compression ratio but has a combustion chamber designed for regular fuel. The hot version of this engine, the Monza option, has 9.0:1 compression ratio, special cam and lifters, and a heavy-duty clutch; it produces 102 hp.

Three- and four-speed manual transmissions and Powerglide are available on all models, but the Positraction rear end is not available on station wagons, any 3.27:1 rear axle ratio, or on any high-performance engine using Powerglide. ●

Formerly called the Lakewood, the Corvair station wagon is now designated as the "700" series four-door, six-passenger wagon.

'62 ANALYSIS

Engines

Cubic Inches	Type	Compression Ratio	Carburetors	Horse-power	Torque
145	6-cyl. opp.	8.0:1	2 1-bbl.	80	128
145	6-cyl. opp.	9.0:1	2 1-bbl.	84	130
145	6-cyl. opp.	9.0:1	2 1-bbl.	102	134

Dimensions Compared (in inches)

	Car	Wheelbase	Length	Height	Width	Front Tread	Rear Tread
1962	Sedan	108.0	180.0	51.5	67	54.5	54.5
	Wagon	108.0	180.0	53.5	67	54.5	54.5
1961	Sedan	108.0	180.0	51.5	67	54.5	54.5
	Wagon	108.0	180.0	53.5	67	54.5	54.5

DRIVER'S REPORT
CORVAIR with RPOs

*The major weakness of the Corvair — the brakes and suspension —
have been cured with Regular Production Options.*   By JERRY TITUS

W E DROVE A MONZA CORVAIR that would undoubtedly out-handle a Porsche Super 90! To those with Corvair experience this may sound like an incredible statement, but, so help us, it's true. Further, the brakes survived three stops from 100 mph, plus several fast circuits around a tight, demanding road course! The ride? We found it even more comfortable than normal since the pillow-soft oscillations of the stock suspension were "firmed-up" to exactly the right point. All this took place recently at the GM Proving Grounds in Milford, Michigan, where every type of road surface and configuration imaginable is available within a few thousand square acres. The machine was a full-optioned Monza of 1961 vintage, with the '62 roadability RPO's installed.

Though an admission is hard to come by, the handling and stopping characteristics of the Corvair have been far from laughing matters around Chevrolet Division even though both have been in the laughable category. This is especially true when the 98-horse Monza is considered. Therefore, they were justifiably proud to display one that is exceptional in both instances. And, after taking printed sidewipes at these factors — the June SCG was one of several instances — we were overjoyed to witness the results Thus eliminated were the only real drawbacks the Corvair had and, from here on, everything is downhill.

So that the reader can appreciate the whole picture, we'll start from the beginning and detail what has happening with the Corvair in a corner. The problem basically centers around the rear suspension design which, roughly, has a modified swing-axle configuration. The inner pivot points of the semi-trailing support arms for the half-axles are in the same horizontal plane as the U-joints of the latter. With the flat-opposed engine and the low-mounted gas tank, the majority of weight is also in the same horizontal plane. Tire roll-under of the "outside" rear wheel is just enough to reduce hub-to-ground height below that

of inner-pivot-to-ground height, resulting in the suspension arm acting as a lever that throws the weight of the rear section upward instead of rolling it downward onto the outside rear wheel. Therefore, the stock Corvair not only oversteers abnormally when cornered fast, it does so with a series of "unloads" that are extremely difficult to correct. In a series of experiments this writer conducted, it was found that adding 170 pounds of weight on the rear floor increased the maximum cornering velocity by twenty percent! The extra weight was enough to induce some negative camber in the rear wheel *and* — more important — canted the suspension arms upward at their outboard ends just enough to eliminate the lever-action resisting normal body roll. Juggling tire pressures, etc., resulted in

only fractional improvements. One thing we discovered — which is natural where adhesion problems are encounteerd — was that the car was very critical to the brand of tire installed since one will have a slightly better bite or lateral stability than another.

Yet another problem with many Corvairs is a tendency to drift around in straight-line cruising. This, however, isn't prevalent in *all* Corvairs (approximately sixty percent of those we've driven had the trait) so we can only conclude that the semi-trailing arms make the car super-snsitive to both front and rear-end alignment and spring height.

What the factory includes in their option kits doesn't alter the basic design but offers the best solution short of that. All springs and shocks are changed, an anti-sway bar is included in the front and limit-straps are installed on the rear suspension arms. What does all this accomplish? Most important are the optional springs; they're of higher rate (i.e., stiffer) but of lower height. Thus, negative camber is induced in the rear wheels to about 1½ degrees. The static angle of the rear suspension arms from their inner pivot point toward their outboard ends is now UPWARD, however. This latter change makes the biggest difference, since it eliminates the "lock" normally set up by the arm, allows the body to roll weight into the rear wheel vertically. Further, the negative camber makes the tire less critical — from a radius standpoint — to roll-under. The increased spring and shock rates eliminate the wobble cornering and stabilize straightline cruising.

The front end of the car is also lowered by installation of the optional springs, to balance out the rear, but wheel geometry is corrected through normal adjustments to bring them back to conventional settings. The anti-sway bar increases roll-stiffness in the front and induces a tendency toward understeer. Thus, what must remain an oversteer vehicle — with the engine mounted aft of the rear axle — is greatly "tamed" by increasing slip-angles at the front and reducing those at the rear.

Presence of the limit or rebound straps on the rear arms helps in two ways. First, it slightly increases roll stiffness in the rear — just enough to aid stabilization. Second, it keeps the inside wheel from dropping down in a hard corner to a point where the unusual geometry of the semi-trailing arms induce considerable toe-in and thereby increase the amount of oversteer. The straps do, of course, increase

the possibility of picking up the inside rear with a resultant traction loss. Yet another option — just announced at this writing — will be a limited-slip differential. Though not installed on the car we tested, this should be enough to nullify any wheel-lifting problems.

Your next question will undoubtedly be, "Why isn't the spring-shock option, at least, made standard on all Corvairs?" The answer, even though the kit is expected to be of nominal cost as an RPO, lies in the fact that the changes incorporate negative rear-wheel camber. With normal load of driver and one passenger, uneven tread wear will be negligible but the inside will definitely wear faster than the outside. With, say, four persons aboard — plus some luggage — the option-equipped Corvair will be ambling down the pike with something like six degrees negative camber, enough to wear tires out very rapidly *and* contribute some handling problems of its own. Therefore, a potential buyer must rationalize how much of the car's operational time will be spent fully laden and sacrifice either handling or tire-wear.

The brake option embodies no sacrifices except increased pedal pressure. The stock drums, etc., are retained and the organic linings simply replaced with cerametalic, segmented linings. This is enough to cure the extremely rapid heat deterioration that occurs when normal Corvair brakes are used hard. Because of the single change — using the metallic lining — the HD brake option should also be an inexpensive one.

All in all, we consider both options very successful, eliminating the two objectionable features we've found in Corvairs. It would have been a lot more satisfying to see the present rear suspension design scrapped and, for example, a low-pivot, long-arm configuration utilized. What they have, however, works extremely well, even though slip angles are a bit high. Further, the options are bolt-on for previous model Corvairs, which should make a *lot* of owners happy.

The 1962 Corvair remains relatively unchanged over the '61. New emblems and little front grills gild the lily a bit, and not too tastefully at that. Undoubtedly the line will enjoy another good sales year. It's possible that the new "in-between-size" cars offered by Detroit will cut into their market a bit, but Corvair remains the FUN car line out of Motor City.

MONZA SPRINT

Blown Corvair engine and modifications to rear suspension and steering make the Monza Sprint a very attractive car for the non-racing motor enthusiast.

● Most people who buy sports cars do so with no intention of racing them and often, for a number of reasons that need no explanation to enthusiasts, become disenchanted with their choice and begin to look around for a car that will carry four people and their luggage yet retain a certain amount of distinction, satisfactory performance and comfort. This explains the soaring popularity of the Grand Touring car with which European and American manufacturers alike have found a fertile seller's market.

The sales success of the Corvair Monza 900 is a prime example of this, but being a car fancier is a disconcerting business. It seems that no matter what you have you inevitably want "a little bit more" whether it be power, comfort or styling extras.

Racing driver John Fitch has recognized all this and is offering for sale his concept of the American G.T. Based on the Corvair, he calls it the Monza Sprint. Our day with it at Lime Rock and bombing around back roads shows he's got the right idea.

The prescription is a simple but effective remedy for curing enthusiasts' wants. John takes the basic Monza (he's presently offering only white ones with black interiors to give the Sprint "identity") and dolls up the bow with a chrome-plated wire-mesh screen running its full width. Serving as a pebble guard for the headlights, it gives spice to the otherwise uninteresting front end. He transforms the roof line by adding a black textured material to give it the appearance of a padded top. A chrome bow at the rear window's top

edge results in a modified notch effect and the rear window is partially masked both for appearance and to cut down on interior glare from headlights of following cars. The capping touch is two dark metallic blue stripes running the length of the car on top of the fenders. The result is distinction without gaudiness; it's tasteful customizing and does improve the looks.

To make sure the car will go as well as it looks, John offers a power kit on the 98 bhp factory optional engine. In the case of the car we tested it was a Paxton blower giving a modest 4 psi boost and dual exhausts providing a pleasant burble in keeping with the restrained changes of the rest of the car.

Handling is improved compared to the stock Monza through use of special rear coil springs which result in 2 degrees of negative camber and a higher spring rate. Coupled with different shock absorbers, the net result is a better-behaved rear end well-suited to fast driving over virtually any surface with comfort and a good feel. On the track, using speeds much higher than

Thanks to effective decambering, cornering power of the Monza Sprint was quite high, even without the front sway bar fitted.

those we ever encountered on the road, the ultimate oversteer of the Corvair was evident, yet with 130 bhp available all that was needed was a flick of the wood-rimmed steering wheel and a steady hard foot on the accelerator to straighten things out. Since Fitch's concept was for a strict touring car (not one designed for G.T. or compact car racing) the changes have all been designed to improve performance without sacrificing tractability. Our lap times at Lime Rock probably could have been improved with adjusted air pressures in the tires (we used the recommended touring pressures on purpose) and a track-designed tire. In even the hardest cornering situations, the rear wheels remained pretty nearly vertical although there was quite a bit of tire deformation.

The blown engine was not at its best until 3000 was registered on the tachometer, with full-throttle use below that figure resulting in a stumbling or a dying feeling under the gas pedal. Over that, the faster the car went, the faster it seemed to want to go as boost climbed. John says 5000 to 5500 rpm is a satisfactory top rev limit for most uses but we found 5800 could be used and acceleration times improved when we did. In starting, the engine made a few revolutions before it burst into life and when the engine got really hot the idle became lumpy.

The Monza Sprint prototype represents a good car made better and more desirable. However, for production models, John said he has decided to scratch the

The driver's view must appeal to every enthusiast. The wood-rimmed aluminum steering wheel is dished for maximum safety.

John Fitch demonstrates how the stone guard which is hinged at the bottom gives easy access to the baggage compartment lock.

manifold and its performance are described in Wayne Thoms's story, "Modified Monza" in the November C/D.

A few goodies in addition to the tachometer and wood-rimmed steering wheel are found in the interior and others are planned. At present all Sprints will come with a Helphos windshield-mounted spotlight, a compass and a radio. Still in the talking stage are headrests and reclining seats. If you cannot recognize the Sprint by its distinctive interior and trimmings, it's spelled out for you on the hood and dashboard in chrome letters.

John says immediate plans are to sell complete cars through selected Chevrolet dealers covering the entire country. Remember, the Monza Sprint will come equipped with the four-carb engine rather than the blown version we tested. The retail price includes a suspension conversion, quick steering, special steering wheel, Radson tachometer, front stone guard, windshield washer, striping, compass, Indicaps (valve caps registering loss of pressure), dual muffler, padded dash, grab rail and the convenience group of accessories. The first series of cars will be built by Dutchess Motors of Millerton, New York and questions regarding local delivery should be addressed to the manufacturer.

If there is sufficient demand, Fitch says complete Sprint conversion kits and individual components may be offered for sale. However there is no such arrangement at this time since attention is being given to preparing the completed cars. Our photos are of the prototype which was a 1961 model. All subsequent cars will be '62s.

For a price just under $3000 the Sprint offers performance and comfort normally associated with cars costing twice that. The basic Monza lends itself well to the thoughtful modifications John Fitch has devised. We feel a good number of driving enthusiasts will agree with us. —C/D

supercharger in favor of a four-carburetor manifold which should give equal performance at a lower price while also improving tractability. In addition, a longer pitman arm will be installed on future models to speed up the steering and a front anti-roll bar will be standard to improve rear-end behavior. The four-carb

---

ROAD TEST
CORVAIR MONZA SPRINT

Price as tested: $3295 ($2995 with four carbs)
Manufacturer:
John Fitch & Co.
Lime Rock, Conn.

ENGINE:

Displacement..............145 cu in, 2372 cc
Dimensions...6 cyl, 3.44 in bore, 2.60 in stroke
Valve gear: Narrow-angle pushrod-actuated overhead valves
Compression ratio..................8.0 to one
Power (SAE)..............130 bhp @ 5000 rpm
Torque..................185 lb-ft @ 4000 rpm
Usable range of engine speeds...3000-5500 rpm
Corrected piston speed @ 5000 rpm...2470 fpm
Fuel recommended................Premium
Mileage......................15-22 mpg
Range on 14-gallon tank.........210-300 miles

CHASSIS:

Wheelbase.......................108 in
Tread..........................54 in
Length.........................180 in
Ground clearance................5½ in
Suspension:
  F: Ind., wishbones and coil springs
  R: Ind., swing axles, trailing wishbones and coil springs
Turns, lock to lock...................2½
Turning circle diameter, between curbs...42 ft
Tire and rim size.............6.50x13, 13x5K
Pressures recommended:
  Normal   F 16   R 26 psi
  High-speed F 20 R 30 psi
Brakes, type, swept area: 9-in drums, 198 sq in
Curb weight (full tank)...............2550 lbs
Percentage on the driving wheels...........62

DRIVE TRAIN:

Gear	Synchro?	Ratio	Step	Overall	Mph per 1000 rpm
Rev	No	3.66	—	13.15	-5.3
1st	Yes	3.65	57%	12.98	5.4
2nd	Yes	2.35	63%	8.34	8.3
3rd	Yes	1.44	44%	5.12	13.6
4th	Yes	1.00	—	3.55	19.8

Final drive ratio...................3.55 to one

ACCELERATION:

Zero to	Seconds
30 mph	4.1
40 mph	6.6
50 mph	9.8
60 mph	12.6
70 mph	16.2
80 mph	21.0
90 mph	25.2
Standing ¼-mile	18.9

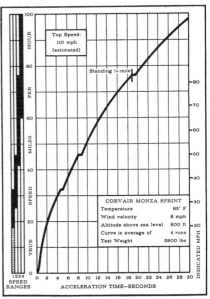

Top Speed: 110 mph (estimated)

Standing ¼-mile

CORVAIR MONZA SPRINT
Temperature ....85° F
Wind velocity ....8 mph
Altitude above sea level ....800 ft
Curve is average of ....4 runs
Test Weight ....2800 lbs

ACCELERATION TIME—SECONDS

"SEE HOW THEY RUN"

24 Hours for a CORVAIR

Automotive testing under the most extreme conditions

Everybody pitched in on pit stops. Here MT's Nerpel (with jack) and Wright (left rear) help on changeover from stock rubber to Goodyear Sports Car Specials.

"**S**EE HOW THEY RUN . . ." is not only a line from the nursery rhyme about the three blind mice, but the real reason for endurance runs. Exposing automobiles to accelerated wear tests is the best way to find out a great deal about a piece of equipment in a very short time. It is also the most practical way to test components — tires, chassis and engines, stock or modified.

Besides that, it provides valuable experience for automotive writers. We all test drive many cars in the course of a year, but 24-hour endurance runs are infrequent, and it is important to maintain authoritative knowledge of such tests by participating in them.

So that is exactly what we decided to do — run some cars under extremes of speed, braking and acceleration for 24 hours to see how they run. We, in this case, were the Petersen Publishing Company, the country's leading publisher of automotive magazines, including MOTOR TREND, Hot Rod, Sports Car Graphic, Car Craft and Rod and Custom; and Carroll Shelby, former national sports car champion and currently head of a high-performance driving school bearing his name.

The test course, Riverside International Raceways, a twisting 3⅓ miles of snake-like esses, reverse-camber turns, and a 6000-foot straightaway, was selected as the site because of the wide variety of road conditions available. The drivers included even *text continued on page* **48**

Experimental Bell helmets worn here by Chuck Nerpel and Chuck Daigh had small, transistorized receiving sets built into them for picking up pit instructions.

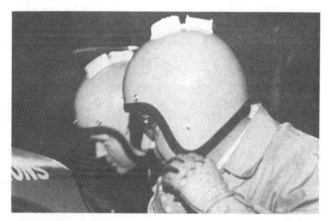

PHOTOS BY BOB D'OLIVO

LUCAS ROAD LIGHTS PROVIDED MAXIMUM AROUND-THE-CORNER ILLUMINATION. LUCAS FLAME THROWERS REPLACED THE STOCK HIGH-BEAMS.

24 Hours for a Corvair

Small-diameter (14½-in.) racing wheel marketed by Carroll Shelby replaced the stock item. Large plastic rim is easy on the hands.

Two five-gallon Moon fuel tanks were used to speed up the fueling procedure and to provide for a more accurate check of fuel consumption. Mobil gas was used throughout test.

Flat cornering at 65 mph plus in tight turn 6 was made possible by installation of EMPI front stabilizer bar, camber compensator and Armstrong shocks.

When the rains came, they came all of a sudden and Chuck Nerpel had the dubious honor of finding out whether or not the Monza would stick on the slick, blacktopped surface.

Just how well the Corvair handled on the greasy-wet surface is evidenced here as Chuck Daigh storms the car into the tricky, reverse camber of turn 8 at close to 60 mph.

Carroll Shelby, road racing champion and head of a high-performance driving school, set up test and shouldered a load of the driving.

Enduro ended at the final stroke of noon, with Chuck Daigh coasting across the finish line as Wally Parks, Petersen Publishing Co. editorial director, gives him checkered flag.

24 Hours for a Corvair

continued from page 45

a wider variety of driving techniques, with Los Angeles metropolitan newspaper auto editors liberally sprinkled in among race drivers and the editors and technical editors of the Petersen Publishing group of automotive magazines.

The car(s) were Corvair Monzas, and the reason for the plural designation is that we had intended to run two automobiles, one highly modified with non-factory power options that were purely experimental; the other, strictly stock except for minor chassis modifications in the interest of safe handling at high speed in the corners. Unfortunately, the highly modified experimental car did not survive — not through any failure of the special cylinder heads, the four-barrel carburetors, the ignition system, or the special cam and valve springs. In fact, it went like the very devil until a human error in assembly, a loose cam gear, sidelined what was a most exciting automobile.

In stock form, the other Monza was also exciting, especially with the chassis tuning by Bill Yeager, who had been selected for the job by Carroll Shelby. The rear wheels were decambered by cutting one coil from each spring and then stabilized by adding an EMPI camber compensator. As the Corvair is not normally equipped with a front stabilizer bar, EMPI's front bar was installed.

Two Moon fuel tanks of five-gallon capacity with easy-filling tops were mounted in the forward luggage compartment to provide a quick method of topping off at each driver-change pit stop. One of Mobil's fuel trucks right in the pit area kept these stops down to 60 to 80 seconds, during which time the tanks were filled, oil level checked, speedometer reading recorded, brake pedal travel checked, wheels, tires and lug bolts inspected, and a fresh driver seated behind the wheel with time to adjust the seat and fasten his Tularoff seat belt.

To light things up for the long night session, a pair of Lucas flame throwers replaced the high-beam lights in the Corvair dual system, and two Lucas road lights were hung low below the front bumper with their beams crossed to give a little more around-the-corner illumination. The low-positioned lights were best appreciated when it began to rain shortly after dark — just a drizzle at first, then a downpour that lasted until dawn, forming puddles and cutting visibility, but not the steady 68 mph set as lap speed necessary to maintain 65 mph for 24 hours.

One of the most impressive and useful phases of the endurance run was an experimental pit-to-car radio communications system under development by the Bell Helmet manufacturers. A short-range, line-of-sight transmitter in the pits was tuned to a small, light, transistorized receiver built right into the helmet. No plugs or cords were necessary, and the driver could hear the pit orders loud and clear as long as the transmitting antenna was in view of the car.

One of the most disappointed men when the modified Corvair retired was Zip Keyes, designer and manufacturer of the Hands Engineering magnesium wheels for Corvairs. Zip had supplied a set of his wheels to be tested against the fatigue of 24 hours of high-speed cornering. These were on the modified car, but Keyes was not to be denied something he deemed necessary to the success of his brainchild, so he rolled his own candy apple red Monza out on the course and invited the waiting entourage of drivers to have at it.

A wide variety of drivers, from automotive editors to drag strip champions, were doing very well with this car with no practice laps, and Zip was smiling broadly when the unscheduled test which ended the test occurred. Jack Chrisman, drag strip champion, was behind the wheel in the early night hours before the rain began. Unfamiliar with the course, especially at night, Jack got into treacherous turn 4 just a little too hard and flipped end-over-end, with the wheels taking a terrific beating in the process.

The impact pulled one rear axle, wheel, hub and brake assembly clear of the housing, but neither Chrisman nor the mag wheels suffered any damage. However, happy as he was over the test of strength of his wheels, Keyes was not smiling so broadly as he surveyed his damaged Monza.

With only one car left running — the stocker — Shelby could not afford to take any chances with the threat of rain hanging over the entire Riverside area. He revised the 19 hours of driving time left to include drivers who knew the course blindfolded and could drive in the rain. This boiled down to race and sports car designer, builder, driver Chuck Daigh; experienced sports car race drivers Carroll Shelby and Paul O'Shea; and MOTOR TREND's editor and technical editor, Chuck Nerpel and Jim Wright.

So the run settled down to a long, hard job with some time to make up because of Chrisman's flip and the midnight and dawn tire changes from racing to stock and back to racing tires. Shortly after daylight the rain stopped and the course began to dry out rapidly. This, and the fact that the Corvair kept running faster and faster down the 6000-foot backstretch as the mileage built up (it was finally running 105 mph), helped to get back on the 65-mph overall average.

Here are the facts and figures:
Total miles traveled: 1549.1
Total gallons of gas used: 94.0
Overall miles per gallon: 16.48
Total quarts of oil used: 1
Total drivers used: 11   /MT

CORVAIR

Continued from page 38

I made a special point of checking on the Corvair's reputed oversteering tendency and found it hadn't been exaggerated. Admittedly, Bruno Chan was running with his back tyres at rather less pressure than the recommended 30lb. per square inch — but even a Volkswagen has nothing on this car when it comes to thrusting one's tail outward on a corner!

There's one thing, though: the Corvair, with its longer wheelbase, breaks away more slowly, so that one is able to correct the helm, and even to engage in tail-end acrobatics, with perfect safety.

The rear suspension, with its swing-axles, is a dream on holes and corrugations, and I would rank the Corvair almost equal to the 220 Mercedes when it comes to handling horrible roads without loss of direction. You can bat this little Yankee over deep ruts and potholes without a shudder being transmitted to the body or to the wheel!

But you have to take things more easily on a loose-surfaced corner.

The shortish drive I had in the Corvair convinced me that it must be one of the most comfortable long-distance autos available. At its 60-70 m.p.h. cruising speed the engine is unobtrusive, the car has lots more response up its sleeve, and the relaxed seating position makes it extremely comfortable to drive.

Pity that it isn't sold in Australia. I'm sure it would find many takers, and it shouldn't be expensive to maintain.

All-up price in Rabaul is £1550 — left-hand-drive models only. ● ● ●

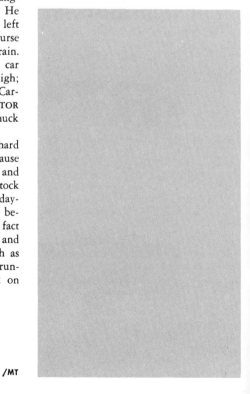

CHEVROLET

CORVAIR MONZA SPYDER

The Corvair Monza Spyder, which has a four-speed gearbox and a full range of sports-type instruments.

Considerable interest is being generated in the United States by the introduction recently of a new sporting version of the popular Chevrolet Corvair. Called the Monza Spyder, it is a beautifully styled 4-passenger convertible powered by a high performance version of the air-cooled Corvair engine, which has been fitted with a turbo-charger to produce 150 brake horse-power.

Also going into production at Chevrolet is a less potent version of the Monza Spyder. It is almost identical in appearance with the Spyder and is called the Corvair Monza Convertible.

These two models are in addition to the other Corvair Monza models already in production — the Monza Club Coupe and the Monza 4-door Sedan. They are not available in South Africa.

"This expansion of offerings in the luxury Monza series is in response to heavy public demand," said Mr. S. E. Knudsen, General Manager of Chevrolet. He revealed that at present the Monza is taking about 65 per cent of total Corvair sales.

The Monza Spyder and the Convertible will have one of the lowest silhouettes of any American production car. With the top down these new cars present a virtually straight line contour from front to rear. Height to the door sill is 33·5 inches, and to the top of the windshield less than 50 inches.

Special features include bucket-type front seats, all vinyl interior trim and ashtrays in arm rests at both sides of the rear seat. A manually operated top, counter-balanced for ease of operation, is standard, but an automatic power top is available as an option.

In addition to the 150 b.h.p. turbo-charged engine, the Spyder features a four-speed gearbox, 3·55 to 1 ratio rear axle, heavy duty suspension and sintered metallic brakes. The underbody has been strengthened to give added rigidity and many of the internal engine parts have been changed to withstand the tremendous power increase.

Directly in front of the driver is a full range of sports type instruments, including 120 m.p.h. speedometer with regular and trip mileage recorders; electric rev. counter calibrated to 6,000 r.p.m.; manifold pressure gauge; cylinder head temperature gauge; fuel level gauge; and circular direction signals. Generator-fan and oil pressure warning lights are retained from the normal production instrument panel. Headlight and ignition switches and main-beam headlight indicator complete the instrument cluster.

The horizontally opposed Corvair engine is extensively changed to provide the increased power output for the Monza Spyder. The power increase is as much as 87 per cent over the 80 b.h.p. of the standard engine.

The big increase in power comes primarily from the fitting of a turbo-charger to force more fuel-air mixture into the combustion chambers. The turbo-charger is a simple but highly effective type of super-charger, and consists of a turbine driven by the Corvair engine's exhaust gases. The turbine drives a centrifugal impeller, which draws the fuel-air mixture from the side draught carburettor and forces it into the combustion chambers.

★

The turbo-charged Corvair engine used in the Monza Spyder develops 150 b.h.p. The exhaust-driven super-charger and side-draught carburettor are plainly visible.

Without any change in the internal dimensions of the Corvair flat six engine, the power is boosted to 150 brake horse-power at 4,400 r.p.m., giving the Monza Spyder an excellent performance. Peak torque is 210 lbs. ft. and occurs through a range of 3,200 to 3,400 r.p.m. The compression ratio of 8·0 to 1 is not high by modern standards, but calls for premium grade fuel.

To withstand the tremendous power boost, the Spyder engine is fitted with structurally stronger pistons, connecting rods and crankshaft, and the exhaust valves and exhaust valve guides are made of high temperature alloys. In addition, a new engine cooling blower is used to reduce inertial forces and improve the life of the generator-blower belt. The new blower is made of acetal resin plastic.

The ignition system has also been revised. A high-capacity ignition coil with approximately 20 per cent greater output is used in conjunction with a block type resistor to provide a hotter spark at the plugs. The distributor has been changed to include an automatic pressure retard device, in place of a vacuum advance, to regulate the spark timing. The clutch has also been strengthened to absorb the increased engine output. ●

Chevrolet's new sports Corvair Monza Spyder gives higher performance to the only rear-engined car made in America.

The instrument panel has cylinder-head temperature gauge as well as a 120-mph speedometer and 6,000-rpm tachometer.

Turbocharged Monza Spyder

Turbocharger boosts Corvair power to 150 bhp in the new convertible luxury sports model from Chevrolet

When Semon Knudsen took over from Ed Cole as general manager of Chevrolet, no statements were made about the future of Corvair models. Chevrolet engineers had long been working on a project to combine a high-performance version of the Corvair engine with a body based on Bill Mitchell's open two-seater Sebring Spyder, which was described in CAR AND DRIVER, November, 1961. Knudsen gave instructions to speed up the program, and the Corvair Monza Spyder went into production at Willow Run in April, with a 150-bhp turbocharged engine. The interest in turbo-supercharging small gasoline engines has had a sudden upswing, and today both Oldsmobile and Chevrolet offer blown models, although highly different (see pages 62-67).

A lightweight engine with a small turbocharger, the new power pack for the Corvair has only two pounds engine weight per developed brake horsepower and offers great promise of performance without any serious increase in fuel consumption. The turbocharger installation on the Corvair consists of an exhaust-driven turbine mounted on the same shaft as a centrifugal impeller drawing an air-fuel mixture from a single side-draft Carter carburetor and forcing it through the crossover which supplies both cylinder banks. The power output is 150 bhp at 4,400 rpm and maximum torque is 210 lb-ft, developed through a range from 3,200 to 3,400 rpm. The compression ratio is eight to one. Internal reinforcements to enable the engine to withstand the added stress include revised pistons, connecting rods and crankshaft, exhaust valves and valve guides in high-temperature alloys, and a new, lighter cooling fan. Camshaft, valve springs and bearings remain the same as used in the 102 bhp twin-carburetor engine. The carburetor is the same single-throat triple-venturi instrument which was fitted to the early six-cylinder Corvette. The compressor has a maximum speed of approximately 70,000 rpm and is made of a three-inch-diameter aluminum die-casting. It has 14 equally spaced vanes. The turbine has 11 blades on a 2.97-inch diameter and is made of high-temperature cobalt-base alloy. The turbine exhaust pipe has 2½ inches diameter, which is maintained through the entire exhaust system.

The muffler was especially designed for the turbocharged engine, and is of oval shape with reverse-flow internal configuration. It is divided into four compartments and, according to Chevrolet, provides a degree of efficiency comparable to that of a straight-through muffler.

The clutch has a 16% stronger pressure plate with improved cooling, and the Chevrolet four-speed all-synchromesh gearbox is standard on the Monza Spyder. The final drive ratio is 3.55 to one. Regular production options for the Corvair that have been standardized for the Monza Spyder include a heavy-duty suspension and sintered metallic brake linings.

The underbody had to be strengthened to provide adequate rigidity with the convertible body, so the Monza Spyder is heavier than the Club Coupé. Bucket-type front seats and all-vinyl interiors are standard equipment, but the power top is optional.

The usual twin-carburetor layout is replaced by the large air filter (top left), turbocharger and special muffler.

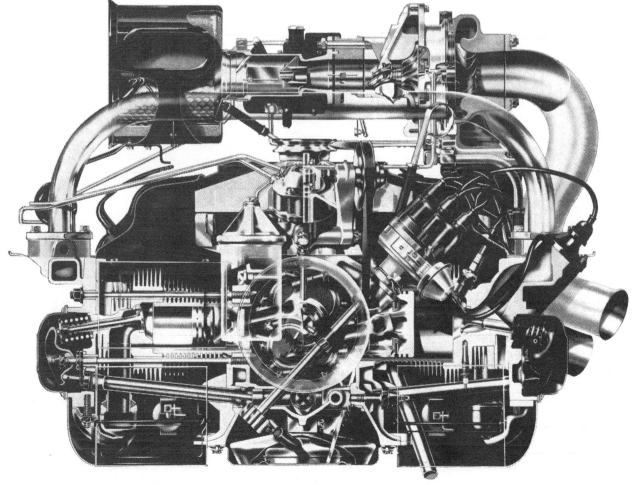

In turbocharged form the Corvair engine remains a highly compact unit delivering over one bhp per cu. in. displacement.

Driving the Corvair Sprint

STORY AND PHOTOS BY HARVEY B. JANES

IN THE FALL of 1959 John Fitch, wearing his General Motors Consultant's Suit, had the unique opportunity to test several models of the brand-new Corvair for two weeks at Lime Rock Park in Connecticut. This pre-public-introduction tryout, attended by much secrecy and a small army of Pinkerton guards, left Fitch greatly enthused about the Corvair's potential as a grand touring machine. Accordingly, he set himself the task of experimenting with an extensive variety of modifications to engine, chassis and body with the idea of coming up with a package that GM could adopt, wholly or in part, for future production models. It is interesting to note that although GM officials refused, in the early production stages, to share Fitch's concept of the Corvair as a sporting car they have lately come around to that point of view, and the subject of this report—the Corvair Sprint, privately produced by John Fitch & Co.—is being forced to compete with the production turbocharged Corvair Spyder.

Before getting on to comparisons or evaluations, however, let's take a look at what the Sprint actually is. The "standard" Sprint, ordered as a complete car, consists of a Monza coupe in which certain pieces of equipment supplement or substitute for various production options. The basic Monza is ordered from the factory with the 102-bhp engine, 4-speed gearbox, 3.55 rear-axle ratio, seat belts, padded dash, and the comfort and convenience accessory group, which includes an outside mirror, non-glare inside mirror, 2-speed electric windshield wipers, windshield washers, etc. Then the Sprint equipment is added, as follows: Two additional Corvair carburetors are installed, for a total of 4, giving, in conjunction with a tuned dual-muffler and dual-pipe exhaust system, 145 SAE bhp [Rather optimistic, we think.—Ed.]. The rear springs and shock absorbers are changed for a set that produce, at static-no-load, 2° negative camber; the steering arms are exchanged for a pair that provide steering with approximately three turns, lock to lock, instead of the five on the stock car. A tachometer, wood-rimmed sports steering wheel and an assist rail make the interior still more sporting. The exterior is enhanced by the addition of a padded, vinyl-covered top (except on convertibles), a Lucas long-distance driving light that replaces one of the left-side sealed-beam units, a hinged chrome stone guard, tasteful striping and a set of Indicaps. For an additional $42 you can have the rear window made smaller, which adds surprisingly to the appearance and is distinctly appreciated in night driving.

The price for all of this (minus the optional rear window treatment) is $563.70, bringing the total cost for the Sprint to $2995 plus transportation charges and any other factory-ordered goodies like a Positraction axle, push-button radio, etc.

This may seem like a lot of money for a Corvair—until you drive the car. Our own evaluations are based on experience in two different Sprints, driven several months apart and, while we were much impressed with the car on the first try, we were even more impressed the second time around because we were fortunate enough at that time to have secured a well-broken-in production Spyder for purposes of comparison.

First we tried both cars for handling. The Spyder was fitted with the optional GM heavy-duty suspension, which includes four new springs and shocks plus a roll bar in front. Fitch leaves the front end of the Sprint completely stock, and the result is a different automobile. Oversteer comes in at a much higher point—only, in fact, when you deliberately provoke it with the throttle. Even then the Sprint is as controllable as any good sports car, thanks to the quickened steering. Further experimentation revealed that, while the GM suspension produces a choppy ride, with frequent bottoming and poor control on rough surfaces, the Sprint rides extremely well, never bottoms and exhibits outstanding traction on all surfaces, even when driven hard. As might be expected, the Sprint is quite stable in cross winds, something that cannot be claimed for any normally-sprung Corvair. In our opinion the roadability of the Sprint is generally equal to, and in some ways superior to, that of the stock Corvette.

Comparing the performance of the Sprint and Spyder is somewhat more involved than comparing the handling. Our test Sprint got to 60 mph in just 12 sec and, although the Spyder is usually considered to be somewhat faster than that, such was not the case with the particular turbo-supercharged car we had. With the four-carb Sprint setup the additional power is felt all along the speed range, and at low to middle revs it is clearly superior to the turbocharged Spyder unit. It proves this by outjumping the Spyder every time from a standing start. Between 4000 and 5000 the Spyder comes on with a mighty rush that is not matched by the Sprint, but this is a lot less usable in the normal driving for which both cars were designed. As a bonus the Sprint is considerably more tractable than the Spyder, requiring much less shifting, and it seems to be quieter. In short, while the turbocharged Spyder is faster than the Sprint in some speed ranges the Sprint is the better performing car in most traffic and highway situations and require less fine tuning and adjusting than the Spyder.

An additional point of information that might have some bearing on long-range durability, especially for those who drive their cars without mercy, is that the Sprint cylinder head seems to maintain itself at a much healthier temperature level. Standard equipment on the Spyder is a cylinder head temperature gauge, and one of these was fitted for experimental purposes to our test Sprint. While the Spyder hovered alarmingly near the 500° mark most of the time, the Sprint never registered over 360. [Ed note: R & T tests show a maximum of 430° F on the Spyder.] We have no experience to indicate what would be a safe level but GM must have been a bit concerned about the Spyder or they wouldn't have fitted such a gauge in the first place. At the very least, the Sprint has a greater safety margin.

On the subject of durability, Fitch pointed out that parts and service should be no problem with the Sprint, as every part that actually wears or requires maintenance is a stock GM part. And if you should need to replace a piece of Sprint equipment this can be done quickly through mail order or by one of the existing Sprint dealers around the country.

Another interesting point that is not generally known about the Sprint project is that the various parts can be purchased separately and installed privately. If, for example, you already have a Monza and would like to make a Sprint out of it you can get all the necessary parts by mail. And if you merely want to improve the handling, or the steering, or the performance on *any* Corvair, Monza or not, you can do that, too. Fitch tells us that he has already made a few Sprint Spyders. To get one of these just order a normal Spyder *without* the optional heavy-duty suspension. Then add the Sprint suspension, steering, etc.

In case you have been wondering if there are any drawbacks to the Sprint modifications of the Corvair, we can see only one. The addition of the two extra carburetors has made it necessary to re-locate the spare tire just a bit, but it's still in back. The only other drawbacks to the car are those that are built-in on all Corvair coupes; we refer to limited rear-seat legroom, difficult access to three of the spark plugs and some fan noise at high rpm. But all things considered, the Sprint is an extremely well balanced, luxurious, complete automobile that provides handling and performance not usually associated with domestic products.

CORVAIR SPRINT TECHNICAL SPECIFICATIONS

List price	$2995
Price as tested	3037
Curb weight, lb	2544
Test weight	2852
Distribution, %	37/63
Bhp @ rpm	145 @ 5000
Torque, lb-ft	188 @ 3600
Steering ratio, o/a	n.a.
turns, lock to lock	3.0
turning circle, ft	38
Axle ratio	3.55:1
Fuel consumption, mpg	16/24
Speedometer error:	
30 mph, actual	29.3
60 mph	60.6
Performance: top speed (est)	112–115
3rd (5500)	75
2nd (5500)	46
1st (5500)	30
Acceleration:	
0–30 mph, sec	3.8
0–40	5.9
0–50	9.0
0–60	12.0
0–70	15.7
0–80	20.4
Standing ¼ mile	18.5
Speed at end	76

SPRINT DEALERS

Dutchess Auto Co., Millerton, N. Y.
Atwood Chevrolet, Bristol, Conn.
Seymour Chevrolet, Greenwich, Conn.
Harry Mann, Los Angeles, Calif.
Bud Gates, Indianapolis, Ind.
Nickey Chevrolet, Chicago, Ill.
Don Allen, New York, N. Y. (and 8 associates)
Cooke Chevrolet, Louisville, Ky.
Don Yenko Chevrolet, Canonsburg, Pa.
Jim White Chevrolet, Toledo, Ohio (and 9 associates)

Two additional Corvair carburetors are installed.

Protective screen hinges to allow access to trunk lock.

CAR and DRIVER
ROAD TEST

Corvair Monza Spyder

Poor Man's Porsche adds a "Super" to the top of the line

High-powered **Spyder** remains flat and stable, if a bit hung-out, on bad surfaces.

N ow that the Chevy II has come along to relieve the Corvair of the responsibility of being "sensible," in the sense of stodgy and mundane transportation, the Corvair has been allowed to swing. Back in the beginning of the great compact revolution, General Motors engaged in some typical thinking, and came up with a carefully implemented misunderstanding: the sales department was under the impression that it was getting a Falcon, and Engineering was under the impression that it had been ordered to build a Volkswagen. The result, in addition to the first Corvair, was a panic that caused the Chevy II to be pushed through as a hysterical reaction, to give Sales something to throw into the battle with Ford.

Interestingly enough, in the interim between panic and Chevy II introduction, the Corvair had been developed into a pretty fine automobile. And, perhaps more interesting, it was done under the aegis of Billy Mitchell and the much-maligned styling department. The top-of-the-line Monza has taken over so much of the Corvair's sales that the lower lines are dropped or ignored. The Chevy II has been a success, but

registrations of that car haven't in any gross way overshadowed those of Monza Corvairs. The success of the factory-entered rally cars in various Canadian events, and a continuing succession of improvements, have made a warm spot for the car among automotive enthusiasts throughout the country. Every option that comes along seems to add to the sporting nature of the little dear. And the latest, the exhaust-driven turbo-supercharger, is per-

haps the largest single step in a sporting direction.

This option, covered technically in C/D in June, 1962, is very simply a small compressor that uses exhaust gases for power and provides a healthy boost in intake manifold pressure for what is basically a very restrictive head design. The result is a jump in horsepower and torque on the order of 50%.

If this explanation seems a bit single-minded, then that is as it

Miserable weather conditions really brought out the charm of Corvair's neat coupe.

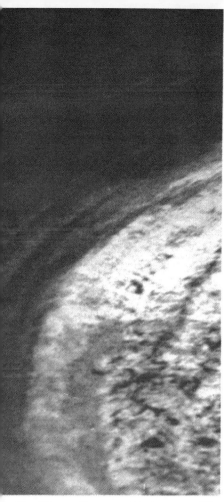

Handling options are chiefly responsible.

should be. The turbo-charger is just as directly straightforward in its approach to the problem, avoiding as many complications as possible and making no compromises at the expense of all-out performance. The Oldsmobile exhaust-driven super-charger, by contrast, is forced to embroil itself in sophistication to give a broad range of response with tractability. The Corvair doesn't bother. There is lag in the throttle response (because of the inertia of the exhaust-driven turbine), there is no boost to speak of until about 2,400 rpm, and maximum boost (about 10 p.s.i.) isn't obtained until 3,400 rpm. Further, to avoid the high-compression-ratio detonation problems that forced Oldsmobile to devise a water-and-alcohol injection system, Chevrolet engineers responded with disarming directness: they simply lowered the compression ratio, from 9-to-1 down to 8-to-1, and got, in the bargain, a more manageable low-rpm engine than the 102-bhp "Hi-Performance Turbo-Air." (They also radically revised the spark-advance curve for the same reasons.)

The package comes as the "Corvair Monza Spyder," from Mitchell's "Sebring Spyder" dream car a couple of years back. The name seems to mean the turbo-charger package, plus some identifying trim and a very handsome brushed-aluminum instrument panel, with 120-mph speedometer, resettable trip odometer, an electric tachometer (which unfortunately crams its 6,000-rpm range into a quadrant, instead of keeping the styling theme of the speedometer, and being incidentally a lot easier to read), a manifold pressure gauge that reads either vacuum or pressure, a fuel gauge, and a cylinder-head thermometer.

Also standard equipment on the Spyder is the 3.55-to-1 rear axle ratio, which is a particularly good choice. Not only does it give a nice compromise for all-round use, but it provides a traditional set of figures for the enthusiast. Fourth gear gives 20 mph per 1,000 rpm, so two times the number on the tach gives the mph. Handy. The ratio does make for a bit of noisy churning, though, particularly when the heater is whistling away at high rpm.

Testing a tried-and-true, already-on-the-market sort of car with a markedly more powerful engine op-tion, the likely thing to remark would be the performance of the combination, in particular the ac-celeration. As it turns out, we found ourselves more intrigued by the virtues of the basic, evolving design than by the performance option. What comes with the blown Corvair is better than the blower.

What came with it on the test car was the four-speed manual transmission, the heavy-duty suspension, the heavy-duty metallic brakes, and Positraction. (What didn't come with it, and isn't available from Chevrolet, to our great disappointment, is faster steering. Despite constant nagging from enthusiast sources, otherwise known as the market, for more than three years, and despite continual improvement in the running gear and handling of the car, Chevrolet still hasn't made faster steering available. The car has the lightest non-power steering imaginable now, so fears of heavy steering could hardly be the excuse. With the Corvair's weight bias and swing axles, it needs quickened steering perhaps more than anything else. Why it isn't available, when other options are, is beyond us.) The handling options to trans-form the car, changing it from a queasy every-now-and-then-you-almost-catch-up-with-it feeling to a solid and positive tautness that gives confidence. It becomes a great car to charge around back-country roads in, which is just what we spent most of our time doing, in the snow.

The surprise of the car, however, is a somewhat negative one, having to do with its complete tractability. On one hand there is the little fun car, great in the snow, manageable and with a trace of fire. On the other, there is the expected liveliness that somehow doesn't materialize, the knowledge that something ought to be going on back there that never makes itself felt (despite the fine acceleration times the car turns in). With the lowered compression ratio, around-the-town plugging below the 3,400-rpm limit of maximum blower effect is pleasanter than in the 102-bhp car with the same (3.55-to-1) rear axle ratio. In fact, given a top limit on the order of 4,000 rpm, it would be easy to come away from a trial run wondering if you hadn't been in the wrong car.

With the accepted lag in blower response, the 3,400-rpm lower limit to maximum boost, and the stump-pulling gearing of the indirect ratios in the transmission, by the time the turbocharger begins to take effect, on a hard acceleration run, it is almost time to upshift. The kick in the back is a mild one, only

Weather equipment worked well once the car was really warm, but warm-up was slow.

MONZA SPYDER

achieved at the very top end of the rev scale, and short-lived at that (we used 5,000 rpm in our test, and the engine wasn't really sharp in the upper ranges). It has its effect, this blower, in acceleration runs. But for the kind of rip-rip quick response on the road (that the car could now handle), it needs low-end punch and reduced weight.

Perhaps with time in the car it would be possible to become accustomed to staying up where the boost comes in. In case this is your custom, you shouldn't have to worry about things staying together, because included in the engine when blower-fitted are heavier connecting rods, different bearing inserts, a specially hardened crankshaft, special pistons and rings, and different materials for exhaust valves and valve guides. Externally there are various modifications to the power plant, mostly for heat protection because of the use of exhaust gases in the engine compartment. The option includes a heavier clutch.

Shift linkage on the fine four-speed all-synchromesh transmission has been improved considerably, and there is no hint of previous second-gear problems that occasionally cropped up in earlier versions. The device is a continuing joy, effortless and yet positive. The much-praised Monza interior is pleasant and plush, the individual seats doing a lot better job of holding and supporting than many of the pure-blooded buckets of the past. A bit more adjustment would be welcome in the seating, but there's room for all but the occasional anomaly (and we've got a staff full of anomalies). The car's very lowness makes entry and exit a bit cumbersome, but we seem to be continually paying that price these days for styling—and a low center of gravity—and smiling about it. All in all, the character of the car hasn't been changed very much, except for a large chunk of capability tacked onto one end.

In that light a particular comparison comes to mind. Corvair has benefited since the beginning from a "poor man's Porsche" whispering campaign. And we are reminded of the Porsche Normal vs. Porsche Super arguments that rage eternally. The "Super" designation on a Porsche is sometimes characterized as 500 rpm, at a dollar apiece, tacked onto the wrong end—for normal street use, that is, since another 500 rpm of redline is not too handy in traffic. The Spyder option on the Corvair Monza is very similar, but only if compared to a Monza that already has the handling options.

Tradition has it that the first

Tiny blower doesn't interfere with spare.

bunch of enthusiasts sprang full-blown and wind-whipped out of MG TCs—a little mythically, perhaps. Another batch has undoubtedly erupted from the Volkswagen, wending their economic way just as enthusiastically and with just as much dedication to the sport. We suspect that the New Wave in sports cars will flow from just the sort of machinery that staid old General Motors is supplying in the Monza. GM must certainly be surprised to see what has happened to its economy car, which is rapidly becoming "too good for the common people." But where else can you buy a four-seater that will break 100 mph, do 0-60 in less than 12 seconds, have all-independent suspension, four-speed all-synchro gearbox, American-car luxury, and reasonable handling for under $3,000? **C/D**

CORVAIR MONZA SPYDER

Price as tested: $2,739.65
Manufacturer: General Motors Corporation
Detroit 2, Michigan

ACCELERATION:

Zero to	Seconds
30 mph	3.9
60 mph	11.7
90 mph	25.7
Standing start ¼	18.5

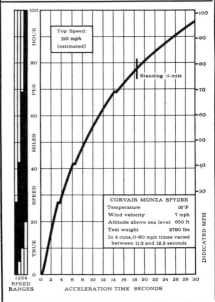

Top Speed: 110 mph (estimated)

Standing ¼-mile

CORVAIR MONZA SPYDER
Temperature 18°F
Wind velocity 7 mph
Altitude above sea level 650 ft
Test weight 2790 lbs
In 4 runs, 0-60 mph times varied between 11.3 and 12.3 seconds

SPEED RANGES ACCELERATION TIME SECONDS

ENGINE:

Displacement	145 cu in, 2,372 cc
Dimensions	6 cyl, 3.44-in bore, 2.60-in stroke
Valve gear	narrow-angle, pushrod-operated, overhead valves
Compression ratio	8 to one
Power (SAE)	150 bhp @ 4,400 rpm
Torque	210 lb-ft @ 32-3400 rpm
Usable range of engine speeds	850-5,200 rpm
Carburetion: Single-barrel sidedraft Carter and Turbo-Supercharger	
Fuel recommended	Premium
Mileage	16-24 mpg
Range on 14-gallon tank	225-335 miles

CHASSIS:

Wheelbase	108 in
Track	F 54.5 in, R 54.5 in
Length	180 in
Ground clearance	7.5 in
Suspension: F: ind., wishbones and coil springs. R: ind., swing axles, trailing wishbones, and coil springs.	
Steering	Recirculating ball
Turns, lock to lock	5
Turning circle diameter between curbs	42 ft
Tire size	6.50 x 13
Pressures recommended	F 15, R 26 psi
Brakes	9-in drums, 198 sq in swept area
Curb weight (full tank)	2,513 lbs
Percentage on the driving wheels	62

DRIVE TRAIN:

Clutch . . . . Single disc dry plate

Gear	Synchro	Ratio	Step	Over-all	Mph per 1,000 rpm
Rev	No	3.66		13.15	-5.3
1st	Yes	3.65	57%	12.98	5.4
2nd	Yes	2.35	63%	8.34	8.3
3rd	Yes	1.44	44%	5.12	13.6
4th	Yes	1.00		3.55	19.8
Final drive ratio				3.55 to one	

Dome behind tire protects it from heat.

Lush Spyder interior, with well-placed controls, makes a very desirable package.

Front anti-roll bar, stiffer springs and shocks of the heavy-duty suspension kit (standard with Spyder engine) reduce positive camber of rear wheels, lower car.

Brushed-aluminum dash is handsome, with nearly complete set of instruments, but markings on tach are too small for quick readings; full-circle dial would help.

CORVAIR MONZA GT

SINCE ITS INCEPTION the Corvair has been classified as the "fun-type" Compact, pleasant and sporty to drive. Chevrolet enhanced this image by coming out with the Monza. The reception has been gratifying and, to keep interest fresh, construction was authorized for two "idea" cars; the Monza GT and Monza SS, the latter a roadster version nearly identical to the coupe detailed here. Bernard Cahier, in the April SCG, described an around-the-block-type driving impression of the coupe when it was equipped with a 200-horsepower three-liter engine. As the design of this machine is a matter of close co-operation between Chevy's Re-

hevy's Forward-Look xercise is in he right direction.

search & Development and GM Styling, several experimental engines have been shuffled in and out. At this writing, a "nearly" stock Corvair is installed.

The sleek, delta-nosed body is the result of wind-tunnel testing based on an increased interest in aerodynamics that has come to Motor City. GM's Styling chose Fibreglass as the skin material for the upper body sections, while the large rocker panels are aluminum, semi-stressed to tie in with the bathtub-type pan, also of aluminum, forming a unitized chassis. The body shell is therefore three pieces; tail-section, canopy, and nose. All three tilt up for access to powertrain, cockpit, and forward section. The canopy, which includes the doors, windows, roof, and windshield, poses an interesting problem when applied to FIA

CORVAIR MONZA GT

GT rules. The latter specifies a door for each side. *This* the Monza GT has — and of legal size, too — but do you consider it one or two doors when they are joined together and open simultaneously?

Speaking of FIA rules, the Monza GT wouldn't quite make the category, but it's a lot closer than you might imagine. The production Corvair Monza would, naturally, qualify for homologation. A special body is allowed on a production series and, in the case of a unit-constructed chassis, a special frame/body is allowed. But sub-frames and all mechanical components have to be in the original model. And here the Monza GT deviates by placing the engine in front of the transaxle and by using different suspension, brakes, etc. than the production car.

The suspension system is full-independent, with the classic unequal A-arms both front and rear. The rears are ball-jointed at the outer end and a third arm — ála Ferrari Formula 1 — attaches to the hub carrier to govern rear-wheel toe-in. Torsion bars provide the spring medium at all four corners. Disc brakes of undetermined size are mounted outboard, behind the 13-inch knock-off alloy wheels. Details of items such as drive axles, front spindles, and many other technical features are not available, "as a matter of Chevrolet policy." We presume this is for two possible reasons; either prototype components are being used or enough changes are being made in experimentation so that no set specifications can be given. It is stated that the car is equipped with a four-speed gearbox with hydraulic-actuated clutch. In some photos of the car, strange bits of hardware can be seen on the engine, but the major difference in appearance is an elaborate cold-air box to the carbure-

Cockpit, left, has a minimum of frills and good instrumentation. Seats are unadjustable; wheel & pedals move to fit driver.

Headlight doors, right, are exotic but Mickey-Mouse due to lack of streamlining in open position as shown. It is dash-controlled.

tors leading from the louvered scoops in the rear quarter-panels of the body. The exhaust system is dual, including mufflers, and kicks up in the air just aft of the engine to exit on each side of the rear deck. Either flexible tubing or special couplings are used so the lid can be raised with the tailpipe extensions remaining in the body.

In both design and space allotment, the cockpit is very racecar-like with long, semi-reclining bucket seats molded into the shell. Adjustment to driver size is made by mounting the pedals on a moveable bracket and including a slip-coupling in the steering column. The wheel, incidentally, is completely removeable to allow ease of entry. More like an armrest than a floor tunnel, a central separator for the seats holds the short gearshift handle and a toggle-type horn "button."

The simple instrument panel is crackle-finished, has the tach and speedometer directly behind the steering wheel, other gauges on the right side but canted toward the driver for easy reading. Switches form a vertical row of toggles in the center. Wide sills on both sides of the cockpit are fully upholstered.

Twin, interconnected gas tanks are placed in the front fenders, just behind the wheels and in a manner not unlike the Lotus 19. The sharp-edged nose contains doors that open right on the leading edge to reveal rectangular headlights. Very aerodynamic when closed, these doors split to open much like a bomb bay and they appear to be the one impractical concession in the car, forming very effective air-brakes when open. There are, of course, other solutions not quite so exotic but far more practical.

Justifiably, the Monza GT has received a lot of attention and, like the Ford Mustang, given rise to rumors that a very similar car is about to be produced. Such, we can assure you, is *not* the case. The purpose of this type of machine is very close to exactly that stated by the factory; an engineering and styling exercise. It also provides a show-type vehicle that's worth its cost in publicity and enables the Sales Dept. to survey public reception to the design for future reference. Most important — from the outsider's standpoint — is that it proves Detroit engineers and stylists are both cognizant and capable of the design and construction of very sophisticated machinery. The knowledge and experience gained on projects of this type will be reflected in the showroom product of the near future. The thinking we find displayed in the Monza GT is indeed encouraging.
— *J.T.*

PHOTOS: GM PHOTOGRAPHIC

A unique gimmick is louvered rear window shown here in both opened and closed positions. It would be more practical if slats were made of Plexiglass, giving vision closed.

Though tight laterally, there's a lot of room for the driver's legs in the small car. Note good hand-control placement.

EMPI-Equipped Corvair Monza

Bolt-On Suspension and Engine Equipment
Can Improve the Monza's "Fun Factor"

CAR LIFE ROAD TEST

THERE ARE SO many excellent qualities inherent in the Corvair that we often tend to completely overlook some of its less acceptable points. Fortunately, the Corvair enthusiasts and the performance accessory manufacturers haven't been so derelict in their attention.

The Corvair has become such a popular vehicle with the younger and sporting type of buyer that a large new accessory market has sprung up around it. The range of additional equipment and dress-up paraphernalia available is far greater than that for any other single car on the U.S. market today.

This market burgeoned because of two factors: A) there were certain specific weaknesses to the Corvair's character, and B) the car's size, appearance and maneuverability have tremendous appeal to the enthusiastic sort of driver —so much appeal, in fact, he's willing to overlook or improve those traits which are displeasing to him.

Closely keeping pace with the trends in this market is EMPI, a Riverside, Calif.-based specialty house which manufactures and markets, both wholesale and retail, a wide variety of nonstandard equipment for the Corvair. EMPI, which stands for Engineered Motor Parts Inc., actually got into busi-

ness by supplying just the same sort of product for the Volkswagen, now happily finds Corvair equipment sales surpassing those of the VW.

To improve the handling ability of the car, EMPI offers a "Camber Compensator" rear wheel stabilizer, an anti-roll bar to be added to the front suspension and replacement steering arms for quicker steering.

Powerplant improvements have been limited to the "bolt-on" variety, which still leaves a wide area of operation. EMPI has done a good deal of work with single-carburetor intake manifolds, replacing the stock units (two, single-barrel) with either 2- or 4-barrel instruments. Results are impressive. EMPI also sells mufflers and muffler systems, transistor ignitions and additional instrumentation.

What do these do for the automobile? Do they really work to improve handling, performance and driver satisfaction? In most cases, either with the items evaluated separately or in confluence, the answer must be a qualified "yes."

Having already driven a large variety of Corvairs, mostly non-modified, the *Car Life* staff borrowed one of EMPI's demonstration vehicles for an examination of the other side of the coin. What a surprise! The EMPI-ized Corvair has a completely different character and displays vastly better manners on the highway. The flavor is far more sporting than before, and, in fact, it exudes more sportiveness than many so-called sports cars.

Perhaps the key to this improved handling is EMPI's own Camber Compensator, a transverse single-leaf spring which links together the independently sprung rear wheels. Pivoting at the differential housing, this spring acts just the opposite to the motion of an anti-roll bar.

Where an anti-roll bar tries to keep the front wheels in similar attitudes during cornering maneuvers, the Compensator tends to pull the inside, unloaded wheel toward the full rebound position, thereby lessening the body roll. This won't do a thing for solid-axle rear suspensions but it does wonders with the Corvair, where the inside rear wheel has a great tendency to "tuck under" during cornering. It also tends to lessen the effect of body roll on the angled trailing arm pivots, which normally causes the inside wheel to assume an understeering, and the outside wheel an oversteering, attitude. The roll oversteer of this vehicle has been one of its most criticized points, so EMPI's device is a real improvement.

TWIN TAILPIPES of EMPI's Bestone system project from under Monza's rear.

In conjunction with this, EMPI's front anti-roll bar works nicely, stiffening up the front roll-resistance to the point where the car appears to corner in a virtually flat attitude. This is the usual type of bar (commonly referred to as a "sway bar" although it has nothing to do with controlling "sway" or "yaw") similar to the one Chevrolet recommends with its Heavy-Duty suspension options. Cost of the bar is $19.95, where the Compensator kit is $24.95, you-install-it.

Our test car also had quick-steering arms and these imparted a much more suitable reaction to steering wheel movement. Slow steering has also been a Corvair complaint and the EMPI arms reduce the number of turns required to turn the wheel from lock to lock from 4.8 to 3.3 turns. This accessory, however, has certain drawbacks: increased turning radius and heavier steering, equivalent to about that of a light front-engined car without power steering. The turning radius reduction manifests itself in slightly lessened maneuverability, particularly noticeable during parking and parking lot activities. Still, at $19.95, a worthwhile addition.

Putting the steering and handling characteristics together, we found excellent compatibility. On dry pavement the car could be whipped around corners without the wheel hop character-

CHROMED, REVERSED wheels and knockoff-type caps add a custom touch; spotlights are dummies, strictly for show.

WOOD-RIMMED steering wheel, console panel are expensive but usable accessories.

EMPI-Equipped Corvair Monza

istic of the standard Corvair's rear suspension. The lack of body roll was especially noticeable. The car seemed quicker through every conceivable cornering condition. In the wet, however, we found that the greater "flatness" lessened the warning of impending rear-end breakaway, which seemed to occur at approximately the same speed as with a normal Corvair. Thus, while the threshold of breakaway has been moved notably upward with the EMPI kits, it would seem that ultimate

cornering force is still determined by the slip angles of the tires.

What effect the reversed (and chrome-plated) wheels had on the cornering power would be difficult to judge. Reversing the wheels gives them more leverage on the springs, thus reducing (softening) the spring action; also, the increased track tends to magnify oversteer (with wider front track) and understeer (wider rear track) effects. Theoretically, the wider the track is in relation to the wheelbase, the more

stable will be the car. The Corvair's track is already 54.1% of the wheelbase, where the popularly called "Wide Track" is only 53.3%. One word of caution about reversed wheels in general: the reversing has to be done by a competent, careful shop, else the wheels will be out of true and out of balance, and the altering of the hub/rim relationship can cause wheel centers to crack out and wheel bearings to fail. We are not at all certain that whatever benefits accrue from the reversing are worth the risk.

Bolt-on engine equipment can be risky, too; the would-be improver of operational efficiency can, through misguided ministrations, completely destroy all versatility or performance potential of his particular plant. But with organizations such as EMPI, the experimentation has been done before the kit is offered to the public. Final and fine tuning, of course, has to be left to the individual and this factor sometimes spells the difference between a successful and an unsuccessful conversion.

EMPI currently offers two types of intake manifolds for the Corvair, one mounting a single Rochester 4-barrel carburetor and the other a Rochester 2-barrel unit. Both carburetors are original equipment on Chevrolet V-8s and are in relatively plentiful supply. The manifold consists of two extension tubes, which bolt to the old carburetor flanges at the heads, and which are connected by a common chamber on which the carburetor is mounted.

Both systems offer certain specific advantages over the stock system and over each other. Both have drawbacks. The buyer must determine whether the advantages overcome the drawbacks.

REVERSED WHEEL widens track, helps handling.

IN ACTION, the Camber Compensator keeps rear wheels aligned.

The stock Corvair comes from the factory with a pair of single barrel, 1.25 in. dia. throat carburetors, which give, when wide open, 2.45 sq. in. of venturi area. Substituting the 2-barrel single unit, albeit at a greater distance from the intake ports and hence slightly slowing engine reaction, gives an increase in area to 3.24 sq. in. The 4-barrel, as is well known, operates on 2 barrels (1.44 in. dia. each) most of the time, but when the primary throttles reach a pre-set position, the secondary pair begins to open, so that when full-throttle is reached, all four barrels, and 6.48 sq. in. of venturi area, are open.

More area means simply better breathing at the top rpm range—hence more power, more rpm.

The drawback, of course, is that large venturis do not operate well at low speed. There's so little vacuum through the venturi that gasoline is not properly vaporized and the engine often starves out. Without the assistance of carburetor heat, it is most difficult to keep the 4-barrel equipped Corvair running at an idle when it is cold. The 2-barrel model we drove, which had a form of carburetor heat, was much better in this respect.

The 2-barrel system actually was a prototype of a new manifold EMPI is announcing shortly. Finished in a black crackle paint, the manifold conducts heat along itself to the carburetor. This probably is not nearly as efficient as ducted hot exhaust gas, but it is far less complicated. This new manifold mounts the carburetor lower and farther forward than other similar setups, thus eliminating the need for modifying the inside of the deck lid.

Checking the performance revealed some definite improvements, although

VISIBLE BENEATH chromed exhaust pipe is EMPI's Camber Compensator.

we can't call them startling. We sampled both a 4-barrel equipped car and one with the 2-barrel; the former needed a tune-up, the latter was fresh and didn't. As a comparison, we list the results from a *Car Life* road test of a stock, 1961 Corvair Monza.

	4-BBL.	2-BBL.	STOCK
0-40 mph	7.0 sec.	7.2 sec.	6.8 sec.
0-60	15.0	15.5	15.5
0.80	21.1	32.5	35.0
¼ mile	19.9	20.3	20.3

Obviously, the benefits to be gained are all at the upper end of the performance scale. This can be interpreted as passing performance, too, since this is the range (3rd and 4th gears, 3000–5000 rpm) most used for

accelerating past slower-moving vehicles. The safety factor is obviously increased. The lower range performance is not improved noticeably, however, and the Corvair has just as much "dig" with the stock carburetion. We must note, though, that the seemingly lumpy idle and bucking characteristics typical of the Monza 102-bhp engine are eliminated by the addition of either EMPI carburetion system.

Another increment in the car's fun factor was notched by EMPI's Bestone dual exhaust system which, while it may not necessarily increase the engine efficiency, does wonders for driver morale. Although quiet enough

BIG CARBURETOR mounts on manifold extensions.

ROCHESTER 4-barrel improves top-end performance, acceleration.

COMPENSATOR attaches to differential housing, suspension arms.

EMPI-Equipped Corvair Monza

to pass inspection by the most un-equivocal law enforcer, the unobtrusively audible exhaust note is just right for the enthusiast.

Interior accessories are also popular and here EMPI offers the gamut. As can be noted from the photos, our test car had EMPI's Instrument Console. This combines cylinder-head tempera-ture gauge, electronic tachometer and an ammeter set into a single panel, which is mounted on top of the regular dash pad between the twin humps. The console is finished in a matching material and blends well into the scheme of things. However, on our test car the tachometer didn't work accurately and the instrument lights

didn't dim with the panel light rheostat. Turn signal flashing caused 2000 rpm fluctuations of the tachometer needle, leading us to believe that a shielded cable should have been used to connect tachometer to coil.

We found the cylinder head temperature gauge to be very worthwhile, particularly during our test runs, where we kept a wary eye out for any temperature rise. It did go as high as 300° F. while we were testing, from a normal cruising temperature of 260°. Head temp gauges should be made standard equipment on all Corvairs.

Headrests, which we can take or leave, and dummy spotlights, which we'll definitely leave, were the finishing, customizing touches.

What does all this cost in terms of money? Our demonstrator had more than $550 in EMPI accessories added to a car which costs $2364 to begin with. Is the game worth the candle? It all depends, as Tom said saltily, upon your taste. ∎

CAR LIFE ROAD TEST

PERFORMANCE

Top speed (4300), mph	93
Shifts, rpm-mph (manual)	
3rd (4700)	70
2nd (5000)	46
1st (5050)	30

ACCELERATION

0-30 mph, sec	4.1
0-40	7.0
0-50	11.0
0-60	15.0
0-70	21.1
0-80	31.5
0-100	
Standing ¼ mile	19.9
speed at end	68.5

FUEL CONSUMPTION

Normal range, mpg	14-16

SPEEDOMETER ERROR

30 mph, actual	29.0
60 mph	57.0
80 mph	75.6

CALCULATED DATA

Lb/hp (test wt)	28.0
Cu ft/ton mile	81.7
Mph/1000 rpm	21.6
Engine revs/mile	2780
Piston travel, ft/mile	1205
Car Life wear index	33.4

PULLING POWER

4th, max gradient, %	8.7
3rd	13.0
2nd	21.1
Total drag at 60 mph, lb	125

CORVAIR MONZA
Empi-equipped

SPECIFICATIONS

List price	$2364
Price, as tested	2914
Curb weight, lb	2530
Test weight	2860
distribution, %	37/63
Tire size	6.50-13
Tire capacity, lb	3600
Brake swept area	197.7
Engine type	flat-6, ohv
Bore & stroke	3.44 x 2.60
Displacement, cu in	145
Compression ratio	9.0
Carburetion	1 x 4
Bhp @ rpm	102 @ 4400
equivalent mph	95.0
Torque, lb-ft	134 @ 2800
equivalent mph	60.5

EXTRA-COST OPTIONS

Camber Compensator, 4-bbl. carb., reversed & chromed wheels, wsw tires, headrests, wood-rim steering wheel, instr. console, Quickshift, dummy spotlights, anti-roll bar, am/fm radio.

DIMENSIONS

Wheelbase, in	108.0
Tread, f and r	54.5
Over-all length, in	180.0
width	67.0
height	51.5
equivalent vol, cu ft	360
Frontal area, sq ft	19.2
Ground clearance, in	6.0
Steering ratio, o/a	n.a.
turns, lock to lock	3.3
turning circle, ft	45.5
Hip room, front	2 x 25.5
Hip room, rear	57.0
Pedal to seat back, max	39.0
Floor to ground	9.0
Luggage vol, cu ft	6.6
Fuel tank capacity, gal	14.0

GEAR RATIOS

4th (1.000), overall		3.27
3rd (1.438)		4.70
2nd (2.350)		7.68
1st (3.647)		11.9

ACCELERATION & COASTING

ELAPSED TIME IN SECONDS

ONZA GT (DREAM)

IT'S only a dream car they say, put on show to tempt visitors away from other exhibits at New York, but is it? The Chevrolet Monza GT introduces a lot of ingenious features, but is a car which could be built in the not very distant future, many of its parts coming from existing Corvair models.

The whole car has been designed around an unconventional cockpit, as used on Bertone's special Corvair exhibit at Geneva Motor Show and illustrated in the April issue of *Sporting Motorist*. Instead of a fixed roof and two hinged doors, there is one structure comprising the roof, a windscreen which wraps right around the body sides, and the panels of what would normally be doors, and this structure hinges forwards to let passengers enter or leave the car. In the high-sided cockpit two seats are fixed, the pedals being adjustable, as also is a telescopic, universally-jointed steering column. One can counter-balance this sort of an opening roof, but one could not open it on a wet day without letting in the rain.

In the manner of modern racing cars, this Monza GT has its engine ahead of the rear axle, the same twin-carburettor air-cooled flat six is used *behind* the rear axle in other Corvair models. Instead of the stressed steel bodywork of other Corvairs, this two-seater has plastic panels on a girder frame, the members of which virtually enclose the engine. At last disc brakes appear on a General Motors car, behind cast light-alloy wheels with centre-lock hubs.

An ingenious form of enclosure is used for two rectangular headlamps which, as on so many dream cars, are mounted unacceptably low down. Each lamp has a streamlined two-piece cover, of which one half hinges up and the other down when the headlights are needed. Tail treatment of the bodywork features the fashionable concave panel for rear lamps and a number plate, is unusual in having adjustable louvres in the manner of a venetian blind to provide ventilation through the steeply sloping rear window.

The Monza GT is only 13 ft 9 in long, on a wheelbase of 7 ft 8 in, and its height is 3 ft 6 in. General Motors Corporation describe the Corvair GT as "part of Chevrolet's continuous programme of building and evaluating new styling and engineering ideas. While they will not be produced, we will be most interested in show visitors' reaction to them." I, on the other hand, would guess that Chevrolet will be building and selling a small brother for the V-8 Corvette Sting Ray, a sports car not unlike this Monza GT, within at most two years.   **Joseph Lowrey.**

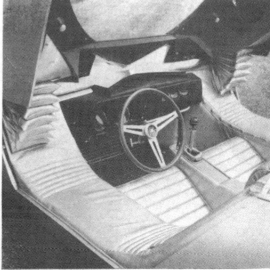

CORVAIR MONZA

Detail refinements, and more sting in the tail.

What the Chevrolet Motor Division of General Motors has done to the Corvair should happen to a lot of cars.

Instead of paying lip service to the routine industry claim of making 'tremendous improvements,' Chevy has actually carried out a program of steady refinements on a basic design. Instead of moving the chrome around a bit or re-hashing the body lines to produce the illusion of newness, the company has instituted a number of mechanical changes. And, instead of a test reporter being forced to search for something to say about innocuous cosmetic applications, those who drive the 1964 Corvair can see *and feel* the difference. (Shades of Volkswagen!)

In fact the company has done exactly what a legion of Corvair fanciers have been crying for and what a vast number have been doing to their own cars for a couple of years. The proprietary modification components from EMPI, Bill Thomas, EICO, John Fitch and so on, which have found a market like that generated by the Ford V8 in 1932, pointed the way. Chevrolet deserves a boost for having the temerity to adopt their approach. It is much easier, and more conductive to sales, to move the chrome.

Two substantial changes have been made for 1964: Engine and chassis.

Of the two, alterations to the suspension are the most significant but the increased engine size makes it even more fun for the modifier.

Externally, and in the interior, you will have to look twice to distinguish the year model. Basically, the bright metal body-sill molding has been smoothed out and a chrome bead is carried around the wheel openings; new tail light bezels and lenses are used; the rear grille is different and the identification name plates have been changed. In addition, Chevy has come up with some actually good looking, non false-appearing wire wheel covers. It takes a couple of glances to determine that these are not the Mc Coy. The individual chromed spokes are remarkably well done and the whole effect is excellent.

Phony Borranis do not a sports car make, of course, nor does a four speed gear box transform a sedan into a Gran Turismo. But the Corvair is approaching the latter if not the former. Best of all, its new handling characteristics will please those who admire GT cars, and make driving a lot safer for the Clyde who thinks that "handling" refers to the charges tacked onto his financing.

There is a good chance that soon Corvairs will no longer lead the statistics in one-car accidents. The new suspension should certainly eliminate many of the 'lost control' phrases in Highway Patrol reports because the car now has a much more conventional feel in many of its cornering attitudes and a lot fewer quick reactions are required. You can still swap ends with it but you have to try a lot harder and the biggest hazard—decelerating at the apex of a sharp turn—is not nearly so conducive to butterflies in the pit of the stomach.

The Corvair is still not going to satisfy the all-out enthusiast who sees his car as the thinking man's Ferrari, it will take a few John Fitch *Sprint* type modifications to achieve that, as it has in the past, but for pleasant cruising on nearly any kind of road. the 1964 model is an outstanding example of the car builder's art.

The 'nearly' is inserted in the preceding sentence only because extremely rough going with lots of deep ruts, chuck holes and high centers is murder with this chassis. Like a Porsche, when you come to the end of the pavement, you slow way down and pick your route carefully to avoid wiping out a large part of your investment. The Corvair is no Jeep, otherwise it is close to impeccable. Much less affected by wind and high speed wander than before, the Corvair will hang on 100 mph (indicated) almost hands-off.

Steering is still a trifle slow but steering response has been improved. The initial moment of oversteer is present in the same degree but it shifts back to a near-neutral feel as the new suspension begins to work and breaks away much later. Body lean is less and there is much less of a need to brace a knee against the door in cornering.

Credit for this improvement goes to a shrewd application of the helper spring principle in conjunction with a front anti-roll bar. Both of these items have been available as accessories for previous models but the reason they work noticeably better on the 1964 model is that the rear spring rate has been reduced. Weight shift diagonally across the chassis is greatly improved and the effect of what amounts to a dual spring rate is highly beneficial as outside rear wheel loading increases. The Corvair still needs improved shock absorbers to take advantage of the suspension's potential, but it is a giant step in the right direction.

Corvair dealer service information bulletins, link the transverse helper spring to the Sting Ray Corvette (which uses a leaf spring) but this seems more like coincidence.

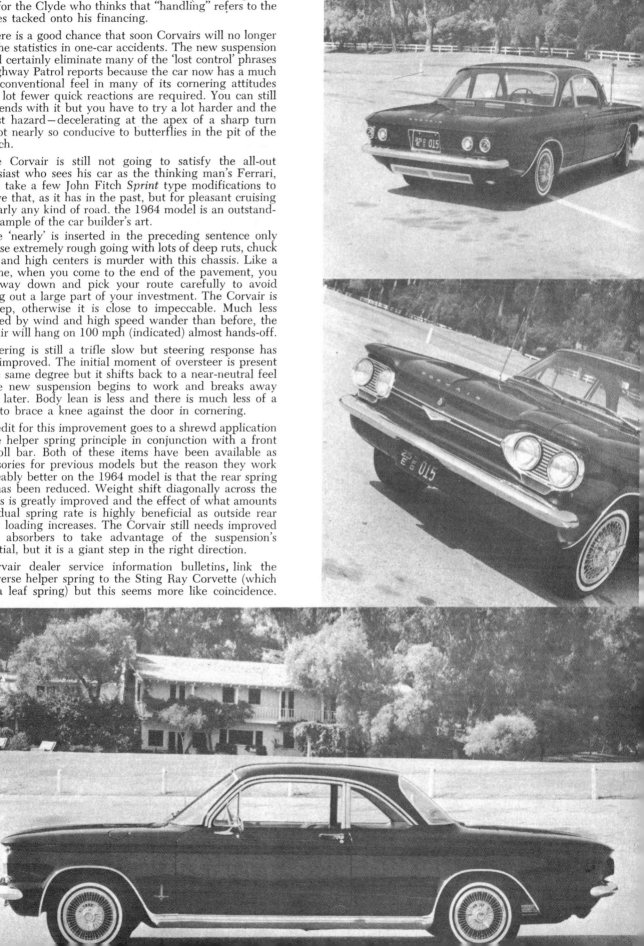

CORVAIR

Porsche has utilized the idea for several years and the whole scheme seems to have stemmed from Joe Vittone's "Camber Compensator." Regardless, the center of the leaf is attached to a mounting flange cast into the trans-axle housing, sandwiched between rubber insulators. The outer ends are drilled and a long bolt passes through the leaf into a bracket on the control arm. Rubber biscuits are used here to lessen the chance of transmitting vibrations to the drive unit. The leaf is curved downward and at design holds the biscuit against the washer and retaining nut so there is no chance that it will rattle.

Engine improvements are more subtle but just as encouraging.

They follow accepted practice of increasing displacement, but in the case of the Corvair the increase has been needed far more than in the full sized Chevy for example. Displacement has been upped from 145 cubic inches to 164 cubic inches by increasing the stroke (from 2.60 inches to 2.94 inches) in both the Turbo-Air and the Turbocharged models. Horsepower rating for the basic engine is now given as 95 bhp. The 'High Performance' engine is rated at 110 but the Turbocharged Spyder is still 150 bhp. The "Monza Powerglide" as a separate engine (94 hp) has been discontinued.

Corvair has returned to the central aircleaner mounted over the cooling blower inlet, as on the 1960 model, but it is a different setup, basically like the "snorkle" units used on water cooled Chevy engines. Carburetors remain the same in venturi size but have been re-jetted and altered to conform with the greater velocity induced by the bigger engine. Linkage is changed somewhat and a mechanical air bleed has been incorporated to improve hot starting and idle. This bleed is a small passage drilled into the throttle bore and sealed by a rubber plug mounted on a piece of spring stock. The plug is unseated and the passage opened by a tang on the fast idle cam to provide a greater amount of air. A spring-loaded float is also used to cure complaints of fuel flooding during hard cornering.

The new longer stroke crank in non-blown engines is now made of the same alloy used in the Spyder shaft (5140), and a Simpson type harmonic balancer is incorporated in all but the base engine when used with a manual transmission. Crank gear and keys have also been strengthened, and an oil slinger has returned to the distributor end.

Premium aluminum bearings are now used on both rod and main journals. Rods are of a new design, like the Turbocharged type in cross section, with altered caps (to provide more clearance in the slightly changed case). Clearance was eked out as much as possible by removing some of the side wall meat, but conditions are still pretty cramped. Tappet bore angle and spacing is different to accommodate revised cam lobes and cylinder barrels are notched to conform with the depression in the case.

Pistons are all new. Compression height and skirt have been changed and the rings are narrower than in previous engines. Compression rings are 1/8 inch thick. Upper compression rings in the Turbocharged engine are full chrome (also in truck engines) and flash chroming is used in the other powerplants.

Heads on all engines have been altered slightly in the combustion chamber area to take care of compression ratio which is still 9.25 to 1 in the High Performance engine and 8.25 to 1 in the base engine and the Spyder. All engines have inner dampers in the valve springs and are up to 180 psi open.

Two new camshafts are employed. The base engine's stick has 98° overlap while the Spyder and High Performance engines share a cam with 19° more duration. Lift is .385 inch versus .390 inch in the two types. All valve seats are high alloy steel with aluminized face on the inlet side, cast chromium steel on the exhaust side.

Improved clutch assemblies are used with the higher output engines coupled to manual transmissions. Pressure plates are pearlitic mallable iron, as used formerly only on the Turbocharged model, and flywheels are thinner and lighter. The housing has also been changed internally to give greater clearance for the clutch unit.

Externally, in addition to the air cleaner, the die cast magnesium cooling blower is the biggest noticeable change. This lightweight fan absorbs less horsepower and should be easier on belts. Although the shape of the blades is the same, the new fan seems less noisy than in the past.

An enlarged capacity oil cooler has also been incorporated and an even bigger type is used on the commercial vehicles. The generator now delivers more output as well.

Minor touches, but all aimed at eliminating customer complaints, include a dust shield around the base of the distributor.

Although the Powerglide transmission remains the same unit as before, it now upshifts at a higher speed and seems more positive in action.

The sum of Chevy's improvements to the Corvair promises more reliability and smoother performance, even though the casually-interested owner may not even be aware of them. Certainly they are the kind of changes an enthusiast likes to see and, subtle or not, will go a long way toward keeping the smart Corvair as a much-desired and appreciated sporty car . . . as well as good family transportation.

CAR: *CORVAIR MONZA*
PRICE AS TESTED: *$2715.65*

SPECIFICATIONS

1. GENERAL CONFIGURATION

Body Material: *STEEL*　Engine Location: *REAR*
Chassis Type: *UNITARY*　Warranty: *24 MO.,*
24,000 MI,

2. CAPACITIES, WEIGHTS AND DIMENSIONS

Fuel: *14 GAL.*　Test Weight: *2780*
Oil: *5 QT.*　Wheelbase: *108"*
Water: *NONE*　Width: *67"*
Tire Size: *6.50 X 13*　Length: *180"*
Turning Radius:　Height: *51.4"*

3. ENGINE

Configuration: *FLAT 4*　Horsepower: *95*
Valves: *O.H.V.*　Torque: *NOT AVAIL.*
Bore & Stroke: *3.43 X 2.94*　Comp. Ratio: *8.25:1*
Displacement: *2523 CC.*　Main Bearings: *3*

4. POWER TRANSMISSION

Gearbox: *AUTOMATIC*　Axle Type: *SWING*
Synchro: *—*　Final Drive Ratio: *3.27:1*

5. SUSPENSION

Front: *IND., COIL*　Rear: *IND., TRAILING*
SPRINGS　*WISHBONE, COIL*
SPRINGS

6. BRAKES

Type: *DRUM, 9"*　Area: *126 SQ."*

7. PERFORMANCE

0-30: *4.0 SECS.*　Top Speed: *100 (EST)*
0-60: *14.7 "*　Mileage Range: *18/25 MPG*
0-90: *31.1 "*　Standing ¼ Mi.: *20.0 SECS*

1964 CORVAIR
Monza 4-speed, 110-bhp

More horsepower and an improved suspension
make the Monza an even more enjoyable car

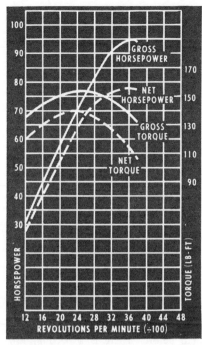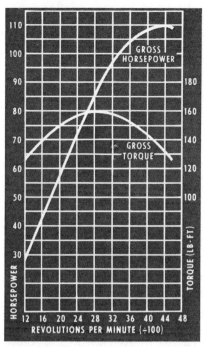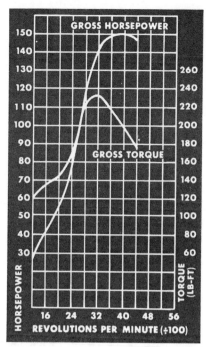

HORSEPOWER AND TORQUE curves for the three engines offered to 1964 Corvair buyers. From left, the curves are: 95-bhp standard, the 110-bhp Super Turbo-Air, Turbocharger; all have 164-cu. in. displacement.

LIKE THE WEATHER that everyone just talks about, few people have ever done anything about air-cooled engines. However, a little over four years ago, Chevrolet did do something about it—by introducing the radical air-cooled Corvair. The success story of this car is emphasized by the fact that more than 1.25 million Corvairs have been built and sold.

A little background on the air-cooled story came out recently in a book by retired GM president Alfred P. Sloan, Jr., "My Years with General Motors." Here Sloan implies that the failure of the ill-fated Chevrolet copper-finned, air-cooled model of 1922 never would have happened except for the fact that overall corporate policy was not yet well organized. (The car was announced and pilot production was underway when it was suddenly dropped.) Yet, in 1959, Chevrolet's then general manager, E. N. Cole, did get corporate approval for his air-cooled car, the compact Corvair, and when Cole writes his memoirs the complete background story on this car may well be one of the highlights of his career.

The success of the Corvair is not due to any one factor; its compact size appeals, its appearance is very good (and the stylists, fortunately, have left it alone) and the air-cooled engine has proved itself practical, reliable and exceptionally long-lived. (One staff-owned Corvair has 90,000 miles on it with no major engine work.) Furthermore, while a buyers' service insists that the Corvair is not a "family car," the fact remains that this respected organization highly recommends the Volkswagen, which is 8% smaller than the Corvair in box volume. The Corvair is a very comfortable car, in sedan form, for a family of four. Taken in that perspective it is, then, a practical economical family conveyance.

Changes in the Corvair for 1964 are highlighted by a larger engine with piston displacement increased 13%. The original concept was an 80-bhp, 80-mph car that would perform on a par with the big 6-cyl. sedan and give about 25 mpg. The super de luxe Monza model, however, showed that buyers would pay extra for plush interiors and more performance. The original "1960½" Monza had a 95-bhp variation on the same size engine (140 cu. in.). The 1961 Corvair offered 145-cu. in. engines, with 98 bhp as an option (later increased to 102 bhp) and for "1962½" a 150-bhp turbosupercharged Spyder option.

With engine size now increased to 164 cu. in. for '64 by increasing the stroke from 2.60 to 2.94 in., the standard engine now has 95 bhp and the optional Super-Turbo-Air unit is rated at 110 bhp. This latter is an increase of only 7.7%, but more importantly, the torque curve has been boosted by 19.4%. This is much more significant and simply means that climbing a long mountain grade of 9% formerly required use of 3rd gear whereas the 1964 Corvair (with 4-speed transmission) can do it in high gear and at a speed of 70 mph, approximately 10 mph faster. It is also noteworthy that the 1964 car develops its peak torque and pulling power at 55 mph in high gear as compared to 62 mph formerly (with optional high-performance, nonsupercharged engine).

For this test we asked for the 110-bhp option with 4-speed all-synchromesh transmission. However, the car turned out to be a convertible, giving test results which are fractionally below what could be obtained from the lighter coupe or 4-door sedan. The actual weights at the curb for the 3 Monza models are:

Convertible	2640 lb.
Sedan	2555 lb.
Coupe	2530 lb.

We have driven enough Corvairs to sense the improvement, even before obtaining the actual test data. In actual figures the story looks like this:

	1963	1964
Test weight, lb.	2840	2940
Axle ratio	3.27	3.27
0-60, sec.	15.5	14.0
SS ¼, sec.	20.5	19.5
SS ¼, mph.	67	70
Top speed	94	98

A portion of this improved acceleration must be accorded to the revised gear ratios in the 1964 Corvair 4-speed unit. Formerly, the 2nd gear ratio left something to be desired and a long gap from 2nd to 3rd. Now both 1st and 2nd have been moved up closer to third (which is unchanged) so that the speeds for shift points change as follows:

	1963	1964
3rd gear ratio	1.44	1.44
mph @ 5000 rpm	75	75
2nd gear ratio	2.35	2.18
mph @ 5000 rpm	46	49
1st gear ratio	3.65	3.20
mph @ 5000 rpm	29	33

An important change in the 110-bhp engine is a new camshaft with slightly more lift and less duration. This, of course, explains why both peak power and peak torque points come at a lower rpm than before. Theoretically, the '64 engine should be a little more tractable at low speeds, but we could detect no pronounced difference; the problem of bumbling and jerkiness below 30 mph in high gear persists. However, the 4-speed transmission is there to be used and 25-mph zones can be negotiated easily in 3rd gear.

Speaking of the transmission, it is notably quiet, perhaps even quieter than before. There is a peculiar low

CORVAIR

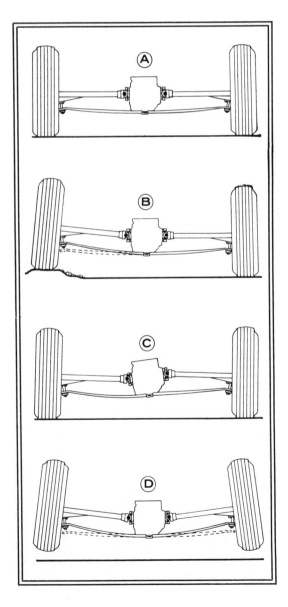

TRANSVERSE LEAF spring addition to the Corvair's independent rear suspension is fastened to differential case and torque arms (A); under bump conditions (B and D) it resists deflection, while in roll conditions (C) it remains neutral.

whistling sound from the gears when first starting out, as well as the typical trouble with getting into 2nd gear without clashing. But once the gear oil is thoroughly warm, the transmission is very good indeed.

Corvair brakes have been improved for 1964 by a new seal design and the rear drums have 40 radial fins added. This emphasis on the rear brakes is opposite to conventional car practice, because the Corvair carries up to 65% of its total weight at the rear when fully loaded. Thus the rear brakes do more work than those in front. Our tests showed that fade resistance has improved and elimination of dirt and water entry is claimed to give the linings a longer life. However, while the brakes are passable, the rate of deceleration is not outstanding and owners who live in mountain areas would be well advised to remove the wheel trim discs to improve anti-fade characteristics.

There are a number of important changes in the suspension and the handling qualities are somewhat improved. The car seems much less susceptible to wind wander and it corners with less roll and no tendency to hop at the rear.

Without going into great detail about the suspension changes, it can be stated that the ride is unchanged. What the engineers have done is to increase understeer by adding an anti-roll bar in front and reducing the rear roll couple in a very novel manner. A single leaf spring runs transversely under the differential housing. This spring (see illustrations) carries 40% of the rear end load while coil springs (not shown) carry 60%. Since the coil springs are softer than before, and the center pivot leaf spring contributes nothing as an anti-roll device, the result would normally be more roll in a corner. But, the heavy anti-roll bar in front more than compensates for this with the excellent results mentioned earlier.

All Corvair engines for 1964 incorporate certain improvements originally specified for the Spyder series only. These include chrome alloy steel for the longer stroke crankshaft, heavier section connecting rods, heavy-duty aluminum bearings, stiffer valve springs with dampers, Stellite-faced exhaust valves, better material for intake valves, chromium-plated top compression rings and a harmonic crankshaft vibration damper. These features will obviously improve the already excellent longevity of this engine.

Another new mechanical feature is a cooling fan cast of magnesium alloy instead of being welded up from stamped steel. It weighs only one-third as much as before and thus helps improve fan belt life.

The sum of these rather extensive changes indicates to us that Chevrolet is going all-out to make the Corvair a top-quality compact and, we feel, this has been made possible by the premium-priced Monza's popularity. ∎

CAR LIFE ROAD TEST

1964 CORVAIR
Monza Convertible

PERFORMANCE

Top speed (4550), mph	98
Shifts, rpm @ mph (manual)	
3rd (4900)	73
2nd (5070)	50
1st (5070)	34

ACCELERATION

0-30 mph, sec	4.6
0-40	6.9
0-50	9.8
0-60	14.0
0-70	19.5
0-80	27.9
0-90	43.0
Standing ¼ mile, sec	19.5
speed at end, mph	70

FUEL CONSUMPTION

Normal range, mpg	19-22

SPEEDOMETER ERROR

30 mph, actual	30.2
60 mph	58.2
90 mph	88.5

CALCULATED DATA

Lb/hp (test wt)	26.7
Cu ft/ton mile	90.5
Mph/1000 rpm	21.4
Engine revs/mile	2800
Piston travel, ft/mile	1370
Car Life wear index	38.4

PULLING POWER

70 mph, (4th) max. gradient, %	9.6
50 (3rd)	14.6
30 (1st)	25.9
Total drag at 60 mph, lb	120

SPECIFICATIONS

List price	$2481
Price, as tested	2736
Curb weight, lb	2640
Test weight	2940
distribution, %	39/61
Tire size	6.50-13
Tire capacity, lb	3340
Brake swept area	198
Engine type	flat-6, ohv
Bore & stroke	3.44 x 2.94
Displacement, cu in	164.0
Compression ratio	9.25
Carburetion	2 x 1
Bhp @ rpm	110 @ 4400
equivalent mph	94.4
Torque, lb-ft	160 @ 2600
equivalent mph	55.7

DIMENSIONS

Wheelbase, in	108.0
Tread, f and r	54.4/55.1
Over-all length, in	180.0
width	67.0
height	51.1
equivalent vol, cu ft	357
Frontal area, sq ft	19.0
Ground clearance, in	5.7
Steering ratio, o/a	25.0
turns, lock to lock	4.75
turning circle, ft	38.2
Hip room, front	2 x 26
Hip room, rear	47.2
Pedal to seat back, max	39.0
Floor to ground	8.5
Luggage vol, cu ft	10.0
Fuel tank capacity, gal	14.0

EXTRA-COST OPTIONS

Wire wheel covers, radio, 4-speed transmission, tinted windshield, seat belts, 110-bhp engine, convenience group.

GEAR RATIOS

4th (1.00), overall	3.27
3rd (1.44)	4.71
2nd (2.18)	7.13
1st (3.20)	10.5

ACCELERATION & COASTING

MPH — ELAPSED TIME IN SECONDS

CORVAIR SPRINT

*John Fitch does much to improve
the breeding of the popular
rear-engined car from Detroit*

SINCE ITS INTRODUCTION in the fall of 1959, the Chevrolet Corvair has attracted a more devoted coterie of followers than any American car since the Model A Ford. One of the marks of distinction that set it off from any other American car now in production is the unusually large number of specially made parts and accessories for the Corvair—everything from pistol grip shift knobs to complete engine conversions—and there are prosperous businesses based wholly on producing these items for an eager following.

There are several good reasons for the devotion of the Corvair buffs. First, it is a fine design, probably the outstanding American automobile design of the past 20 years. Also important is the fact that the Corvair has sufficient technical novelty to be of continuing interest to drivers who regard automobiles as something more than A-to-B transportation. Perhaps equally important is the fact that the Corvair may have been cursed for its shortcomings in power and handling but it has never been guilty of the most terrible of all American car characteristics, that of being dull. It's a car you can get hooked on.

The accessories that have been developed for the Corvair come in three general groups; those to increase the power,

those to improve the handling, and those that are aimed at enhancing its comfort and appearance. By using combinations of these, it is possible, within reasonable limits, to tailor the Corvair into virtually whatever you want of it whether it be a pretty decent little drag racing machine, a good handling touring machine or a wildly customized eye-catcher.

Our test car, a "Sprint by Fitch," is an example of what is being offered to the Corvair driver who wants a decent amount of all three—more power, better handling and customized appearance. The Sprint has been developed by John Fitch, a driver whose credentials need no endorsement, and there are now about a thousand Corvairs around the country using Sprint conversions. The car we tested was loaned to us by William F. Nolan, the writer, who has found the Sprint an excellent compromise between the all-out sporting characteristics of fondly remembered 2-seaters and the creature comforts of an American sedan.

The history of Nolan's Sprint is typical of the experience of the average owner. The car was ordered from Detroit through Don Allen Chevrolet in mid-town New York, then taken to Fitch at Lime Rock, Conn., for Sprintification. Since being driven to the West Coast, where Nolan lives, it has been attended to by Fitch's West Coast Sprint dealer, PAM Foreign Car Service, Manhattan Beach, Calif. The Corvair ordered from the dealer by Nolan was a Monza club coupe with the optional 110-bhp engine, 4-speed all-synchro transmission and limited-slip differential in addition to the usual optional extras such as radio, padded dash, seat belts, wire wheel covers, and so on. Then, after delivery to Fitch's shop in Lime Rock, the conversion to full Sprint specifications was accomplished. For power, the 2-carburetor, 110-bhp

Chevrolet engine was converted to 155 bhp by the addition of two more carburetors and a tuned dual exhaust. The handling conversion included exchange of the factory-furnished tires for Michelin X, speeding up the steering ratio, adding a steering damper, and making changes in both the front and rear suspension. The "customizing" features, which include both convenience and appearance items, account for such things as a heel-and-toe bracket attached to the accelerator, Radson electric tachometer, Lucas driving light, headlight high-beam flasher, seat track extension to give the tall driver more leg room and a short-throw gearshift conversion. There are also such things as a wood-rimmed steering wheel, vinyl panel covers, luggage deck carpeting and so on. The

Sprint customer may opt for any or all of these things, of course, and either have them done by Fitch or one of his dealers or do them himself. Virtually the only Sprint items not to be found on Nolan's car are the tilt-back seat, headrests and vinyl trim on the top.

Nolan had his own ideas about the appearance of his Sprint and the combination chosen, a deep gold lacquer with two red stripes, is striking. Driving it, we soon became aware of the heads that were being turned and no car we have driven lately got a larger number of looks from bee-hived nymphets than Nolan's Sprint. Obviously, Humbert Humbert would have loved it. In more "normal" trim (Nolan admits that Fitch winced on hearing of the gold and red), the Sprint

CORVAIR SPRINT
AT A GLANCE...

Price as tested............................$3627
Engine...............Flat 6, ohv, 2689 cc, 155 hp
Curb weight, lb..........................2540
Top speed, mph (mfg).......................120
Acceleration, 0-60 mph, sec.................11.9
Passing test, 50-70 mph, sec.................7.4
Overall fuel consumption, mpg.................18

CORVAIR SPRINT

is distinguished by vinyl covering above the waistline, racing stripes, Michelin X tires, chrome stone guard (which is frowned upon by the law in some states) and the "Sprint by Fitch" identification flashes on either side. Unmistakably, it is still a Corvair, but to a Corvair buff a Sprint is considerably more than just another Corvair.

The Sprint is a very satisfying car to drive. The seat-track extension offers an improved driving stance, the short-throw gearshift takes less shoulder work, the dished "real tree" steering wheel has a business-like feel and the increase in power is apparent the first time you release the clutch. Getting off from a standing start, the Sprint demonstrates that it is not a drag race machine as the bite from the Michelin X tires doesn't permit enough wheel spin to keep the revs up. Once under way, however, the Sprint shows its breeding and, given its head on a winding road, brings one a feeling that no Corvair ever handled so well.

Other changes include relocating the spare tire from the engine compartment to the luggage compartment. Unfortunately, however, nothing has been done to improve the brakes, which is probably the Corvair's greatest weakness. A car with the performance potential of the Corvair, with or without the Sprint options, deserves something more in the way of stopping ability.

The philosophy of the Sprint suspension conversion is to minimize the natural oversteering characteristics of the tail-heavy car (62% of the weight on the rear wheels) by increasing roll resistance at the rear and decreasing it at the front so a higher percentage of weight transfer takes place at the front, a characteristic of understeer. This is accomplished in the Sprint by leaving the factory springs and shocks in place at the front of the car but removing the anti-sway bar to reduce the roll resistance. At the rear, the suspension is decambered and the roll resistance is increased by using heavier coil springs and specially made adjustable shock absorbers. These suspension changes, plus the contribution by the Michelin X tires with 20 and 30 psi, front and rear, result in handling that is so good that handling is no longer a problem—and this is saying quite a lot for any car with the weight distribution of the Corvair.

In the simplest terms, the Sprint can be driven hard without the necessity for developing the special "toss it and catch it" driving techniques required by the normal Corvair. It may take away a certain amount of the exhilaration which comes from driving a lively oversteerer, but it adds immeasurably to the driver's feeling of security. If you like Corvairs, you'll really like this one.

Engine conversion includes use of four carburetors.

Folded seat and carpeting offer nice touch.

ROAD TEST
CORVAIR SPRINT

SCALE: 10" DIVISIONS

PRICE

List, West Coast.............$2394
As tested, West Coast......$3627

ENGINE

Engine, no. cyl, type...Flat-6, ohv
Bore x stroke, in......3.44 x 2.94
Displacement, cc...........2689
 Equivalent cu in...........164
Compression ratio.........9.25:1
Bhp @ rpm...........155 @ 5000
 Equivalent mph...........102
Torque @ rpm, lb-ft...202 @ 3600
 Equivalent mph...........74
Carburetor, no., make..4 Rochester
 No. barrels—diameter..one-1.25
Type fuel required.....Premium

DRIVE TRAIN

Clutch diameter & type...9.12 in,
 diaphragm
Gear ratios, 4th (1.00).......3.55
 3rd (1.44)..........5.11
 2nd (2.18).........7.74
 1st (3.20)........11.36
Synchromesh..........on all four
Differential, type & ratio: Limited
 slip, 3.55.
Optional ratios: 3.27, 3.08, 3.89.

CHASSIS & SUSPENSION

Frame type: Integral body-chassis.
Brake type.................Drum
 Swept area, sq in.........198
Tire size................640-13
 Wheel revs/mi...........830.4
Steering type....Recirculating ball
 Turns, lock to lock.........3.3
 Turning circle, ft..........38
Front suspension: Independent with
 A-arms, coil springs, tube shocks.
Rear suspension: Independent with
 swing axles, coil springs, trans-
 verse leaf helper spring, tube
 shocks.

ACCOMMODATION

Normal capacity, persons.......2
Occasional capacity...........4
Hip room, front, in........2 x 25
 Rear..................57.0
Head room, front..........38.5
Seat back adjustment, deg.....0
Entrance height, in..........48.0
Step-over height...........14.2
Floor height..............8.5
Door width, front/rear.......43.0
Driver comfort rating:
 for driver 69-in. tall........95
 for driver 72-in. tall........95
 for driver 75-in. tall........75

GENERAL

Curb weight, lb............2540
Test weight................2920
Weight distribution
 with driver, percent.....38/62
Wheelbase, in.............108.0
Track, front/rear.......54.4/55.1
Overall length............180.0
 Width................67.0
 Height................50.9
Frontal area, sq ft.........19.0
Ground clearance, in.........5.4
Overhang, front............30.3
 Rear...................41.7
Departure angle, no load, deg.14.5
Usable trunk space, cu ft....11.4
Fuel tank capacity, gal......14.0

INSTRUMENTATION

Instruments: 100-mph speedometer, 8000-rpm tachometer, fuel
 gauge.
Warning lamps: Temperature, oil
 pressure, generator, turn signals.

EXTRAS

"Sprint" package includes Michelin
X tires (exchange), 4-carburetor
engine conversion, dual-muffler
tuned exhaust system, rear suspension conversion, tachometer,
quick steering conversion, wood-
rim steering wheel, chrome
stone guard, driving light, grab
bar, luggage deck carpeting
short-throw shift, seat track extension, panel covers, steering
damper, heel-and-toe bracket,
high-beam flasher—$665.
Optional extras ordered from
 dealer include 4-speed transmission, limited-slip rear end,
 chrome wheel covers, etc.—
 $340.85.
Custom paint—$225.

CALCULATED DATA

Lb/hp (test wt).............18.9
Cu ft/ton mi...............95.7
Mph/1000 rpm (4th).........20.4
Engine revs/mi............2948
Piston travel, ft/mi........1445
Rpm @ 2500 ft/min........5100
 Equivalent mph..........104
R&T wear index............42.6

MAINTENANCE

Crankcase capacity, qt........5
Oil filter type..........full-flow
Lubrication points............4
Lube, oil and filter change
 interval, mi..............6000
Tire pressures, front/rear, psi.20/30

ROAD TEST RESULTS

ACCELERATION

0–30 mph, sec...............3.5
0–40 mph..................6.2
0–50 mph..................8.3
0–60 mph.................11.9
0–70 mph.................16.4
0–80 mph.................21.6
Passing test, 50–70 mph......7.4
Standing 1/4 mi, sec........18.4
 Speed at end, mph........74.5

TOP SPEEDS

High gear (5900), mph.......120
3rd (6000)................85
2nd (6000)................56
1st (6000)................39

GRADE CLIMBING

(Tapley Data)

4th gear, max gradient, %.....10
 3rd...................16
 2nd...................23
Total drag at 60 mph, lb......130

SPEEDOMETER ERROR

30 mph indicated....actual 29.0
40 mph.................38.6
60 mph.................57.0
80 mph.................76.2
100 mph................95.0

FUEL CONSUMPTION

Normal range, mpg........15–20
Cruising range, mi.......210–300

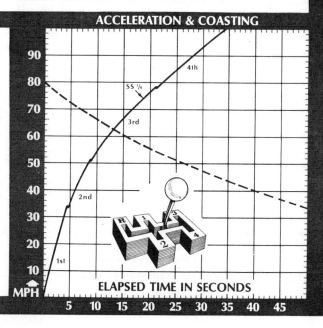

ACCELERATION & COASTING

ELAPSED TIME IN SECONDS

Although the changes aren't sensational,
they do make a great deal of difference!

'65 Corvairs

FOR MANY MONTHS WE'VE LOOKED FORWARD IN ANTICIPATION TO A VIEW OF THE 1965 CORVAIR. As early as December of last year there were rumors from reliable sources that Chevy's air-cooled Compact would undergo its first major styling change. In view of the forthcoming Mustang and other possible sporty-type models from competitors, it was scheduled to have a very definite sports car appearance. We expected something like the Super Spyder show car. Rumor had it that there were two versions under consideration — a tame, tasteful restyle and a really far-out version. Chevy is well-aware that many of its Corvair buyers are extremely interested in sports cars and sports car activities. Small, flexible, economical, and easy to drive, Corvairs number high among the entries at any rally, gymkhana, or slalom. Apparently, Chevy brass got cautious at the last minute and nixed the far-out version, as the heredity of the '65 Corvair is more than obvious. The styling is definitely tame, but entirely successful; it almost completely removes the box-like appearance of previous Corvairs and the hardtop models — the Corsa coupe and the four-door exhibit the beautiful balance and smooth lines of a top-flight European design, if viewed in profile. There's little point in delving further into a description of the body lines; everyone will have full opportunity to see them.

High on the list of things new for Corvair is the full-independent rear suspension. As you know, '64 and earlier models had what might best be described as a semi-swing axle setup. The camber changes were drastic during wheel travel and a definite problem existed where weight-center, roll-center, and camber-change all combined in getting the Corvair around a corner. That setup also had a built-in tendency to wind-wander. At a sacrifice in tire wear, the car could be lowered and a few degrees negative camber cranked in to improve stability and handling, but this was a makeshift correction at best, and had several other drawbacks. What Corvair has adapted is pretty much the Sting Ray rear suspension, where the half-shafts form the upper arm, the lower arm is a single tube, and the trailing torque-arm is a healthy stamping fixed solidly to the hub carrier and pivoting in a large rubber bushing at its forward end.

There are a few innovations all Corvair's own, however. First, due to the 13-inch wheels, it was necessary to kink the outer end of the lower arms for ground clearance. While camber adjustment on the Sting Ray is accomplished by an eccentric bolt at the inner pivot of this arm, the eccentric is placed at the outer end on the Corvair. As all the arm lengths are shorter in the Corvair, the rubber bushings on the torque arms are more flexible and an additional rod extends transversely from the forward end of the transmission to the pivot end of the torque arm. Threaded adjustment on these rods govern rear-wheel toe-in. Thus, back-end geometry can be adjusted with speed and simplicity. Coil springs are used instead of the Sting Ray transverse-leaf setup.

Next on the list of important news is the Corsa model; an evolution of the Monza Spyder coupe. It's a very smooth-looking hardtop and sports a 180-horsepower Turbocharged engine. The output figure seems to us to be *very* optimistic, but the boost is definitely higher and there are many minor improvements in the turbocharger. An option for the 500 and Monza series is a 140-horsepower engine that sports four single-throat carburetors. All models can be ordered with either three- or four-speed transmissions, but you can't get a Powerglide with the Corsa. Other new options include an adjustable steering column with three-inch travel and a power-top option for the convertible models; both Corsa and Monza.

Brakes are an important item on the new Corvair. They're still drum-type, but are now the same size as the Chevy II and Chevelle (9½-inch diameter), and have 268.6 square inches of swept area. In previous models, it was far from a difficult trick to run them completely out of brakes. There is now plenty of stopping power for almost anything but out-and-out competition.

Our test of the new car took place within the confines of the GM Proving Grounds at Milford, Michigan. They have a small section there known as the Handling Course, very tight and gymkhana-like in the beginning and opening onto a faster series of curves. It provides ample opportunity to evaluate handling potential. We made several laps in a Corsa convertible and a Monza hardtop. Prior to these rides, the best-handling Corvairs we've driven were pretty well doctored with accessories that made them quite stiff and flat. If they swept around a corner at near the limit they did a diagonal dance on the suspension that one Chevy engineer termed "corking." This was especially true if there were any deviations in the road surface. The new Corsa, without any options

Engine air intake on the '65 is located just behind the top in the rear deck, shown above.

All closed models of the Corvair are hardtops. Prototype two-door, right, is missing some trim.

The four-door hardtop has excellent lines and balance; strong, rigid chassis makes it work.

PHOTOS: BOB D'OLIVO & JERRY TITUS

'65 Corvairs

Turbocharged engine, at left, has roughly the same configuration as last year. Boost pressure and hot cam raise output to listed 180 hp. Tunnelled instruments in the new model, above, are both attractive and legible. Below is the new rear suspensions. Advantages include lower roll center and a drastic reduction in camber change through wheel travel. Rods extending outboard from the front transmission mount govern toe-in adjustment of the rear wheels.

or wild camber changes, goes around a corner just as well and without *any* evidence of corking. It is also vastly improved from the standpoint of wind-wander. Steering has been quickened a bit on all models and this, too, is a very desirable improvement. About the only item they left pretty much unchanged is the long throw on the gearshift. The handle has been stiffened, however, and makes the length a lot less noticeable.

Completely docile, the turbocharged engine will, on demand, get the Corsa under way in a hurry, attaining 0-60 mph in 9.7 seconds and holding good acceleration rates right up to its top speed of just under 120 mph. It takes a few rpm to get sufficient charge built up, then the pressure increases constantly and smoothly. Our test took place on a 95°F day; not one you'd imagine conducive to good turbocharger performance, but there was no apparent effect on output and the car started easily after being left standing hot. Good signs of trouble-free motoring.

The body package has been stiffened in many areas to make sure there is no flexibility with the hardtop design. Now included are inner fender wells over the rear wheels. Though it's difficult to accurately judge noise-level im-

provements by ear without an older model right along-side, we'd venture that the new Corvairs are definitely quieter in terms of road and engine noise. They were quite pleasant in this respect and cannot remember being able to say the same in past years; the engine noise was enough to be noticed at all times, and many individual road surfaces produced drumming in the passenger compartment. Some of this was corrected in 1964 and it seems to now be improved below any objectionable level.

As with the Mustang, the Corsa attempts to provide the man that wants a sports car but needs a sedan with an answer. While the Corsa does not offer the super-performance options the Mustang does — when you can get 'em, that is — it is much less a Compact in many ways. Because of current corporate policy, it won't receive the performance image it possibly should, but this won't stop it from being a hot seller. Matter of fact, we feel it's destined to bring an additional amount of head-scratching in Detroit about the potential of a sporty-type car on the market. At least that's the way we hear it At any rate, the new Corvair is an impressive, enjoy-able automobile. Get a test hop in one, even if you aren't in the market for new wheels. — *Jerry Titus*

CHEVROLET CORVAIR CORSA-CONVERTIBLE ROAD TEST 16/64

PERFORMANCE:

0-30	3.1 sec.	0-70	12.3 sec.
0-40	5.0 sec.	0-80	16.8 sec.
0-50	7.2 sec.	0-90	22.7 sec.
0-60	9.7 sec.	0-100	31.9 sec.

Standing ¼ miles .... 15.6 sec. @ 78 mph
Top Speed (av. two-way run) .... 119 mph

Speed Error		30	40	50	60	70	80	90
Actual		30	40	50	59	69	78	88

Fuel Consumption
Average: .... N.A. mpg   Max. 1st .... 32 mph
Recommended Shift Points   Max. 2nd .... 53 mph
    Max. 3rd .... 83 mph
RPM Red-line .... 5500 rpm
Speed Ranges in gears:

1st	0 to 32 mph	3rd	15 to 83 mph
2nd	8 to 53 mph	4th	22 to top mph

Brake Test: 72 Average % G, over 10 stops. Fade encountered on 7th stop.

Vehicle .... Chevrolet Corvair
Model .... Corsa Convertible
Price (as tested) .... N.A.
Options .... Radio

ENGINE:
Type .... 6-cyl., flat-opposed, air-cooled
Head .... Alloy removable
Valves .... Ohv, pushrod/rocker, hydraulic lifters
Max. BHP .... 180 @ n.a. rpm
Max. Torque .... n.a. lbs. ft. @ n.a. rpm
Bore .... 3.4375 in. 87 mm
Stroke .... 2.94 in. 74.6 mm
Displacement .... 164 cu. in. 2685 cc.
Compression Ratio .... 8.25 to 1
Induction System .... Single-throat, side-draft Carter, turbo-charged
Exhaust System .... Two manifolds to turbocharger, single muffler
Electrical System .... 12 V. distrib. ignition

CLUTCH:
Single disc, dry, diaphragm plate
Diameter .... 9.12 in.
Actuation .... Cable

TRANSMISSION:
Four-speed, full-synchro
Ratios: 1st .... 3.20 to 1
     2nd .... 2.19 to 1
     3rd .... 1.44 to 1
     4th .... 1.00 to 1

DIFFERENTIAL:
Transaxle, hypoid
Ratio .... 3.55 to 1
Drive Axles (type) .... Open, 2-joint half-shafts

BRAKES:
Shoe-type, self-adjusting
Drum Diameter .... 9.5 in.
Swept Area .... 268.6 sq. in.

CHASSIS:
Frame: .... Unit construction with sub-frames
Body: .... Steel, integral
Front Suspension: .... Unequal arm, coil springs, tube shocks, swaybar
Rear Suspension: ...... I.R.S., single lower, axle upper, trailing torque arm, coil springs
Tire Size & Type: .... Tubeless 6.40 x 13

WEIGHTS AND MEASURES:

Wheelbase:	108 in.	Ground Clearance	5 in.
Front Track:	55 in.	Curb Weight	2665 lbs.
Rear Track:	57.2 in.	Test Weight	2990 lbs.
Overall Height	51.5 in.	Crankcase	4 qts.
Overall Width	69.7 in.	Cooling System	Air
Overall Length	183.3 in.	Gas Tank	14 gals.

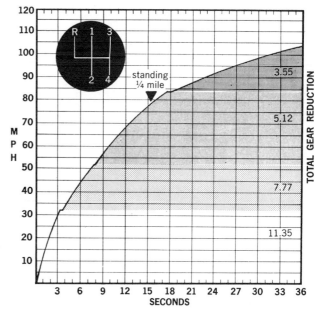

REFERENCE FACTORS:
Bhp per Cubic Inch 1.1
Lbs. per bhp 16.25
Piston Speed @ Peak rpm .... N.A.
Sq. In. Swept Brake area per Lb. 0.101

CORVAIR CORSA

Corvair's design breakthrough sets a milestone in performance handling combined with comfort, space, economy, and price

REVVING THE ENGINE, THEN POPPING THE CLUTCH PRODUCED NECK-SNAPPING ACCELERATION OFF THE LINE, WITH VERY LITTLE WHEELSPIN.

by John Ethridge, *Technical Editor*

THE NEW CORSA reigns as Corvair's top-line offering for 1965. It marks the spot formerly held by the Monza (which now occupies second place). The Corsa is GM's answer to American demands for a low-priced Europeanish performance/economy car — but with a touch of luxury and more seating capacity and luggage space than you normally find in imported cars. This may sound like a large order to fill, and it is, but we were amazed at how well such conflicting requirements were carried out on one set of wheels.

Our test Corsa was ordered with the 180-hp turbocharged engine and four-speed transmission (in place of the standard 140-hp Turbo-Air and three-speed box). With the exception of air conditioning, the car had all the high-cost options plus the usual, numerous low-cost accessories.

Our car's interior was tastefully and luxuriously finished. The Corsa provides comfortable seating for two, plus occasional seating for two more adults for short jaunts. In a car like the Corsa, which is capable of developing high cornering forces, we feel the front seats should give more side support to the back and shoulders. In fact, the seats can best be described as being individual (rather than bucket).

The optional telescoping steering wheel on the test car, together with seat adjustment, will provide a comfortable position for all sizes of drivers. Over-six-footers will find they have to lean forward to reach third gear when they have the seat moved back to accommodate their long legs.

In-town driving was very pleasant. The light, reasonably quick and precise steering, together with a small turning circle, is a boon to the city driver for parking and maneuvering through traffic. In driving the car on wet streets, which we were anxious to try, we found the car free of the handling vices normally associated with rear-engined designs under these conditions.

Gas mileage can have some wide variations, depending on how you drive the car. Around town, our average was just under 15 mpg. On a 100-mile trip that included freeways, small towns, and some mountain driving — all within posted speed limits — the average was 22 mpg.

The exhaust-driven supercharger, which incidentally makes no audible noise above the cooling fan's, didn't become effective on the test car until we reached a rather high rpm. Our 50-70-mph times were two full seconds faster than our 40-60-mph times.

The Corsa's new, larger brakes really work, giving short stopping distances. Under panic braking, the rear wheels tended to lock first, but the car was always controllable, with little tendency to pull to one side. Moderately hard braking in the mountains produced no detectable fade.

Before we get into a discussion of the 1965 Corvair's performance handling — with its obvious appeal to enthusiasts — it may be well to point out the fact that the car's improvement in this area hasn't reduced utility or general acceptability one bit.

Under cornering, steering was perfectly neutral until we

ZIGZAGGING THROUGH PYLONS AT 40 MPH GAVE VERY LITTLE BODY LEAN, PROVED AN EASY TRIUMPH FOR CORSA'S LIGHT, QUICK STEERING.

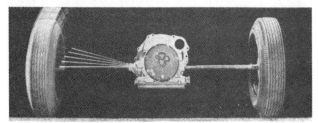

Corvair's old swing-axle setup (1960-64) had U-joint at the inboard end of halfshaft only. Camber compensator was added in 1962. This old system gave a good deal of jacking effect.

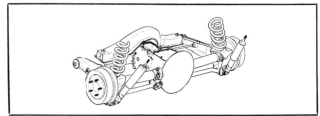

For 1965, all Corvairs have fully independent rear suspension, with a second joint at outer end of halfshaft. There's also a control arm—one piece of equipment missing in old design.

PHOTOS BY PAT BROLLIER, BOB MCVAY

Corsa was very stable at high speeds. Driving twisting back-mountain roads turned out to be a one-handed affair. Even un-

paved and gravel surfaces didn't leave any doubt that Corsa has the superior handling of a car bred for performance driving.

reached a rather substantial speed. Then we noticed a mild understeer that increased with speed. At this point, in anything but the tightest of turns, the car was moving at a truly ridiculous velocity. There wasn't enough excess power available to induce power-controlled oversteer on dry surfaces. (The Corsa would need a considerable increase in power to do this, because of the excellent bite of the rear wheels.)

What accounts for the uncanny good handling of the 1965 Corvair? A physical description of the new suspension was given in our October, 1964 issue. To understand the improved function of the new setup, let's first take a look at Corvair's old swing-axle arrangement that's widely used for independent rear suspensions on production cars. It's what *was* used on all earlier Corvairs.

Swing axles have several things to recommend themselves as opposed to solid rear axles. Among the most important are low unsprung weight and independent action, with reasonably good geometry of the outside wheel under body roll. But the Achilles' heel of swing axles is camber change associated with a jacking effect. This happens when you corner hard. Forces under these conditions tend to make the car

rise, and, since the axle droops, the outside wheel tends to fold under the car, causing the tail end to swing out in a sudden and sometimes catastrophic manner.

Various remedies have been used with swing axles to get rid of this: camber compensators and low-pivot, single-joint designs. While these are definite improvements, none is 100% successful. This fact caused Corvair chassis engineers to look elsewhere for a solution to the problem.

The new Corvair still has a tendency to heist its tail when cornering hard— due to the same jacking effect (lessened somewhat by a lower roll center). But camber change is minimal with the extra joint and control arm. This is to say that the wheels (especially the outside one) maintain a nearly constant angular relationship to the ground, in this case negative camber, throughout the range of wheel travel and body roll. Since, in the case of the Corvair, the rear wheels carry most of the weight and also push the car forward, what happens to them on rough roads, cornering, or a combination is the major factor in the way the car handles. The nearly constant camber held by the new setup is what's led to its being called a *fully* independent rear suspension.

Of course, Corvair engineers didn't stop at the rear sus-

Rear seat folds down, provides room for items too bulky to be carried in front trunk. Seat-back cover seems a bit flimsy.

Spacious luggage compartment under hood can be gotten to from sides as well as front, holds very reasonable amount of goods.

Telescoping steering wheel can be adjusted to any position in a three-inch range. Cog at horn button loosens and tightens it.

Engine compartment layout remains virtually unchanged from last year. Extra horses come from different carb and blower.

Corsa's tinted rear window proved effective in controlling the interior temperature at back seat: 10° difference inside and out.

STEERING SENSITIVITY STAYED ABOUT CONSTANT THROUGHOUT SPEED RANGE, AND CORSA WAS VERY STABLE RIGHT UP TO ITS TOP LIMIT.

CORVAIR CORSA ROAD TEST

pension. Both front and rear suspensions have to be coordinated to get good results. To get the stable, basic understeering characteristics, the Corvair's front suspension has to provide most of the roll stiffness. So the Corvair got a very stiff chassis to transmit the roll torque and anti-roll bar at the front to counteract it.

If, by any chance, you're feeling by now that you may have missed a point or two in the foregoing explanation, don't feel too dismayed. One automotive writer, when discussing exactly the same basic setup on a race car, labeled it "a trick suspension . . . containing too many compromises . . . ," solely, we feel, because he didn't understand it.

We noticed that our test car tended to be slightly affected by grooves in the road and by streetcar tracks. It took some steering correction to hold a given direction. This is a common characteristic of all cars with wider tread in the rear. It's no real problem, though, and it's a small price to pay for the extra stability gained by going to the wider rear tread. If you mount some square-shouldered tires (cheater slicks, for instance), you can expect the effect to be magnified.

Now. . . nothing is ever good enough for some people, and they'll be looking for ways to improve an already good thing. Look for Corvairs on the road with larger wheels (the new five-lug pattern will fit other sizes). You can also expect to see a variety of suspension settings tried, because the rear is now adjustable.

Special accessory manufacturers will have a field day with this car, as they've had with previous Corvairs. Even Chevrolet plans to offer a handling kit. The factory's starting the ball rolling by offering four different engines ranging from 95 to 180 hp. We're hesitant to speculate on what can be done with these, but rest assured — you haven't heard the end of it. All of this is precisely what's so endeared the Corvair to enthusiasts. You can own one, tailored to your personal tastes, that's not exactly the same as any other on the road.

The new Corvair, although restyled and redesigned, keeps its character. It's a rare occurrence when such a car can be changed to broaden its appeal and please its established hard-core following at the same time. It still won't lose a single old friend. And, because it's a vastly improved car, it'll gain many new ones. /MT

CORVAIR CORSA
2-door, 4-passenger coupe

OPTIONS ON CAR TESTED: 180-hp engine, 4-speed manual transmission, radio, telescoping steering wheel, whitewalls, misc. access.

BASE PRICE: $2519
PRICE AS TESTED: $3229.90 (plus tax and license)
ODOMETER READING AT START OF TEST: 2257 miles
RECOMMENDED ENGINE RED LINE: 5800 rpm

PERFORMANCE

ACCELERATION (2 aboard)

0-30 mph	3.5 secs.
0-45 mph	6.7
0-60 mph	10.9

PASSING TIMES AND DISTANCES

40-60 mph	7.1 secs.
	520 ft.
50-70 mph	5.0 secs.
	439 ft.

Standing start ¼-mile 18.1 secs. and 79 mph

Speeds in gears @ 6000 rpm

1st	36 mph	3rd	79 mph
2nd	52 mph	4th	114 mph

Speedometer Error on Test Car

Car's speedometer reading	31	47	52	61	70	80
Weston electric speedometer	30	45	50	60	70	80

Observed miles per hour per 1000 rpm in top gear .... 19 mph

Stopping Distances — from 30 mph, 32.25 ft.; from 60 mph, 146.0 ft.

SPECIFICATIONS FROM MANUFACTURER

Engine
Ohv, horizontally opposed 6
Bore: 3.4375 ins.
Stroke: 2.94 ins.
Displacement: 164.0 cu. ins.
Compression ratio: 8.0:1
Horsepower: 180 @ 4000 rpm
Horsepower per cubic inch: 1.1
Torque: 232 lbs.-ft. @ 3200 rpm
Carburetion: 1 single-barrel side-draft
Ignition: 12-volt coil

Gearbox
4-speed manual, all-synchro; floorshift

Differential
Transaxle
Installed ratio: 3.55:1

Suspension
Front: Independent, coil springs with upper and lower control arms, direct-acting tubular shocks, and anti-roll bar
Rear: Independent, half-shaft acting as upper control arm, single lower control arm, coil springs, direct-acting, tubular shocks

Driveshaft
None used

Steering
Recirculating ball
Turning diameter: 35.5 ft.
Turns lock to lock: 5.2

Wheels and Tires
5-lug, steel disc wheels
6.50 x 13 tubeless, low-profile whitewall tires

Brakes
Hydraulic, duo-servo, self-adjusting; cast-iron drums
Front: 9.5-in. dia. x 2.0 ins. wide
Rear: 9.5-in. dia. x 2.5 ins. wide
Effective lining area: 168.9 sq. ins.
Swept drum area: 268.6 sq. ins.

Body and Frame
Unitized
Wheelbase: 108.0 ins.
Track: front, 55.0 ins.; rear, 57.2 ins.
Overall length: 183.3 ins.
Overall width: 69.7 ins.
Overall height: 51.3 ins.
Curb weight: 2540 lbs.

CORVAIR MONZA

□ There is no doubt that the 1965 Corvairs came as a thoroughly pleasing shock to just about everybody, for here is a Corvair unlike previous Corvairs; in fact unlike any other car. When the Mustang came out people began saying: "What is Chevrolet going to do now?" Well the answer is Corvair for 1965, undoubtedly the sexiest-looking of all the domestic crop for '65, and in our opinion ranks with the world's best-looking cars. We might as well confess right now: we love this new Corvair. But the new Corvair is not just new looks. Its handling puts it into a class higher than many sports cars. The promise that the old Corvairs were "almost" sports cars was not quite true. When the back-end let go there was little or no warning. Of course this didn't happen in normal everyday driving but once the old Corvairs were pushed passed their limits of traction — and few drivers could tell where those limits were — you had a really nice heart-stopping situation on your hands. The Corvair was supposed to be the American answer to Volkswagen and when it first appeared in 1959 it was the first time the North American buyer had a choice other than a full-size Detroit product or an economy import. But up until now the Corvair was not exactly a car whose performance an enthusiast would wildly brag about—not that is, without spending a considerable sum on options. But Corvair '65 is a different story.

coachwork

In our opinion the styling is absolutely first-class. While retaining its Corvair identity it obviously owes a lot to some of the best in domestic and foreign styling. The result is a simple and very elegant design that will undoubtedly become a pacesetter. The overall effect suggests Karmann-Ghia but it's only a suggestion. There are also touches from the Buick Riviera, the Monza GT and a touch of Italy's best, but the outstanding thing about this year's Corvair is the beautiful proportions — difficult to achieve in a rear-engine car. There's no doubt whatsoever that on styling alone the '65 Corvair is going to attract a lot of people.

CORVAIR MONZA

interior

The interior shows little change from the '64 models. Our test car, the Monza, was top of the line last year but is now second to the Corsa — a nicely trimmed sports coupe with a standard 140 bhp, four-carb engine or optional 180 bhp turbocharged engine. The interior styling is in keeping with the outside: simple but elegant. The bucket seats are comfortable but don't give all the support needed for fast cornering. Fore-and-aft adjustment of the seat is not enough to get a straight-arm driving position, but frankly it isn't needed with the tighter steering this year (from 25 to 25.5:1 dropping turns lock-to-lock from 4.75 to just over four.) However, an optional telescoping wheel is available. There is a slight gain in shoulder room and entrance height and two adults can manage reasonably well in the back seats. For additional storage the rear seat folds down and forms a substantial extra storage area. Black front seat belts are standard on all Corvairs but the fastidious can order color-keyed belts to match upholstery.

instruments

The dash is finished in black crinkle paint and slopes away towards the front of the car. The instruments — speedometer on left, escutcheon or optional clock in centre and combination fuel gauge and "idiot" lights on the right — are centered over the steering column and deeply recessed. The instruments can be read easily and all the dash-mounted controls are simple to operate and within easy reach. Heating controls are centered beneath the instrument panel within easy reach.

engine

Our test Monza was equipped with the optional 110 hp engine which reaches that horsepower figure at 4,400 rpm and puts out a healthy 160 lbs./ft. torque at 2,800 rpm, more than adequate in our opinion, although the optional 140 hp should make it a real bomb. As it is, the 110 gave us a best figure of 13.5 seconds for 0 to 60 mph, with the average being just over the 14 second mark. Top speed we could manage was just over 110 mph. Generally, we found the 110 engine a nice compromise between the standard 95 hp engine and the powerhouse 140. Response was smooth and willing at all times.

trunk

The luggage compartment under the hood can be loaded from both sides as well as the front and holds a very reasonable amount. Total useable space is seven cubic feet, more than enough for most occasions. When the rear seat is folded down a very roomy cargo platform comes into use. The hood is spring mounted, of course, and the lock protected by a movable panel in the centre of the hood crest.

handling

Handling is excellent and completely different from the earlier models. Both front and rear suspension are new. The front spring rates have been lowered from 182 lbs./in. to 130 lbs./in. (150 on the Corsa). The front track has been widened from 54.5 to 55.2 in. and roll stiffness and anti-dive effect increased considerably. What really makes a big difference is the adaption of the Sting Ray rear suspension, but using coil springs instead of transverse leaf. This new four-link rear suspension allowed a drop in rear spring rates and eliminated the transverse leaf spring necessary on the Sting Ray. Other complicated but highly effective changes have greatly improved stability and cornering and provide a very wide range of almost neutral steering characteristics. Only when really pushed hard on a corner does the typical understeering characteristics become noticeable, but the whole process is steady and perfectly predictable, as it should be in any good sports car. To get the rear-end sliding out you've really got to push hard. The new, improved brakes are outstanding and even under panic braking with locked rear wheels the car is completely controllable. Continuous hard braking showed no signs of fading. The clutch and steering are incredibly light and require almost no effort to operate. The floor-mounted, four-speed gearshift has been strengthened and the linkage shortened so that third gear is no longer a knuckle scraper on the dash. We found the gearbox to be very smooth and only during really snap-shifts did the synchromesh baulk a little.

performance

Although the Monza with the 110 engine won't break any records it will give most sports cars a run for their money. With one up we hit on average of 3.5 seconds for 0 to 30 mph, 14 seconds from 0 to 60 mph and 25 seconds from 0 to 80 mph. The Monza will cruise effortlessly at 90 mph. Top speeds in the gears: 34 mph in 1st; 49 mph in 2nd; 70 mph in 3rd and a maximum of just over 110 mph in top. At 60 mph there is bags of reserve of passing and only a Pontiac GTO fanatic would complain.

summary

The list of options allow the owner to pretty well custom-order his Corvair and the Corsa with optional 180 hp engine should leave a lot of stunned faces behind the wheels of higher-priced machinery when the owner stomps his foot on the gas. As it is, the Monza with the 110 is a fast piece of work. As we said earlier, we love this '65 Corvair and if a little bit of that has crept into our report I'm afraid that all we can say in defence is : go try it for yourself and then maybe you'll forgive us. Old Corvair enthusiasts will really go wild when they try this one and for the many new friends this little beauty is undoubtedly going to make, the introduction will be a pleasurable experience and one that will be hard to duplicate. Personally, we can't wait to get our itchy fingers on a full-blown Corsa.

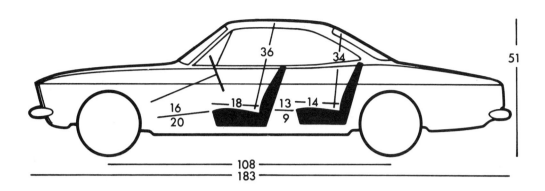

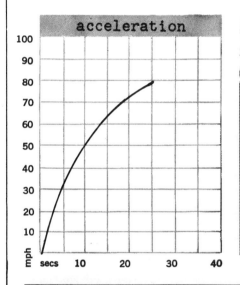

acceleration

performance

ACCELERATION
0-30— 3.0 seconds
0-40— 5.9 seconds
0-50— 8.5 seconds
0-60—14.0 seconds
0-70—17.9 seconds
0-80—25.0 seconds

SPEEDS IN GEARS
1st— 34 mph
2nd— 49 mph
3rd— 70 mph
4th—110 mph

PASSING SPEEDS
30-50—10.0 seconds
40-60— 9.8 seconds
50-70—10.2 seconds
60-80—14.0 seconds

CORVAIR MONZA

**TEST CAR COURTESY
GORRIES DOWNTOWN CHEVROLET**

ENGINE—
Location:	rear
No. of cylinders:	6
Head type:	OHV
Compression ratio:	9.25:1
Carburetors:	2 one-barrel down draft
Cooling:	air
Bore:	3.4375''
Stroke:	2.94''
Displacement:	164 cc's
BHP:	110 @ 4,400 rpm
Torque:	160 lb. ft. @ 2,800 rpm

TRANSMISSION—
No. forward speeds:	4
No. synchro:	4
Gear ratios:	1st: 3.20:1; 2nd: 2.18:1; 3rd: 1.44:1; 4th: 1.00:1
Axle ratio:	3.27:1 (optional 3.55)

DIMENSIONS—
Wheelbase:	108''
Track f and r:	55''/57.2''
Length:	183.3''
Width:	69.7''

Height:	51.3''
Ground clearance:	6''
Fuel capacity:	11.8 imperial gallons
Weight, curb:	2,525 pounds
Tire size:	6.50x13

STEERING —
Type:	recirculating ball
Turns lock to lock:	4
Turning circle:	36 feet

SUSPENSION—
Front:	independent unequal length wishbones, coil spring and stabilizer bar
Rear:	independent trailing arms, lateral location rods, coil springs

BRAKES—
Front:	9.5 inch hydraulic
Rear:	9.5 inch hydraulic

STANDARD EQUIP.—95 hp engine, 3-speed floor-shift; back-up lights; seat-belts; vinyl upholstery; bucket seats

PRICE AS TESTED— $3,157

The Chevrolet Corvair

David Phipps gives road impressions of the promising new version of GM's rear-engined "baby"

MY first new car of 1965 was a bronze-coloured Chevrolet Corvair, which I collected, appropriately enough, on January 1. I had the Corvair for four days, and wherever I went it attracted more attention than anything else I have driven in the past few years—and that includes several models which I tried when they were still officially on the secret list. Most people didn't know what it

Crisply-contoured Corvair contrasts with the rugged stonework of Rochester Castle

was but almost all commented favourably on its appearance —"beautiful" being the most commonly-used adjective— and everyone who travelled in it was impressed by the comfort of the ride, the amount of window space and the efficiency of the heater.

Taken all round, the Corvair is the smallest car currently made in the United States. The Mustang is 2 inches shorter and 3 inches narrower but weighs more and has a bigger engine. The Falcon and Rambler are also a little shorter (2 inches and 6 inches respectively) but larger in every other dimension, and the Chevy II is available (but rarely seen) with a smaller engine. It is also the only "off-beat" car made in the United States, with air-cooled, rear-mounted flat-6 engine and advanced all-independent suspension. (All the others have water-cooled, front-mounted engines, and all except one of them—the Corvette—have live rear axles).

The original Corvair, unveiled in 1959, was strictly an economy car, an American Volkswagen, with performance and handling to match. However, it was very good looking by late fifties standards and was widely flattered by imitation, two of the most obvious examples being the Hillman Imp and the NSU Prinz—both of which now look a little dated. As the years went by, Chevrolet followed the lead of the American tuning shops and produced a range of performance options—including an exhaust-driven supercharger—though until 1965 they did precious little about roadholding and stability. But now, in one fell swoop, the Corvair emerges with completely new styling and completely new twin-transverse-link rear suspension, and is transformed into one of the world's best handling saloon cars, irrespective of engine position. Handling, in fact, is *the* feature of this car, and its almost unique neutral steering characteristics will be a tremendous surprise to anyone acquainted with earlier Corvairs. I drove a turbocharged Monza round the Rouen circuit in 1962 and it seemed quite fun until I got to the hairpin and the back end broke away in a slide which was far too vicious for the ultra-slow steering ($4\frac{3}{4}$ turns lock to lock). Then the rear wheels had $16\frac{1}{4}$ degrees of camber change in $6\frac{1}{2}$ inches of travel. Now they go through only $8\frac{1}{2}$ degrees in $7\frac{1}{2}$ inches. Softer springs and quicker steering make the difference even more noticeable.

Although the Corvair is technically so different from all other transatlantic products, it is unmistakably an American car both inside and out. In the first place it *looks* American, and General Motors American at that, with smooth, harmonious, functional lines—so different from the bechromed apparitions of six years ago. It also smells American, and has the quiet, restful ride of the larger American cars. Finally, it is incredibly easy to drive. Both three-speed and four-speed gearboxes are available, but the test car had two-speed "Powerglide" automatic transmission with a very simple R-N-D-L "gate" controlled by a facia-mounted switch. Selection of D at the start of the journey and N at the end of it are the only calls made upon the driver as far as the transmission is concerned, though he can recall low at speeds up to about 30 mph by flooring the accelerator in the usual manner. Both up- and down-shifts go through imperceptibly in normal driving, and are scarcely noticeable even at full throttle. Wider availability of such refined equipment would quickly convert many European sceptics to two-pedal driving, but unfortunately such advanced automatic transmission is

The very flatness of the flat-six allows the spare wheel to be accommodated in the space so often wasted on rear-engined cars

not generally obtainable on this side of the Atlantic.

Cold starting is taken care of by an automatic choke, and is instantaneous. The warming-up period is shorter than on most water-cooled cars, and the engine shows no tendency to stall, as is so common on European cars with automatic transmission. Admittedly there is some "creep" —in fact "gallop" would be a better word—while the engine is on fast idle, but this can easily be contained by the brakes.

Ah! yes, the brakes, a non-typical American item of equipment on the Corvair in that they work well and require fairly firm pressure on the pedal. In most American cars a panic stop locks all four wheels the first time you try it, but subsequently has very little effect until everything has cooled down again. The pressure required in the Corvair may be a little too high for some tastes, but should at least prevent the ejection of passengers through the windscreen if a heavy left foot is inadvertently slammed on a non-existent clutch. The handbrake is tucked away under the fascia but is less inconvenient than most of its type and notably easy to release.

In the steering department the Corvair has the great advantage of a nice 15-inch wood-rimmed wheel as a standard fitting. The recirculating ball mechanism is ex-

Interior space is good and access in the four-door version tried is excellent. A two-door model is also available

Though better than most, the forward luggage compartment suffers from too many protuberances

There are two snags about the Corvair as far as the British market is concerned—the price, and the fact that it is only available with left-hand drive. Of these the former is by far the biggest objection, and must result in the car remaining a rarity in this country. There are, of course, people for whom an unusual motor car—especially a beautiful one like the Corvair—has a great fascination. Such people will also enjoy the expressions on the faces of hotel porters who try to put luggage in the "boot", only to find the engine there. (The fact that the spare wheel is in the engine bay further increases the confusion.) Perhaps the best we can hope is that the styling and handling of the '65 Corvair will be reproduced at a more realistic price by British manufacturers; that really would be something!

P.S. The locals are *still* talking about it, though normally they only remember the noisy ones.

tremely light at all speeds—even for parking—and well insulated from road shocks. Because of the basically neutral handling characteristics, most people turn the steering wheel too much for their first few corners. However, it doesn't take long to get the hang of things and once it is realised that the back end won't break away suddenly it is possible to go extremely quickly on twisty roads with very little effort. (Only by driving a car like the Corvair can one realise just how much exertion is involved in conducting a typical understeering car).

The performance of the Corvair Monza is comparable with that of the Ford Zephyr 6 (or the confusingly-similarly named Corsair in GT form). Its best aspects are effortless cruising at 75-80 mph and good acceleration for overtaking in the 40-60 mph range. Driven hard the automatic Monza does 15-20 mpg.

For those who want a little more performance there is the Corsa (as distinct from the Monza) with four carburettors and 140 bhp or turbocharger and 180 bhp, the latter (which is available only with manual transmission) providing a maximum speed of 112 mph and acceleration from 0-50 mph in 6.8 seconds. The Corsa is available only in 2-door form (saloon or convertible) and has slightly stiffer suspension than the Monza as well as better instrumentation (including rev. counter) and trim. Fuel consumption in this case is 13-18 mpg.

CHEVROLET CORVAIR
Brief Specification

ENGINE: All-aluminium air-cooled flat-six.
BORE: 87 mm.
STROKE: 75 mm.
CAPACITY: 2688 cc.
COMPRESSION RATIO: 9.25 to 1 (8.125 to 1 with turbocharger).
POWER OUTPUT: (SAE) Monza 110 bhp at 4400 rpm, Corsa 140 bhp at 4800 rpm; Corsa with turbocharger 180 bhp at 4000 rpm.
TRANSMISSION: 3-speed (3.22, 1.84, 1.00) or 4-speed (3.20, 2.19, 1.44, 1.00) manual, or Powerglide 2-speed automatic.
FINAL DRIVE: 3.27 or 3.55.
BRAKES: 9½ inch drums all round.
STEERING: Recirculating ball, 4 turns lock to lock.
TURNING CIRCLE: 34 ft.
TYRES: 6.50 x 13.
WHEELBASE: 9 ft 0 in.
TRACK: 4 ft 7 in front; 4 ft 9.2 in rear.
LENGTH: 15 ft 3 in.
WIDTH: 5 ft 9.7 in.
HEIGHT: 4 ft 3.3. in.
GROUND CLEARANCE: 6 in.
KERB WEIGHT: 2520 lbs.
WEIGHT DISTRIBUTION: 41/59.
PERFORMANCE:

				Monza 110 (automatic transmission)	Corsa with turbocharger
0-30 mph	..	..	..	5.4 sec	2.8 sec
0-40 ,,	..	..	..	7.8 ,,	4.7 ,,
0-50 ,,	..	..	..	11.2 ,,	6.8 ,,
0-60 ,,	..	..	..	15.6 ,,	10.2 ,,
0-70 ,,	..	..	..	22.6 ,,	13.5 ,,
Maximum Speed:	..	..		90 mph	112 mph
Maximum Speed in low gear:				45 mph	
FUEL CONSUMPTION:				15-20 mpg	13-18 mpg

Neatness of the outside is echoed within, where European influence on dash layout, steering wheel is evident

SPRINT

A Custom Corvair for Under $3000

The Corvair Sprint, developed by former race driver John Fitch as an ideal personal car, is a combination of mechanical features usually reserved for thoroughbreds. It has the response of a Porsche, a Jeep's traction, Italian high style, a Mercedes road-holding, Volkswagen practicality, American comfort, and a unique character of its own.

Now in its fourth year, the Sprint has won high reputation among discriminating car buffs, but with the redesign of the basic 1965 Corvair it has become a sure blue-ribbon winner.

Aside from a dozen major mechanical improvements, a striking "fastback" treatment in fiberglass shades the rear window and sweeps down to the tail in a distinctive conformation resembling the exotic racing model Ferrari 250 LM and the Porsche 904 road-racing champion.

Power is demonstrably increased, and the suspension is ingeniously transformed by the use of patented auxiliary biscuit springs in rubber of the type used on the most advanced European racing cars, yet the Sprint remains a comfortable and practical touring sports car for four to five persons. In fact, it is the only touring car made in America with rear engine and sophisticated four-wheel independent suspension. Phenomenal traction makes it a favorite among skiers and all sports-minded adventurers. The steering gear is changed to a more responsive ratio for safe control in emergency, yet the prime objective of an easily maintained, practical and serviceable car by U.S. standards is scrupulously sustained. Refinements and luxurious touches are carried beyond mere convenience and approach the entertaining — but they are useful.

Sprints are seen in increasing numbers in the smarter circles (Manhattan's East Sixties harbors a dozen), and no wonder. An automobile that looks and delivers performance like no other for as little as $2600 is a good thing in any neighborhood. ∎

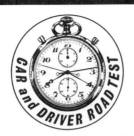

CORVAIR SPRINT

It's real grand touring
on a shoestring, thanks to the
old pro, John Fitch

John Fitch has the sort of wispy gentleness more often associated with a high school English teacher than a great racing driver. He's tall and slightly round-shouldered, with a shock of thinning hair and the brand of articulate good manners that makes it difficult to accept his credentials as one of the finest road racing drivers ever produced in the United States.

The passing years and the press of business have ended Fitch's racing, but nevertheless he still drives superbly, with the same effortless, almost casual style that made him so successful with the Cunningham and Mercedes-Benz teams. Should you ever be driving through the rolling country of northeastern Connecticut, with its monotonously picturesque white clapboard colonial houses, you might be overtaken by a nasty-sounding Corvair with a flat black deck-lid and a rakish roof line. Don't bother trying to keep up, because it may be John Fitch out running in a Corvair

Sprint—one of the nicest custom styling and performance packages available in today's growing automotive accessory market.

Fitch produces the Sprint in a nondescript four-bay garage in the tiny community of Falls Village, a few miles from the Lime Rock race track. He's been in the business several years now, and the demand for both separate components and completely outfitted cars has reached a point where a small but active staff is being supplemented by a dozen special suppliers in both the United States and Great Britain.

Operating on the thesis that the already-impressive Corvair makes the basis for an outstanding American tourer, Fitch markets a line of nearly 40 special options designed to make the car run faster, corner better, stop more efficiently and look racier. These devices can be purchased individually for any Corvair, but they are specifically intended as the parts of a whole package that transforms a standard 140-hp Corsa two-door coupe into a Corvair Sprint.

Eleven items make up the basic Sprint package. They range from a $24.00 engine modification job, which adds 15 horsepower, to a free pair of spiffy polished aluminum nameplates. It all costs $383.65 installed, $306.40 if you want to do it yourself.

The engine modifications are simple and effective. Four small air cleaners and a slightly altered crankcase breather are the basic components, though the three degrees of ignition advance which Fitch & Co. add doubtlessly contributes to the increased poke.

The GT suspension—at $56.00 installed—really works. Included for the front and rear suspension are four progressive-rate, auxiliary rubber springs similar to the aeon units used on some Ferraris, and a pair of adjustable Gabriel shock absorbers for the rear. The front suspension is set at four degrees positive caster and a quarter-degree positive camber. The rear camber is reset at one and a half degrees negative.

Special, shorter steering arms that have been heat-treated and Magnafluxed come with the Sprint package for $46.00. They cut the ratio to 15:1 (from 23:1) and, when utilized with the optional steering damper ($29.50), turn the Corvair steering into a thing of beauty. The damper is the Delco unit employed on the Sting Ray, with special mounting brackets. Should you desire both the damper and the special steering arms, they can be purcashed at a unit cost of $59.00, installed.

Everybody knows that GT cars *have* to have wood-rim steering wheels, and John Fitch makes one available with holes in the tempered aluminum spokes and everything. It will cost you $59.00 and, though it isn't going to make you a Jim Clark (he uses a leather-covered wheel—Fitch sells those too, for $9.95) it will do wonders for the interior of your Corsa.

Another $9.95 will get you a Lucas Flamethrower driving light installed in place of the regular left-hand high-beam unit. Our test car had a pair of Flamethrowers painted with Holt's "Fog Cote" yellow dye for continental driving and the tint added an extremely distinctive note to the front of the car.

When anybody starts to grump about the Corvair, they sooner or later get around to the rather shabby interior appointments, and Fitch has taken several steps to cure this deficiency. The wood-rim wheel, coupled with the fairly adequate Corsa instrument panel (entirely visible tachometer, but no oil pressure gauge or ammeter) takes care of the driver's seat quite nicely, but the back compartment remains a bit stark. He offers, for $21.95 installed, deep-pile carpeting for the back of the folding rear seat and the exposed rear panel. In addition to adding a note of elegance, Fitch claims some sound damping is provided, while the rug's surface prevents objects from sliding around during heavy cornering.

A neighbor of Fitch's, and a fellow car nut, the famous and successful illustrator, Coby Whitmore, assisted in the design of the "Sprint Fastback 904 Ventop" which
*(Specifications overleaf; Text continued on page **99**)*

PHOTOGRAPHY: TOM BURNSIDE

CORVAIR CORSA SPRINT

Manufacturer: John Fitch and Company
Falls Village
Connecticut
Price as tested: $2983.15

ACCELERATION

Zero to	Seconds
30 mph	3.2
40 mph	5.1
50 mph	7.2
60 mph	9.8
70 mph	12.8
80 mph	15.9
90 mph	23.3
Standing ¼-mile	79 mph in 17.0

CORVAIR SPRINT
Top speed, estimated 110 mph
Temperature 75° F
Wind velocity 10 mph
Altitude above sea level 400 ft
In 4 runs, 0–60 mph
times varied
between 9.8 and 10.3 seconds

ENGINE

Air-cooled flat six-cylinder, aluminum block, 4 main bearings
Bore x stroke......3.44 x 2.94 in, 87 x 75 mm
Displacement................164 cu in, 2688 cc
Compression ratio..................9.25 to one
Carburetion...Four single-barrel Rochester Hs
Valve gear. Pushrod-operated overhead valves, hydraulic lifters
Power (SAE)............155 bhp @ 5000 rpm
Torque............202 lbs-ft @ 3600 rpm
Specific power output......933 bhp per cu in, 59.5 bhp per liter
Usable range of engine speeds. 1000–5500 rpm
Electrical system...12-volt, 44 amp-hr battery, 444W generator
Fuel recommended...................Premium
Mileage.......................16–22 mpg
Range on 14-gallon tank.......224–308 miles

DRIVE TRAIN

Clutch................9.12-inch single dry plate
Transmission........4-speed, all synchromesh

Gear	Ratio	Over-all	mph/1000 rpm	Max mph
Rev	3.66	12.99	5.65	−31
1st	3.20	11.36	6.36	35
2nd	2.18	7.74	9.33	51
3rd	1.44	5.11	14.14	77
4th	1.00	3.55	20.36	110

Final drive ratio...................3.55 to one

CHASSIS

Wheelbase........................108 in
Track............F 55.0, R 57.2 in
Length........................183.3 in
Width..........................69.7 in
Height.........................51.2 in
Ground clearance..................5.4 in
Dry weight...................2450 lbs
Curb weight..................2540 lbs
Test weight..................2925 lbs
Weight distribution front/rear....40/60%
Pounds per bhp (test weight)..........19.0
Suspension F: Ind., unequal-length wishbones and coil springs, anti-sway bar, telescopic shocks
R: Ind., articulated link-type, coil springs, telescopic shocks
Brakes............9.5-in drums front and rear 268.6 sq in swept area
Steering.............Recirculating ball
Turns, lock to lock.....................3.8
Turning circle.......................38 ft
Tires and wheels....6.40 x 13 on 5.0-in rim
Revs per mile...........................830

CHECK LIST

ENGINE
Starting.....................Good
Response.....................Good
Noise........................Fair
Vibration....................Good

DRIVE TRAIN
Clutch action.....................Good
Transmission linkage........Very Good
Synchromesh action................Good
Power-to-ground transmission......Good

BRAKES
Response.........................Fair
Pedal pressure...................Good
Fade resistance..................Good
Smoothness.......................Good
Directional stability............Good

STEERING
Response....................Excellent
Accuracy....................Excellent
Feedback.........................Good
Road feel........................Good

SUSPENSION
Harshness control..................Fair
Roll stiffness...............Excellent
Tracking.........................Good
Pitch control....................Fair
Shock damping...............Excellent

CONTROLS
Location.........................Good
Relationship.....................Good
Small controls...................Good

INTERIOR
Visibility.......................Good
Instrumentation..................Good
Lighting.........................Good
Entry/exit.......................Good
Front seating comfort..........Excellent
Front seating room...............Good
Rear seating comfort.............Good
Rear seating room................Fair
Storage space....................Fair
Wind noise.......................Fair
Road noise.......................Good

WEATHER PROTECTION
Heater...........................Good
Defroster........................Good
Ventilation......................Good
Weather sealing..................Fair
Windshield wiper action..........Good

QUALITY CONTROL
Materials, exterior..............Fair
Materials, interior..............Fair
Exterior finish..................Good
Interior finish..................Good
Hardware and trim................Poor

GENERAL
Service accessibility............Good
Luggage space....................Fair
Bumper protection................Fair
Exterior lighting..............Excellent
Resistance to crosswinds.........Good

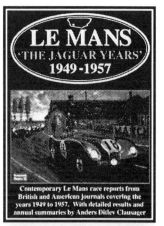

SPRINT *(Continued from page* 97*)*

costs $102.00 installed and painted in black satin. The single most expensive item in the Sprint package, the "Ventop" or whatever you want to call it, makes for a striking change in the car's appearance. While it in no way interferes with visibility or aerodynamics, the top gives the car a hunched, mean-looking contour that we think is a real gas.

Add to this milieu of go and show items a $3.75 Sprint gear shift knob of genuine "rich Brazilian Rosewood" and you've got the basic Sprint ensemble. You can buy another 20 or so items; everything from rear-seat sound insulation at $4.50 to a $184.00 special racing suspension. The car we tested had the regular Sprint equipment plus a passenger seat headrest ($18.95); a $5.95 headlight flasher; $35.00 worth of flat black front-deck paint; a $12.95 seat bracket to give tall drivers more foot room and a set of four 13 x 5-inch Hands aluminum wheels ($198.00).

We liked the looks of our Sprint from the start. It was silver, and, with the flat-black trim, plus the Hands wheels and the tinted driving lamps, it snared second glances wherever we took it. It had 9500 miles on the clock, much of it rugged test driving—including Denise McCluggage's round trip to the Bristol Drags (see page 55)—yet we were impressed with the general tightness of the components.

You know right away that this isn't a stock Corvair. The steering, which requires some huffing and puffing at low speeds, is an immediate giveaway. We were also convinced John had done some extensive monkeying with the shift linkage to make it so positive, but he informed us later that a few minutes of simple aligning and tightening make the difference. The cost of the operation is so negligible he does it on all of his conversions for free.

The cornering efficiency is considerably better than the stock Corsa, though the stiffer suspension injects a harshness into the ride that we really didn't expect. As in the production version, oversteer is practically undetectable, and we were able to fling the Sprint around corners with nothing more than faint evidences of understeer. The car had an irritating weakness for road seams, bumps and expansion joints, and contact with any rifts in the highway would cause it to veer off course. Fitch claims that the as-delivered tires bear full guilt for this ugly habit and recommends the installation of Michelin X or Pirelli Sempione rubber as an instantaneous cure.

The brakes were stock, without the optional $47.00 metallic linings. They seemed to work fine, snubbing the car down from its effortless 70-80 mph cruising speeds without fade or pull. Our only complaint centered on a slight pause between the time the pedal was pushed and the brakes took hold. Fitch claims the problem existed only on our test car (possibly a faulty master cylinder), and, being something less than the optimum, was therefore unsatisfactory to Fitch on principle—and he's taking steps to insure that the problem won't recur.

The 15 extra claimed horsepower were maybe the most amazing additions to the entire Sprint package. They gave the little GT machine tremendous flexibility throughout the rev range and we found the engine capable of healthy acceleration from 2000 rpm in fourth gear. The power is most appreciated in the 50-70 mph range, where a downshift is required for safe passing with the stock version. The Sprint has plenty of steam from 45 mph in fourth up to its top speed of 110-115 mph. Acceleration is more than adequate, and 0-60 times in the high nine-second bracket are within the car's potential. This is impressive, especially when it is recalled that the turbocharged Corsa available from the factory at considerably higher cost won't do any better. The beauty of the Fitch package is its reliability at high revs—in marked contrast to the turbocharged setup, which isn't noted for peak rpm strength.

John Fitch set out to create a distinctive driveable GT car from the Corvair and he has succeeded without letting the price get out of hand. Obviously, the appeal of the Sprint increases in direct proportion to the quantity of accessories that are added, but the basic package is a tempting bargain. We would probably go for the optional tires, but otherwise the Sprint in the form that we tested it is perfectly suited for high-speed touring and is utterly deserving of the appellation "GT car".

We can't think of anything within $1000 of the Sprint's price range that will do what it will do with comparable handling, silence, maneuverability, economy and comfort. As far as the stock Corvair Corsa is concerned, take it from the quiet gentleman from Falls Village, Connecticut; you most certainly *can* gild the lily.
    C/D

CHEVROLET CORVAIR

ROAD TEST AWARD WINNER · OUTSTANDING MODEL IMPROVEMENT

In the initial issue of ROAD TEST we prefaced the 1965 Corvair test by saying: "The Corvair is a unique automobile for more reasons than one. First introduced as a compact competitor to imports in 1959, the image changed when GM discovered that the car had more appeal to sports car enthusiasts than to the economy-minded. Today, the Corvair is the darling of the enthusiast, not because it is such a wonderful automobile, but more because it is the one American make in years which has dared to be different . . . . In 1965, as previously, we doubt that the Corvair will make much of a dent in the economy car market, but sports car enthusiasts will approve of it."

Now, a year later, we must say that the Corvair deserves to be admired not because it is different but simply on the basis of outstandingly good handling, brakes and road manners. Secondarily, it offers far more roominess and utility than the average sports car but satisfies a majority of those requirements which make a good sports car.

The improvement over previous models in this regard is notable and Chevrolet is to be commended on making the changes which resulted in such happy driving qualities.

During 1965, staff members and consultants carried out a continuous program of testing. As you will recall from Vol. I, No. 1, we stated that it was one of the nicest handling cars we'd ever tested. It bothers us to make such broad statements. So, at the risk of proving ourselves wrong, we lived with the car, worked with it and generally did everything we could think of to make it do something bad. We're pleased to report that we were unsuccessful in our endeavor to produce bad results. The fact is, we found that the more we pushed this car and the more we became familiar with it, instead of finding any hidden faults, we began to notice more and more subtle favorable qualities.

The Corvair is easy to maneuver at low speeds but has no tendency to wander or search at high speeds.

Corvair's handling ability is well demonstrated in photo taken during cornering of short-radius turn. Low roll centers and low slip angle insure rear wheel traction. Previous model would lift inside rear wheel under same conditions. In this situation, car is under complete control.

Its ride is smooth and vibration free regardless of the road surface quality. At freeway speeds the car will cruise along over warped cement slabs showing remarkable ability to absorb the motion without any of the rocking or pitching so common to sports-touring cars. Even when driving at high speeds with the front and rear tires of one side passing back and forth over the road edge, the car has little tendency to leap sideways.

IMPROVED CORNERING

Cornering the Corvair at maximum speed produces the kind of results one would expect from an out-and-out sports car. Everything that happens is entirely predictable. When driving into a corner too fast, the car will understeer, like a front-engine car. But when the corner is entered at the proper speed and accelerated out its characteristics go from neutral to oversteer, according to the amount of throttle applied.

This is the behavior pattern which most drivers find acceptable. It provides an added degree of security because the natural reactions to excessive speed, (ie: lifting the foot off the throttle or even applying the brakes), do not produce additional handling problems.

Experiments with tire inflation disclosed that the new Corvair is tremendously less sensitive to tire pressures. This is another laudable characteristic because, unless the owner is a real enthusiast who regularly checks pressures himself, it is easy to become a victim of the service station attendant's eager innocence. Brands of tires, tire tread and carcass design are also less of an influence on the Corvair's handling than in previous models.

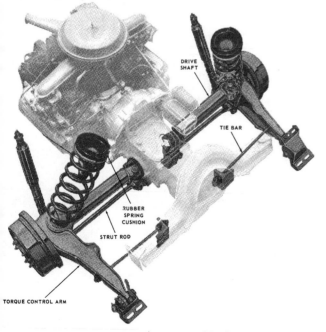

Corvair's independent rear suspension is derived from Corvette, gives car outstanding rear end adhesion.

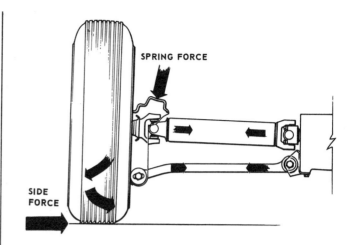

Diagram illustrates how cornering forces are handled by rear suspension.

NEW SUSPENSION

This tremendous improvement has been brought about without scrapping the original premise of the light weight, air cooled, rear engined car by a complete re-design on the suspension system, front and rear. The highly successful independent rear suspension arrangement of the Corvette, modified to utilize helical coil springs rather than a transverse leaf type, has been adopted. A sizeable anti-roll bar at the front and springs with a rate more nearly equal to those in the rear combine to produce 11% more roll stiffness and eliminate the fore-and-aft pitching motion.

The new independent axle rear end has a roll center nine inches lower than the previously-used swing axle set up. Combined with the front suspension's roll center, the vehicle's roll axis is about half the angle of the earlier model. With a low c.g. and tires with a lower cord angle, the car stays flat and 'sticks' in corners in excellent fashion. On more than one occasion over mountainous roads the Corvair clearly demonstrated its handling superiority over the staff-owned Mustangs.

Wider track and reduced track variations of the track during bounce and rebound movement of the rear wheels give improved stability, with no tendency for the rear wheels to "steer" the car. A sharper turning angle of the front wheels reduces turning circle by three feet and the steering ratio itself has been speeded up. The new low profile tires which are standard help steering and directional stability also.

LARGER BRAKES

Increased brake drum size merits special mention. The new brakes are 9½ inch diameter, the same as those used on the larger Chevelle, with 169 square inches of lining area (34% more than earlier models). The larger drum mass provides a better heat sink and an extra flange contributes dissipation of heat. The end product is a remarkably effective set of brakes, quite the best of any conventionally-braked cars in this category.

Finalizing a year of testing of new cars, it was the unanimous opinion of the group that the Corvair was easily the most genuinely improved automobile it had encountered and that it deserves serious consideration as one of the best-engineered cars in production today.

"Hands off" hot brake test results show that Corvair decelerates in straight line under adverse conditions. Car is easy to control in all maneuvers.

Optional adjustable steering wheel permits straight-arm driving position favored by many sports car buffs. Absence of front floor tunnel adds to interior spaciousness.

Recessed instruments are completely visible through two-spoke steering wheel.

Sports car performance characteristics combined with roominess make Corvair attractive to enthusiasts. Car has outgrown "economy" label because of sophisticated engineering not found in other domestic compacts.

Panic-stop brake test reveals that front and rear wheels have equal traction. Lack of nose-dive is evident. Increased brake capacity of new Corvair is one of reasons given in making special award.

IECO CORVAIR

Even the Lily Improves with Gilding

BY JIM WRIGHT

WHEN CHEVROLET designed the 1965 Corvair the engineers seemed to have thought about, and included, just about everything it would take to make the car appeal to the widest range of buyers. They did an excellent job and the resulting "class-by-itself" car *is* accepted by both economy-minded as well as enthusiast-oriented buyers and drivers.

The Corvair's soft, rounded, clean-lined exterior styling might have come right from any one of the great Italian studios. This flair is carried through to the interior, especially in the top-of-the-line Corsa which offers complete and attractive instrumentation. This is also evident in the optional, competition-type, two-spoke steering wheel mounted at the end of an adjustable

column. Not to be overlooked on manual shift models is the precise, quick-shift linkage. This is an item that the owner used to have to buy from an accessory house and either install himself or have installed.

In the past, the Corvair has been a better-than-average handling car—in the hands of a competent driver. With the redesigned, 4-wheel, *full* indepen-

103

IECO CORVAIR

dent suspension system the 1965 Corvair becomes one of the better handling production sedans in the world.

Another feature of the new chassis is an increase in brake size. The drums are increased from the previous 9-in. diameter, 1.75-in. wide units that were used all around to 9.5 x 2.0 front, and 9.5 x 2.5 rear drums. The swept lining area is increased from 197.7 sq. in. to 268.6 sq. in. This gives a car weight to area ratio of approximately 10:1 which is as favorable as found in most any drum-braked car. It should also be noted that brake effectiveness is split 46% front and 54% rear which means that most of the work is done at the rear to take advantage of the 63% rearward weight bias. The resulting stops are smooth and straight, accompanied by a minimum of nose-dive and a minimum of wheel correction—as long as the brakes are in good adjustment and aren't overheated.

Four engines are offered, ranging from a mild 95 bhp up to the exhaust-supercharged 180 bhp. In between are the 110 and 140-bhp versions. All four engines share the same 3.4375 in. x 2.94 in. bore and stroke and 164-cu. in. displacement. The 95 and 110 engines breathe through two single-barrel carburetors, while the 140 has four singles with progressive linkage, and the 180 is force-fed via the exhaust-driven centrifugal supercharger pulling through a single, side-draft carburetor. The 95 and 180 share an 8.25:1 compression ratio and the 110 and 140 share a 9.25:1 c.r. Valve timing is 44-88, 78-54 with 0.403 in. lift for the 95; 55-105, 97-63 with 0.3907 in. lift for the 110 and 140, and 82-

110, 110-70 with 0.3741 in. lift for the 180. The 140 uses 1.72 in. diameter intake and 1.36 in. diameter exhaust valves as opposed to the 1.34 and 1.24 in. valves in the other three engines.

Transmission offerings include an unfortunate 2-speed automatic, a 3-speed manual with synchromesh second and third gears, and a 4-speed, all synchro manual. In our estimation the 4-speed is by far the best suited to the small-inch displacement of the Corvair engine.

Viewed collectively, the many features add up to one conclusion: The final product, with an intelligent assist from the option list, leaves very little room for improvement. This is a fact evidenced by the increasing number of speed equipment and accessory manufacturers who are either phasing out or de-emphasizing their Corvair lines—usually in favor of Mustang goodies for which there is now a greater demand.

Luckily there are a few die-hard Corvair specialists left in the country. Notable among these is long-time speed merchant R. F. "Sonny" Balcaen and his Induction Engineering Co. (IECO), which either manufactures or distributes items designed exclusively for the Corvair. In addition to being president of IECO, Balcaen's credentials include a stint at campaigning what was, and still is, the fastest GMC-powered fuel dragster in the country. He is noted as a racing mechanic, a trade he learned at an early age from Pete Clark, who was the immortal Rex Mays' mechanic. He has also worked for Jim Hall and Carroll Shelby back in the days when they were partners and later was with Reventlow Automobiles Inc., along with such notables as

Travers and Coons, and Troutman and Barnes.

At present, Balcaen also functions as a personal consultant to Shelby in the accessory division of Shelby Enterprises. He continues to specialize in Corvairs because he thinks they're the most exciting cars in America. His personal car, which also functions as a rolling test bed for IECO equipment, is a good example of how just a few well-designed, relatively inexpensive accessories can make a satisfying car even more so. And that's why we chose it to put through the wringer.

The test car is basically a Corsa hardtop originally equipped with the 4 x 1, 140-bhp engine, a 4-speed manual transmission and 3.55:1 Positraction rear axle. Convenience items include bucket-type seats, adjustable steering wheel and the full instrument panel.

Before Balcaen installed any of his equipment the car was properly broken in and then subjected to a series of tests and evaluations. These included determining maximum power output on a Clayton chassis dynamometer, on-the-road fuel economy checks and evaluation of both handling and braking characteristics on a road course. In this way, both the capabilities and limitations of the car in stock form were established as base points for evaluation of any future modifications.

In the search for increased performance only two engine changes were made and these were both of the "bolt-on" variety. One was the replacement of the stock dual exhaust system with an IECO-designed and Cyclone-manufactured megaphone-extractor, tuned dual exhaust system. This system consists of a pair of straight-through 'glass-pack mufflers and resonators

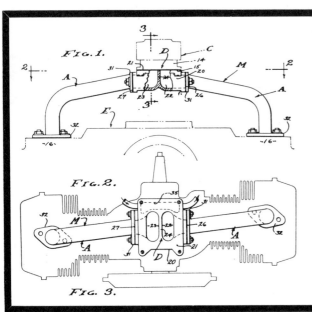

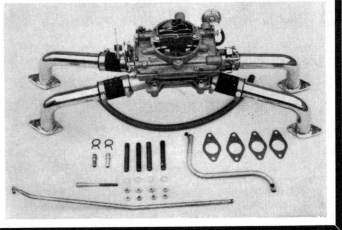

PATENTED MANIFOLD developed by R. F. Balcaen separates 4-barrel induction into two separate elements—one primary and one secondary feeding each bank of cylinders. Separation is achieved by use of a wall in the chamber under the carburetor. At right, IECO Ram Kit for 1965 Corvairs (which have two ports on each head instead of one).

feeding through 4-ft. long extractor exhaust pipes. Tests have since shown the system offers little back-pressure throughout the engine rpm range with its tuned length being most effective from 3500 rpm on up.

The other change was the replacement of the stock 4 x 1 carburetion system with an IECO-designed and *patented* 1 x 4 Ram Kit. This kit consists of a single 4-barrel carburetor, centrally mounted on a cast-aluminum manifold which, in turn, is connected to the intake ports in the cylinder heads by four chromium-plated steel ram tubes.

In detail, the cast manifold section is divided in half by an internal bulkhead which allows one set of primary and secondary throttles to feed one side of the engine and the other set to feed the other side of the engine. This system was originally invented by Balcaen for the early 2-port Corvair engine and, while the patent search was being made, several copies of the system were put out by other companies. Since the Balcaen patent covers the bulkhead feature the other companies have tried to circumvent it by either removing the bulkhead or modifying it in such a way that the effect is destroyed. The system doesn't work nearly as well without the bulkhead, which explains why so many people have been unhappy with 1 x 4 conversions.

In effect, the IECO system functions as two separate 2-barrel carburetors feeding two, separate, 3-cyl. engines and is a true, balanced, 180° induction system. The effective length of the ram tubes is approximately 20 in. and their effect is felt strongest in the 3500-4000 rpm range.

The carburetor which has worked best is the Carter AFB 3858S. It features 1.1875-in. primary venturis and 1.3125-in. secondaries as opposed to the 1-in. venturis of the stock singles. The 4-barrel has a total venturi area of 4.92 sq. in. which is an increase of 1.78 sq. in. over the four singles. The most important part of carburetor modification is not to over-carburete: If the venturi area is too great, the velocity of the mixture through the carburetor will slow down to the point where, when the throttles are opened suddenly, the engine will actually starve. The AFB 3858S is as big as this engine can handle. The secondary throttles are progressively actuated by mechanical linkage on this model so that the transition from 2- to 4-barrel operation doesn't cause an over-carbureted condition. The only modification necessary to the AFB was to go one step leaner on the metering rods.

With the engine changes completed, the car was tested again on the Clayton chassis dynamometer (same dyno, same

IMPROVED HANDLING afforded by IECO modifications to the stock Corvair turns it into a curve-stormer. Wider rim, 14-in. wheels are impressive additions.

operator). Also, just for comparison, a stock, tuned, turbo-charged Corsa was tested. The results of all were:

STOCK 4 X 1	IECO 1 X 4	TURBO-CHARGED
3000 rpm 65 bhp*	82 bhp*	112 bhp*
3500 rpm 72	86	125
4000 rpm 75	106	125
4500 rpm 90	106	110
5000 rpm 86	102	80

(*available rear wheel horsepower)

As the dynamometer shows, the modifications resulted in a substantial power increase throughout the whole usable range. The increase is especially large between 3500 and 4000 which is where the ram effect is greatest. The usable power range above 4000 rpm is also extended over the stock system because of the additional venturi area. The power of the turbo-charged model shows a rapid fall-off after 4500 rpm because of excessive cylinder head temperature and detonation—an inherent weakness of the system that shows

up more readily on the stationary dyno.

When we drove the test car, we were very favorably impressed with the quick throttle response of the 1 x 4. The car could be idled along in any gear and, when the throttle was mashed, it would accelerate smoothly and quickly without a trace of hesitation or bucking. The performance is much improved and in a standing start match between a 1 x 4 and a 4 x 1, the 1 x 4 will easily run away from the other. It will also stay ahead of a turbo-charged version up through a quarter-mile to about 85 mph due to the fact that although the turbo version puts out more power, it takes longer to build it up.

Balcaen claims fuel economy tests show the 1 x 4 gets better mileage than the 4 x 1. He claims that this is because of better distribution plus the fact that the four singles are hard to

IECO CORVAIR

synchronize and harder still to keep in synchronization—a problem that doesn't exist with a single 4-barrel. His actual figures show that his 4 x 1 Corsa averaged 14.8 mpg around town and 21.9 mpg on the highway. When the single four was installed (along with the IECO exhaust system) these figures went to 17.3 mpg in town and 26.1 mpg on the highway.

The chassis was modified by the installation of an IECO handling package. But it was first determined if any improvement could be made in handling by juggling the front and rear suspension geometry. At the front it was found that ½° positive camber with 0.125-in. toe-in and 2½° positive caster produced the best results. At the rear 1° negative camber and 0.0625 in.

toe-in worked best. The overall result was increased directional and cornering stability.

After the optimum geometry was established, the modifications were made. The steering arms were replaced with shorter, stronger units which speed up the steering from the standard 4.7 turns between locks to approximately 2.8 turns between locks. The traditionally light Corvair steering doesn't suffer from the change and is improved quite a bit by the increased maneuverability and precision afforded by the shorter arms. The standard shocks were also replaced by heavy-duty units that are especially calibrated for Corvairs to offer increased control of both jounce and rebound. There is nothing wrong with the stock spring rates that the HD shocks won't cure, so they were left alone. The last item in the handling package was a set of sintered metallic brake linings. These formerly were offered as a factory option but since 1964 have been unavailable. They are actually worth their weight in gold because their performance is almost equal to discs. Water doesn't affect their efficiency and, if you've got the leg power to keep on pushing the pedal, they'll keep on stopping long after standard lining material has disappeared in a cloud of smoke.

The IECO test car came to us with another chassis improvement that wasn't a part of the handling package. This improvement was the result of installing a set of Cragar alloy center/steel rim wheels. The stock wheel di-

mensions are 13 x 5.5 while the customs are 14 x 6. (Any larger 1965 Chevrolet wheel will fit, too; they all have the same, 4.75-in. diameter, 5-bolt lug pattern. However, tire/fender clearances should be checked carefully before installation.) Larger, 7.00-14 Goodyear Powercushions were mounted and, by virtue of putting more rubber on the ground, added to the car's cornering and braking power.

We pushed the test Corsa over some of the hairy, twisting roads to check it out and came away believers. Its sticking power is greater than one can find in any American car, excepting the Corvette. Of course, the stock Corvair is above average, too. The inexperienced or disinterested driver probably wouldn't notice the difference between a Corvair with the IECO handling package and one without it because even the stocker is capable of cornering faster than a majority of drivers have the nerve to try. Another impressive point is the rapidity and ease with which the car recovers if you inadvertently get it out of shape. Truth is, it's a hard car to get out of shape in the first place. You have to do it on purpose because it's virtually impossible to spin-out in this car.

From 80 mph, or above, quick (26 ft./sec./sec.), straight-line stops are possible without experiencing either fade, pulling, or sudden lock-ups. The brakes require somewhat more pedal pressure than those with organic linings, but it's not excessive and it's doubtful if they could ever be heated to the point where the average driver

SPECIAL megaphone-extractor exhaust system was designed by IECO, manufactured by Cyclone, uses straight-through 'glass-packs.

JIM WRIGHT PHOTOS

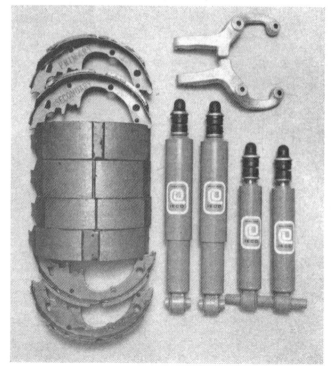

HANDLING PACKAGE includes set of metallic brake linings, quick-steering arms and four new special-duty shock absorbers.

would have trouble applying them.

As an interesting side-note, when we picked up the car from IECO, Balcaen was in the process of running some tests with the stock carburetion system installed. It took him exactly 20 min. to completely install the 1 x 4 Ram Kit. Also, unlike earlier Corvairs, the '65 has enough clearance over the carburetor so that the inside of the deck doesn't have to be cut to clear the air cleaner. As we mentioned earlier, the kit is strictly bolt-on and requires neither welding nor cutting.

By today's standards—the high cost of horsepower and everything—the IECO Corvair can be duplicated for a relatively small outlay. Once you buy the basic car, the rest is easy. The complete exhaust system goes for $39.95; the Ram Kit (less Carter AFB which lists for $55 but which can often be picked up cheaper in a wrecking yard) is $59.95; and $85 for the handling package (steering arms, four shocks and sintered metallic brake linings). If you like those wheels, they add on another $204 (including special lug nuts).

All told it accounts for $443.90. If ordered separately, the steering arms are $17.95, the brakes $31.95 and the shocks $35.95. If you wanted to go all out, IECO also stocks Koni shocks at $25 apiece.

In any event, each and every accessory adds value in terms of owner satisfaction and driving pleasure. Chevrolet knows this now and has released an optional handling package with higher-rate springs, stiffer shocks, 14:1 steering gear and linkage which reduces turns to three, lock to lock. ∎

CAR LIFE ROAD TEST

1965 CORVAIR
IECO-Modified Corsa

SPECIFICATIONS

List price	$2519
Price, as tested	3169
Curb weight, lb.	2540
Test weight	2900
distribution, %	36.8/63.2
Tire size	6.95-14
Tire capacity, lb. @ 24 psi	3680
Brake swept area	268.6
Engine type	flat-6, ohv
Bore & stroke	3.44 x 2.94
Displacement, cu. in.	164
Compression ratio	9.25
Carburetion	1 x 4
Bhp @ rpm	156 @ 4400
equivalent mph	86
Torque, lb.-ft.	170 @ 2800
equivalent mph	55

EXTRA-COST OPTIONS

140-bhp engine, 4-speed, non-slip diff., smog device, radio, seat belts, IECO Ram & handling kits, Cragar wheels, 6.95-14 tires.

DIMENSIONS

Wheelbase, in.	108.0
Tread, f & r	55/57.2
Overall length, in.	183.3
width	69.7
height	51.2
equivalent vol., cu. ft.	378.5
Frontal area, sq. ft	19.8
Ground clearance, in.	5.9
Steering ratio, o/a	23.5
turns, lock to lock	2.7
turning circle, ft.	38.2
Hip room, front	2 x 24
Hip room, rear	56.1
Pedal to seat back, max.	41.0
Floor to ground	9.5
Luggage vol., cu. ft	n.a.
Fuel tank capacity, gal.	14.0

GEAR RATIOS

4th (1.00) overall	3.55
3rd (1.44)	4.97
2nd (2.19)	7.77
1st (3.20)	11.36

CALCULATED DATA

Lb./bhp (test wt.)	20.7
Cu. ft./ton mile	98.3
Mph/1000 rpm	19.6
Engine revs/mile	3060
Piston travel, ft./mile	1500
Car Life wear index	45.9

SPEEDOMETER ERROR

30 mph, actual	27.9
60 mph	58.8
90 mph	90.0

FUEL CONSUMPTION

Normal range, mpg	n.a.

PERFORMANCE

Top speed (5400), mph	106
Shifts, @ mph (manual)	
3rd (5000)	68
2nd (5000)	45
1st (5000)	31
Total drag at 60 mph, lb	110

ACCELERATION

0-30 mph, sec.	3.8
0-40	5.8
0-50	8.4
0-60	11.4
0-70	15.3
0-80	20.6
0-90	30.5
Standing ¼ mile, sec.	18.1
speed at end, mph	76

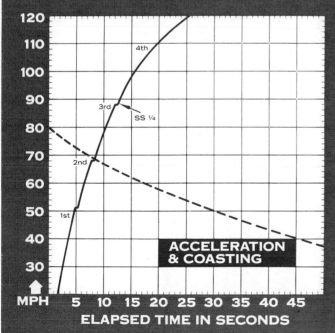

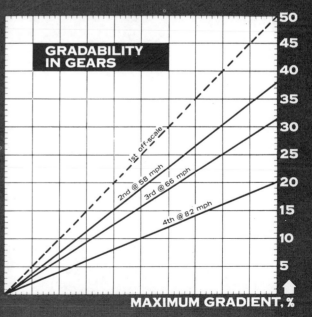

107

ram
INDUCTION

WHEN Chevrolet first introduced their air-cooled economy car, late in 1959, no one would have thought it would become what it is today. Late in 1960 the factory came out with the Monza coupe. It began the revolution! The **little** car lent itself very well to the sportsman, hotrodder and the average driver.

After 1961, several companies were making various accessories for the Corvair. They ranged from wood rimmed steering wheels to full blown racing engines. The enthusiast did not have to look far to find most anything he needed. IECO (Induction Eng. Co.) was the first to introduce a performance item for the car. They patented a "ram induction" system, utilizing a small four barrel carburetor. Since their first accessory came out in 1961, IECO has made items ranging from do-it-yourself tune-up kits to its unique four-tube ram induction for the 140 horsepower model.

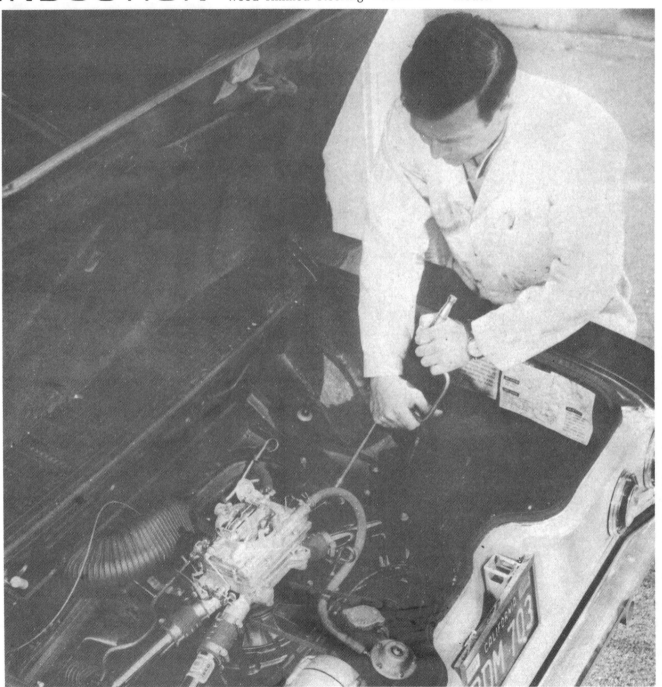

IECO President Sonny Balcaen installs Ram Induction Kit.

FOR THE CORVAIR

Corsa 140 engine ready for Ram Kit installation. Everything stock remains, except carburetors, fuel line and linkage.

The people at IECO have what they call their "rolling test bed." This is a 1965 Corsa 140 with four speed transmission. We decided to test the converted car to see what could be done with a few bolt-on accessories on one of Chevrolet's tame sixes. We thought the best test would be to really feel the car's handling, braking, and performance under all driving conditions. So instead of setting up a planned course for the road test, we drove the car through every condition possible.

All Corvairs lend themselves to chassis geometry changes; however, the 1965-66 models have fully independent suspension, which allows a greater area of adjustment. The IECO Corvair had a special handling kit installed which consisted of metal (powdered) brakes, constant pressure shock aborbers, and quick-ratio steering arms. Part of this package includes a detailed set of instructions which show how to set your chassis geometry for maximum cornering power. Sonny Balcaen, IECO's President, also suggests the addition of 700 x 14 tires and wheels which were installed on the test car. He claims this gives the car more surface contact, and also increases its stability. We tried the car over a winding California road, and must say it truly was a sports machine. The car would enter a corner at a "half drift" angle, and hold it completely until the accelerator was either lifted or depressed. This gives the driver full control in a cornering

Holding the "line" on a left hand corner with gentle "throttle pressure."

Kit makes a simple clean looking engine out of the Corvair six. Note expansion rubber hoses.

IECO Corvair is put through a hard right hand corner, and goes through it like it is on rails.

situation. The short ratio steering helps hold the "line" with little wheel movement. The metal brakes let one get the car deeper into the corner and really slow it down in a hurry! They seem to do this with absolutely no heat fade.

It is surprising how much extra performance can be obtained from the Corvair engine with a few bolt-on accessories. IECO's engine changes consist of a patented four tube ram induction manifold (which utilizes a Carter AFB carburetor), a modified ignition system, and an "extractor tuned" exhaust system. This combination works wonders for the flat six. Power gains as high as 40 per cent were obtained at 4000 rpms. Gasoline mileage was increased because the progressive linkage on the AFB allows a cruising speed with just primary butterflies opened. The kit also smooths out the ill idling characters of the stock system. We ran some acceleration figures on the car before and after the installation. They were as follows:

The completed unit with all the chrome goodies.

Balcaen inspects metal brake after testing. They showed little wear.

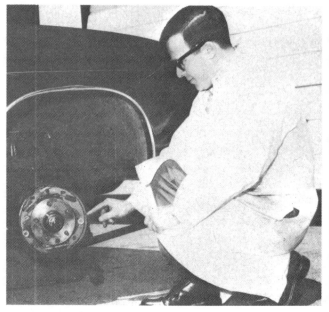

Acceleration:
- Stock: 0-30 — 3.2 sec.
  - 0-60 — 11.4 sec.
  - 0-80 — 20.4 sec.
  - Quarter mile —
    - 19.7 @ 75 mph

- IECO: 0-30 — 2.9 sec.
  - 0-60 — 9.8 sec.
  - 0-80 — 16.1 sec.
  - Quarter mile —
    - 16.9 @ 80 mph

Passing Speeds:
- Stock: 40-60 mph — 8.6 sec.
  - 50-70 mph — 9.1 sec.
- IECO: 40-60 mph — 5.9 sec.
  - 50-70 mph — 6.1 sec.

The Ram-equipped car had none of the hard cornering carburetor flooding associated with the stock system. Another point: since the AFB has a single common float bowl instead of four, the car is not subjected to gummy and stale gasoline in the secondary throttle valves as it is in stock form.

The IECO Corvair was indeed a real experience in sports driving. The people at IECO have become true specialists at transforming the Corvair into an individual's automobile. The chassis corners with great speed, the car stops in short distances, and the acceleration is like no other Corvair. People who are interested in more information may write to: IECO, 1541 Third Street "A", Santa Monica, California 90401 ∎

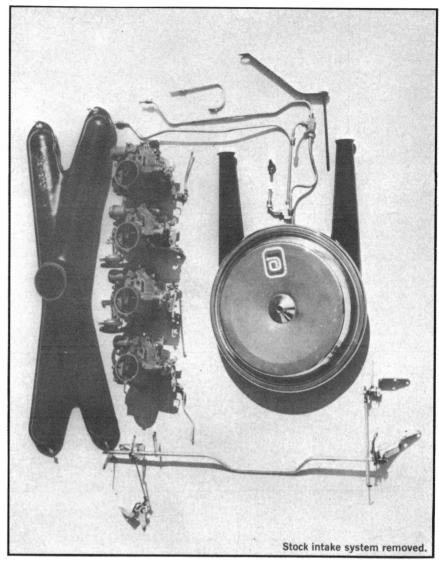

Stock intake system removed.

Fourteen inch wheels with Goodyear "Power Cushion" tires set off the Corvair Corsa.

By JOHN LAWLOR

There are countless thousands of motorists who would enjoy owning and driving the Corvair Corsa — if they hadn't been enticed away from it by the Mustang, or frightened away by the misunderstood pronouncements of so-called "safety experts."

The Corsa provides an exceptional combination of sportiness and practicality. It performs well, handles better than many highly-touted sports cars and looks as good as anything on the road, yet it's spacious and comfortable enough for family use. It's an ideal compromise for the man who wants something interesting, enjoyable and sophisticated, but who also needs sensible everyday transportation.

Unhappily, though, it has lost its appeal to the buying public. As we write, Corvair sales have dropped 50 percent compared with the same period last year. And, if the car continues to lose ground in the marketplace, Chevrolet is expected to phase it out of production by the end of the 1967 season. With that, American car buyers will have lost the opportunity to own one of the most intriguing little automobiles ever offered them.

In our view, the decline of the Corvair began when Ford introduced the incredibly successful Mustang. The Ford product, too, blends stylishness and sophistication with everyday practicality. But it does so with more powerful engine options than the Corvair offers and with a conventional, straightforward chassis layout.

The hottest Corvair engine has 180 horsepower, while choices in the regular Mustang extend to 271 and in the special Shelby GT-350 version to 306.

But, even if the Mustang weren't available with more power than the Corvair, it would still have an edge.

The American motorist seems to mistrust anything out of the ordinary. Given a choice between the Corvair's rear engine and fully independent suspension and the Mustang's perfectly orthodox chassis design, the U.S. car buyer is apt to prefer the latter. Never mind that the Corvair is a better, safer handling car than the standard Mustang. Its engineering doesn't follow the established norm and is, therefore, suspect.

As if to confirm such feelings, the original Corvair has become one of the most controversial automobiles in history. Its handling qualities have been so thoroughly criticized and condemned that much of the public is apparently convinced the combination of a rear engine and independent suspension is inherently dangerous.

From 1960 through 1963, the Corvair was built with swing axles at the rear, shafts that were U-jointed to the final drive assembly but were attached directly to the wheels they operated. Such a layout permitted the wheels to vary considerably in their angles, or camber, on the road surface. This, in turn, affected the slip angles of the tires, the prime factor in a car's directional stability, and allowed the vehicle to oversteer — that is, the rear tended to come around a corner faster than the front.

These characteristics were hardly unique to the Corvair. Several European cars — the Volkswagen and Renault Dauphine, for example, and the earlier Porsche — have had swing axles and consequent oversteering tendencies. In fact, drivers who came to the Corvair from such imports felt right at home and had no difficulty adjusting to the Chevrolet product.

But such a background wasn't necessary. Anyone with reasonable driving ability found the car's behavior within predictable and controllable limits.

Unfortunately, others with less experience and competence began getting into trouble. Failing to understand the

Corvair, they found themselves incapable of controlling it. And, when they became involved in accidents, they wouldn't take the blame. No, they accused the factory of faulty design — some of them actually going so far as to file suit for damages against Chevrolet.

Last year, these malcontents found an articulate and persuasive champion, a young attorney named Ralph Nader, who published a book called *Unsafe at Any Speed.* In it, Nader denounces the original Corvair's oversteering tendencies and suggests that drivers don't have any obligation to understand the behavior of their cars, that they don't have a responsibility to learn how to handle their vehicles properly.

To give the devil his due, Nader confines the brunt of his attack to the 1960 through 1963 Corvair. In 1964, Chevrolet added a compensator spring to the swing axle setup, a device that kept the rear wheels more nearly parallel in normal driving situations. But this didn't eliminate oversteer by any means. It just minimized it at lower speeds. On a given turn, the 1964 Corvair would go into final oversteer and breakaway at the same speed as the earlier models.

In 1965, the car was completely redesigned. The rear suspension became fully independent and articulated, with U-joints at both ends of each axle shaft, so that the extreme camber variations allowed by swing axles no longer occurred. The angles of the rear wheels could remain constant and, as a result, the slip angles of the tires provided more stable control. Oversteering tendencies were, for all practical purposes, eliminated.

Nader concedes · that the 1965 Corvair had excellent handling qualities. Unfortunately, the distinction seems to have been lost on much of the public. Those who haven't actually read *Unsafe at Any Speed* — and all too many who have — know that he condemns the Corvair as an unsafe automobile and they

ALL WASHED UP?

THE TRAGEDY OF BAD PUBLICITY

seem to assume that he means all Corvair models, not merely the ones he specifies.

In brief, Nader decries the handling of the earlier Corvair as a serious weakness – which we don't feel it was – and the public appears to have accepted and extended his criitcism to cover all Corvair models, including recent ones with totally different characteristics.

Fortified by Nader's opinions, the inherent public suspicion of the unconventional becomes a prejudice that Chevrolet can't overcome.

More's the pity, because the current Corvair is an excellent little automobile.

The basic design introduced in 1965 has been continued for 1966 with virtually no modifications. And it will probably go into 1967 in the same form. To be sure, next year's version may incorporate some new safety features, such as a collaspible steering column and a dual braking system, but the basic overall concept is likely to remain unchanged.

That's as it should be. We think the car is just fine as it is.

Any faults we were able to find with the 1966 Corvair weren't related to its particular engineering layout. Assembly quality was disappointing, for example, but that's a problem Chevrolet has been fighting throughout its entire line and not one confined to the Corvair.

And the manual shift linkage was poor, as is usually the case in rear-engined cars. Shift gates were vague and hard to find and the linkage itself operated very stiffly.

Corvair styling, rates among industry's very best. Fully independent suspension, rearward weight bias give smooth ride, excellent traction on unpaved surfaces. Front end, is clean, tasteful, functional.

But, what's important, the vehicle's road behavior was excellent. Setting aside some limited-production sports cars, such as the Corvette Sting Ray and the Shelby GT-350, the current Corvair handles as well as anything made in this country.

Even the incompetents who couldn't control the 1960 through 1963 models would have no trouble with the new one. Poured into a turn, the car displays a slight understeer. But a touch on the throttle overcomes it and, with further applications of the accelerator, the driver can induce a fully-controlled oversteer. That's exactly how most front-engined vehicles with adequate power will react under the same conditions.

In other words, the Corvair may still be unconventional in its engineering but it certainly isn't in its over-the-road characteristics.

140-horsepower engine is standard in Corsa, 180-horsepower turbocharged unit optional. Powerplant is air-cooled, opposed six with aluminum block.

From the first 1960 model, the Corvair has had an extremely smooth, light driving feel. Happily, the recent chassis changes haven't affected that quality one bit. The car still maneuvers smoothly and easily in traffic, surprisingly so for one without power assists on its steering or brakes.

The driving position is quite comfortable, though we'd recommend the optional, adjustable steering column. The standard placement of the wheel is a bit too close for our taste.

The top-of-the-line Corsa series has one of the most remarkable instrument

Forward luggage compartment has plenty of space for weekend luggage. Note deep recess front and center. Spare tire is carried in engine compartment.

panels in any current car. It has six different gauges, yet also incorporates red warning lights for four items!

A large, legible speedometer and a matching tachometer flank four smaller dials, including a clock and gauges showing fuel level, cylinder head temperature and manifold vacuum. One warning light registers generator discharge or fan belt failure, while another indicates unsatisfactory oil pressure or, as a check on the cylinder head gauge, excessive engine temperature.

The instrument panel may not be the most vital part of a car but, here, it's an obvious example of the thoroughness and thoughtfulness thats' gone into the latest Corvair. No other standard production automobile, at least in this country, has as informative a collection of gauges and lights. Even the warning lights are acceptable in this case because they alert the driver immediately

ROAD TEST DATA: **CORVAIR CORSA**

Base Price: $2519

Price as Tested: $2830

CHASSIS

Wheelbase: 108 inches

Tread: 55 inches front, 57.2 inches rear

Length: 183.3 inches

Width: 51.3 inches

Height: 51.3 inches

Tire Size: 6.50 x 13

Suspension: Independent coil springs, front and rear

Steering, lock-to-lock: 4.7 turns

Curb Weight: 2570 pounds

PERFORMANCE

Standing Quarter-Mile: 19 seconds @ 73 mph

ENGINE

Type: Opposed four-cylinder

Bore and Stroke: 3.4375 x 2.94 inches

Displacement: 164 cubic inches

Horsepower: 140 @ 5200 rpm

Torque: 160 @ 3600 rpm

Compression Ratio: 9.25-to-1

Carburetion: 4 x 1-bbl

DRIVE TRAIN

Transmission: 4-speed manual

Rear Axle Ratio: 3.55-to-1

ROAD TEST: **CORVAIR CORSA**
VALUE RATING CONSENSUS

	EXCELLENT	GOOD	FAIR	POOR
RIDE	X	XX	XX	
HANDLING	XXX	XX		
ACCELERATION		XX	XXX	
PASSING ABILITY		XXX	XX	
BRAKING		XXX	XX	
SEATING COMFORT: Front	XXX	XX		
Rear			XXXX	X
NOISE LEVEL: Wind		XXXX	X	
Road	X	XXXX		
INSTRUMENTATION	XXXXX			
CONTROL ACCESSIBILITY	XXX	XX		
PAINT QUALITY		XXXXX		
PANEL AND TRIM FIT: Exterior		XXX	XX	
Interior		XX	XXX	
FUEL ECONOMY		XXXX	X	
LUGGAGE SPACE		XXX	XX	
STYLING	XXXXX			

TEST AT A GLANCE

	EXCELLENT	GOOD	FAIR	POOR
PERFORMANCE		XXX	XX	
ECONOMY		XXXX	X	
VALUE	X	XX	XX	

Dual exhausts peek from beneath rear of 140-horsepower Corsa. Car provides appealing blend of sporting, practical qualities, deserves more popularity.

Dual exhausts peek from beneath rear of 140-horsepower Corsa. Car provides appealing blend of sporting, practical qualities, deserves more popularity.

of any serious engine problem, any difficulty requiring that the ignition be turned off *now*. They're supplements, not substitutes, for proper instrumentation.

The standard Corsa engine is a 140-horsepower version of the opposed, 164-cubic-inch Corvair six. Optional is a 180-horsepower, turbocharged unit.

The lower-priced series, the Monza and the 500, have a modest 95-horsepower engine as standard and a 110-horsepower unit as option. They're also available with the 140-horsepower Corsa setup but not with the turbocharged design.

With either the 140- or 180-horsepower engine, a manual transmission is obligatory. Only the lesser Monza and 500 powerplants can be obtained with Powerglide.

The standard three-speed manual has ratios of 3.11 in first, 1.84 in second and direct drive in third, while the four-speed has 3.20 in first, 2.19 in second, 1.44 in third and direct drive in fourth. In the two-speed Powerglide, the converter stall ratio is 2.6, while first is 1.82 and second is direct.

Only two axle ratios are listed, 3.55 with the higher-powered engines and 3.27 with the two lesser ones. Both can be had in standard or limited-slip form.

Quicker steering, metallic brake linings and heavy-duty springs and shocks are also listed as options. Beyond that, it's necessary to turn to specialized suppliers to gain further increases in horsepower or to capitalize on the already outstanding roadability.

Before the Mustang appeared, there were dozens of firms offering Corvair accessories and equipment. But, with the advent of the Ford's little sporty car, most of them abandoned the rear-engined Chevy and jumped on the new, horse-drawn bandwagon.

Fortunately, there are a few diehards who've stuck with the Corvair. In their own way, they're doing for the Corsa what Carroll Shelby and his GT-350 do for the Mustang, transforming a good car into an even better one.

One of them, in fact, R. F. "Sonny" Balcaen of Los Angeles, has been affiliated with Shelby's enterprises but happens to prefer the Corvair to the Mustang. Under the IECO trade name, short for Induction Engineering Company, Balcaen markets excellent intake and exhaust manifolding and special heavy-duty chassis equipment.

Better known, perhaps, is John Fitch of Falls Village, Connecticut, who produces a true *gran turismo* version of the Corsa he calls the Sprint. Fitch converts complete cars and also sells engine and chassis and even restyling components separately to the Corvair owner who wants to build a Sprint on his own time — and budget.

Most ambitious of all is **Don Yenko,** a Chevrolet dealer of Canonsburg, Pensylvania, who ignores General Motors' refusal to take part in any form of racing and produces the Stinger, a modified Corvair that has qualified in its own right as a D/Production sports car under the rules of the Sports Car Club of America. Yenko builds the Stinger in three forms, mild street, wild street and full sports-racing.

Ralph Nader and his misguided following have cast something of an evil eye on the Corvair. Intentionally or not, they've led the public to believe that it isn't a satisfactory automobile.

In a literal sense, they're right. It isn't merely satisfactory. It's excellent.

Against the hard, cold look of Nader, men like "Sonny" Balcaen, John Fitch and Don Yenko continue to have faith in the Corvair. And, after driving the new Corsa, so do we.

Aluminum paint across rear distinguishes Corsa from other Corvair series, 500 and Monza. Vehicle has one of best standard suspensions in any U.S. car.

The Corvair Corsa, a car far removed from other General Motors products both in design and appearance.

Chevrolet Corvair Corsa

DURING the past year, General Motors must have begun to doubt the old adage that there's no such thing as bad publicity. The Chevrolet Corvair has suffered a series of slashing attacks both by Ralph Nader and in court by various people who have sought to attribute the responsibility for their accidents to the designer rather than to the driver. Certainly the Corvair which we tested in 1960 had a marked oversteer which, because of its very low geared steering, it was wiser not to invoke by excessively fast cornering and it was very sensitive to tyre pressures which most owners treat with casual indifference.

But all this fuss has obscured the fact that the Corvair, a car which is almost unknown in this country, underwent design changes two years ago so drastic that criticisms of the earlier version could not reasonably be extrapolated to current models. We felt we ought to bring our acquaintance up to date and since the nearest car available was at General Motors in Antwerp, this involved going abroad to make a test of limited scope and duration in Belgium and Holland.

It is worth recapitulating some of the features which make the Corvair entirely different from any other American car. For a start it has a flat six-cylinder air-cooled light alloy engine mounted at the rear—originally of 2.3 litres capacity but now grown to nearly 2.7 litres. Secondly, it has independent suspension on all four wheels; these two features together distinguish it from any other production car in the world except the Porsche 911.

The Corvair, of course, was one of the original American compact cars and, although it has grown, it remains a compact by U.S. standards with external dimensions comparable with those of a Vauxhall Cresta or a Ford Zodiac. It grew (longer, wider and lower) in autumn '64 when it had its first major styling change; at the same time it acquired much bigger brakes and, most important of all, the swing axle rear suspension (modified in the meantime) was replaced by a fully articulated system with a low roll centre (shown in the accompanying photograph) which is very similar to that used on the Corvette sports car.

The 1966 models in ascending order of price were the 500, Monza and Corsa, the first two available in two- or four-door coupé or sedan form with 95, 110 or 140 b.h.p. (SAE) engines and with three- or four-speed manual gearboxes or automatic transmission. The Corsa was the top model of the range, a two-door four-seater coupé normally fitted with the four carburetter 140 b.h.p. engine but available also with a 180 b.h.p. unit supercharged by means of an exhaust-driven turbo-blower.

It is announced this week that the Corsa, the model we tested, will be dropped from the 1967 Corvair range and so will the 140 and 180 b.h.p. engines. This elimination of the faster models may possibly be a General Motors reaction to so much ill-directed criticism. If so it seems a pity; we are still publishing this test partly to show that we found nothing dangerous about its handling characteristics and partly because the Corsa is basically so similar to the remaining Corvair models that most of what we have written is still directly applicable to them.

In America the Corsa cost about £925; in Belgium, where sales were considerable, about £1,350 without tax; in England it was obtainable only to special order (with left hand drive) at about £2,300 although we don't think that any were imported.

Corvair rear suspension. Fixed length, double jointed halfshafts, lower transverse links and fore and aft radius arms to take brake torque.

An intake grille below the rear window betrays a flat-six air-cooled rear engine which is notable for its low overall height. The photograph of the power unit shows a flat air cleaner over the four carburetters (two to each bank) and, just visible below it, the multi-blade horizontal fan which forces air round the closely cowled finned heads and block.

The facia follows a trend which can be seen on other GM cars—a high mounted instrument panel with round, sunken dials. As well as the usual instruments it has a cylinder head thermometer, a tachometer and a a manifold pressure gauge. An extra control, fitted for the Belgain market, is a foot-operated headlamp flasher alongside the foot dipswitch.

Performance and transmission

Air-cooled engines tend to be noisy but this isn't a criticism that can be levelled at the Corvair flat six even in this high output form. There is a subdued burble from the exhaust when accelerating hard from low speeds but if there is any mechanical clatter it doesn't penetrate to the inside of the car—probably because it enjoys the luxury of hydraulic tappets.

The 140 b.h.p. engine has a camshaft with long opening periods and considerable overlap which makes it just a little bit flat below 2,000 r.p.m.; above this it really gets into its stride and revs very freely right up to the red sector on the tachometer which starts at 5,500 r.p.m. (preceded by a yellow warning band from 5,200 r.p.m.). At low engine speeds it pinks a little on Belgian premium fuel which, like ours, has an octane rating of 97-99 R.M. The compression ratio is 9.25 to 1 and the presence of a cylinder head temperature gauge on the facia serves as a reminder that air-cooled combustion chambers run hotter than the water-cooled variety. In point of fact it indicated about 400°F when cruising continuously around 90 m.p.h. on the motorways; there is no indication of the maximum temperature permissible but we never reached it; otherwise we should have been warned by a light in the tachometer dial and also by a buzzer connected to it.

So it pays to use the gearbox even though the engine remains smooth and tractable at low speeds. With a maximum speed of 104 m.p.h. and acceleration from rest to 50 m.p.h. in 8.8 sec., the performance is very similar to that of an MG B and rather better than that of most European touring cars in the 2- to 3-litre class. Our car had the all-synchromesh four-speed box which is a slightly more expensive alternative to the standard three-speed. Its ratios are not ideal, the upper three gears being rather widely spaced and bottom very close to second; the gearchange is rather notchy and heavy but the gears are quiet except for a little growl at very low speeds. The clutch is smooth and light but has a long travel.

For the whole test, which comprised a mixture of fast driving or very heavy traffic, not unlike that of our road tests at home, we averaged 20.6 m.p.g.—a very creditable figure for a car of 2.7 litres capacity. This gives a range of 200–240 miles on a tankful of fuel.

Performance

Conditions

Weather: Dry, warm, little wind.
Temperature: Approx. 65°F.
Surface: Dry tarmacadam.
Fuel: Premium grade, 98 octane (R.M.).

Maximum speeds

	m.p.h.
Mean two-way maximum	104.0
Best one-way kilometre	104.5
3rd gear	75.0
2nd gear	50.0
1st gear	35.0

Acceleration times

m.p.h.	sec.
0-30	3.8
0-40	6.2
0-50	8.8
0-60	12.1
0-70	16.4
0-80	23.0
0-90	32.6

m.p.h.	Top sec.	3rd sec.
10-30	—	6.6
20-40	11.0	5.9
30-50	11.0	6.5
40-60	10.3	6.9
50-70	11.6	7.7
60-80	12.8	—
70-90	16.2	—

Fuel consumption

Overall	20.6 m.p.g.
	(=13.7 litres/100 km.)
Total test distance	510 miles
Tank capacity (maker's figure)	11¾ gal.

Steering

Turning circle between kerbs	35 ft.
Turns of steering wheel from lock to lock	4.8

Speedometer

Indicated (k.p.h.)
20 30 40 50 60 70 80 90 100 110 120 130 140
True (k.p.h.)
21 30 40 51 61 71 81 91 101 112 123 134 146

Distance recorder	2% slow

Weight

Kerb weight (unladen with fuel for approximately 50 miles)	23½ cwt.
Front/rear distribution	38/62
Weight laden as tested	27 cwt.

Wheel arches, fuel tank, suspension and steering all combine to make the boot an irregular shape but its total volume is impressive.

Although the rear cushion is rather short and flat, the Corvair is a practical and comfortable four-seater. All four seats are fitted as standard with safety belts.

Chevrolet Corvair Corsa

Handling and brakes

Before we had even left Antwerp after collecting the car one suspension characteristic became obvious—the Corsa rides over pavé with remarkable quietness and stability. Following other cars with orthodox rear axles it was often possible to see daylight under their rear wheels but the Corvair i.r.s. felt well glued down and the whole integral body/chassis structure has an extremely solid, shakefree feel. Road noise generally is low and the front seat ride very comfortable although on bad roads there is some pitching which leaves the front occupants very little affected but contributes to an appreciably less comfortable ride in the back.

This is one of the few American cars which doesn't offer optional power steering and which doesn't need it. The front wheels carry only about 9 cwt. of the unladen weight and the steering is low-geared—4.8 turns for an indifferent lock—so it is never heavy, not even for manoeuvring. An optional "Sport Handling Package" is available which includes harder springs and dampers and a steering gear giving about three turns lock to lock. Unlike the earlier Corvair, it is only mildly sensitive to cross-winds (less so than some front-engined cars) and normally feels extremely stable right up to maximum speed unless you try to drive along a narrow road of changing camber at speeds in the region of 80–90 m.p.h. when it starts to wander appreciably. This, of course, is a very severe test for any car.

Certainly, the steering feels much higher geared than it is for a number of reasons which collectively confer on the Corvair an un-American degree of activity in response to the controls. By this we don't mean that it is in any way twitchy—it isn't—but it lacks the exaggerated understeer built into so many of its compatriots. The real question, though, in view of the GM court cases, is whether it has the unstable degree of oversteer attributed to the earlier swing axle models and the answer is an emphatic negative.

Its cornering, to European hands, feels practically neutral. There is little roll, the tyres don't squeal easily and the car follows a pre-determined line without steering correction. Wet or dry, you can use heavy acceleration on a bend without beginning to unstick the rear tyres and in the hands of a heavy-footed driver this is a real safety factor. In the absence of a closed test-track and in the presence of so many Dutch weekend motorists we couldn't press it over the limit to see what happened—all we can be sure about is that you can drive it fast for well over 500 miles and never experience anything but impeccable behaviour.

The brakes were less satisfactory. They use self-adjusting duo-servo shoes inside large drums without power assistance; we found them quite adequate in the dry—they were heavy but they stopped you well if you pressed hard enough and they continued to do this without fade when used frequently and hard (in, of course, a flat country). But they seemed unduly sensitive to water and on several occasions when cruising fast on wet motorways we found that a first application would reveal a considerable pull to one side or, sometimes, very little deceleration at all.

Apart from this we would say that the current Corvair is a very safe and roadworthy car. **M**

Specification

Engine

Cylinders	Horizontally opposed 6
Bore and stroke	87.31 mm. × 74.68 mm.
Cubic capacity	2,683 c.c.
Valves	o.h.v. (pushrods) with hydraulic tappets
Compression ratio	9.25:1
Carburetters	4 Rochester single barrel downdraughts
Fuel pump	Mechanical
Oil filter	Full flow
Max. power (S.A.E.)	140 b.h.p. at 5,200 r.p.m.
Max. torque (S.A.E.)	160 lb. ft. at 3,600 r.p.m.

Transmission

Clutch	9¼ in. dia. s.d.p. with diaphragm spring
Top gear (s/m)	1.00
3rd gear (s/m)	1.47
2nd gear (s/m)	2.20
1st gear (s/m)	3.11
Reverse	3.11
Final drive	Hypoid, 3.55 to 1
M.p.h. at 1,000 r.p.m. in:—	
Top gear	20.1
3rd gear	13.7
2nd gear	9.1
1st gear	6.5

Chassis

Construction	Unitary

Brakes

Type	Self-adjusting duo-servo drum brakes with hydraulic operation
Dimensions	9.5 in. dia. × 2¼ in. wide
Friction areas:	
Front	84.5 sq. ins. of lining operating on 134 sq. ins. of drum
Rear	84.5 sq. ins. of lining operating on 134 sq. ins. of drum

Suspension and steering

Front	Double transverse wishbones, coil springs and anti-roll bar
Rear	Fully independent using fixed length half shafts, lower transverse links, longitudinal radius arms and coil springs
Shock absorbers:	
Front and rear	Telescopic
Steering gear	Saginaw recirculating ball
Tyres	6.50—13 4 ply
Rim size	5½J

Coachwork and equipment

Starting handle	None
Jack	Screw scissor type
Jacking points	Four, under door sills
Battery	12 volt negative earth, 44 amp. hrs. capacity
Number of electrical fuses	6 and one circuit breaker
Indicators	Self-cancelling flashers
Screen wipers	Two speed electric
Screen washers	Electric
Sun visors	Two
Locks:	
With ignition key	Ignition and door locks
With other keys	Boot and glove locker
Interior heater	Direct supply from engine cooling air plus adjustable cold air vents
Extras	Automatic transmission, radio, air conditioning, tilt wheel steering
Upholstery	Plastic
Floor covering	Carpets
Alternative body styles	Convertible coupé

Maintenance

Sump	6 pints S.A.E. 10W/30 (plus 2 pints for filter)
Transmission	6½ pints S.A.E.80
Steering gear	Chevrolet lubricant 5263437
Cooling system	Air cooled
Chassis lubrication	Every 6,000 miles to 10 points
Minimum service interval	6,000 miles (or 60 days, if shorter)
Ingition timing	18° b.t.d.c. at 650 r.p.m.
Contact breaker gap	0.019 in.
Sparking plug gap	0.028 to 0.033 in.
Sparking plug type	AC 44-FF
Tapper clearances	Zero (hydraulic adjustment)
Valve timing:	
inlet opens	55° b.t.d.c.
inlet closes	105° a.b.d.c.
exhaust opens	97° b.b.d.c.
exhaust closes	63° a.t.d.c.
Front wheel toe-in	¼ in.
Camber angle	½—1½°
Castor angle	2½—3½°
Kingpin inclination	6—7°
Tyre pressures	21 lb. front, 25 lb. rear (plus 7 lb. for continuous speeds of over 90 m.p.h. on motorways)

is the Corvair REALLY Unsafe?

By Tom McCahill

CHEVROLET'S Corvair was given a bad time in 1966 because a character named Ralph Nader hit it pretty hard in a book he wrote titled Unsafe At Any Speed. Overnight, dozens of lawsuits against Chevrolet popped up, blaming injury and death on the design of the Corvair. To this writing Chevrolet hasn't lost a suit for faulty design, which is a tribute to our courts for not being as stupid as some people might think.

The general public (not MI readers) is pretty easy to stampede one way or the other, especially about engineering designs. Since it is the general public that buys most of the automobiles, when

the word got around that the Corvair was unsafe and had design defects, sales started to nose-dive and one of the best compacts in the country was looking extinction right in the eye.

As we have written on these pages before, thousands of guys in this country can get killed peeling a banana and there are thousands of others who shouldn't be on the highways in the second place. The Corvair called for a different handling technique when driven hard because it was different from the typical front-engine automobile. This made it a perfect Patsy for the screamers when people got hurt in it.

The fact that more people got killed

every year in regular Fords, Chevrolets and Plymouths had little influence with those who clamored about Corvair calamities. The Corvairs were different. Rear-engine cars do handle differently in hard cornering but this characteristic is not necessarily a defect. The fact that you may have soloed in a Piper Cub doesn't mean you are ready to pilot a 707 jet and the small outboard owner may not be capable of docking the Queen Mary without tugs.

The popular VW for years was one of the easiest cars to flip in hard bends, not because of poor design but because it had to be treated differently from front-engine cars. And some drivers

were not too hip in separating the difference. The Porsche used to be an easy-to-flip candidate, especially in road races on rough courses. On one circuit where the cars had to race across a railroad crossing, which often caused them to become airborne, the rear wheels tucked under. When the car hit the pavement again it often flipped to the right or left, depending on which wheel touched ground first.

By late 1959, when the first 1960 Corvairs were introduced, most flipping tendencies in rear-engine cars had been licked through suspension changes, snubbers and more-advanced steering geometry.

Here's a quote about the car's handling from the November 1959 MI:

"At first I tried gentle side whips, breaking the rear away slightly around bends. The car steers like a feather and is extremely quick. In 15 minutes I was putting the Corvair into full broadslides. Then came the most crucial test of all. I threw it into spins and drifted off course onto dirt and gravel, then back onto the asphalt again. I feel absolutely certain that if I had done this with some other rear-engine cars I'd have been grasping a lily in a mahogany box before the next sun-up. This Corvair is a magnificent-handling automobile. If it has any killer tendencies, I couldn't find them—and I tried every trick in the book."

That was written by me about the car and model that Mr. Nader felt so strongly about in his well-promoted book.

When my report was written it was assumed that the driver was fairly well-rounded and experienced and not the holder of a mail-order license. If there was an error by the boys at GM it was in underestimating the talent of the typical automobile licensing bureau for turning so many out-and-out kooks loose on our highways. The holder of a license who doesn't have enough intelligence to understand that the Corvair has a rear engine and that the handling might be different from Gramp's old Model A shouldn't be allowed to drive a Dodgem at a county fair.

Up until now we have been referring to the early-model Corvairs. Since then many improvements have been made, however, and if you'd really like a Corvair that will forgive all but the stupidest mistakes, John Fitch of Lime Rock, Conn., sells suspension equipment, especially designed for Corvairs, that will tolerate outrageous handling goofs. Keeping in mind that you can kill yourself by an over-indulgence in aspirin tablets or from smoking in bed (both poor grounds for an industrial lawsuit) let's take the latest Corvair—the '67 —and see how it runs around.

Our '67 test car, as red as a Chinese fire engine and as neat as new money, was delivered to me in Florida. After several weeks of using it for general chores, such as trips to the opium den or to my friendly mortician who was running a sale, the car was ready for a wring-out.

Before testing, it was evident that the engine, sporting 24 more cubic inches than our original Corvair back in '59, had a lot more performance going for it. Also remembering my original test, where I deliberately tried to wreck the car, I decided to take another tack. I pretended (and this didn't take too much pretending) to be good old Joe Bubblehead—long on throttle-beating and short on brains.

As even the most amateurish rear-engine drivers know, the easiest way to get in trouble with such a car is to come into a rough corner too fast where there are bumps in the road to interrupt a slide. If you're going to flip, this is one of the easiest ways to do it. I found a freshly graded country dirt road that led into a dirt corner where, due to heavy rain plus some logging-truck activity, the surface was extremely dangerous for devil-may-care driving.

I charged this corner several times at speeds between 65 and 70—threw the car into a slide and hit the ruts broadside. This got sportier the harder I cut in but the car responded immediately to the mildest of correcting. In less than two fast wrist flicks of the steering wheel the car was back in line again and charging down the roughed-up dirt road.

I feel certain that when I cranked it into the original slide fast if I had remained rigid like the Statue of Liberty I probably would have up-ended when I slammed into the ruts—but then I could easily have up-ended many conventional front-engine cars the same way. If you know what you're doing this car will take a lot of abuse in handling and you won't need the knowledge of a champion Grand Prix driver—just some common driving sense.

After leaving the dust roads I headed for an interstate. It was shortly after daylight and the only other thing on the road was a raccoon that I had a little difficulty in missing. Absolute top speed through my secret measured mile was 94.1 mph.

After these runs I went to the Daytona Speedway for acceleration runs and a couple of high-speed laps. Because of the way the 31° Speedway banks sop up cubic inches and horsepower, top speed around the circuit was down to 90.3 mph. In the acceleration runs 0 to 60 averaged 13.9

[Continued on page 140]

Corvair

TOM gives the lean test to the engineless front end of what he calls a very decent rig.

When Nader's book came out berating the Corvair's handling qualities, especially the early models, I dug into my files to check what my first impressions had been.

I remembered going to GM's Proving Grounds with an MI editor and taking a Corvair before introduction to give it a wring-out. I was looking for flip-and-roll characteristics mainly because some of the famous rear-engine race jobs of the past (principally the German Auto-Unions before World War II) had the reputation of being killers.

The Auto-Unions were designed by Dr. Porsche (who also designed the great P-wagons (as they were known in honor of Dr. Porsche) before you were well into a slide. Even the great Nuvolari, the master of slides and skids, was scared to death of them and almost lost his life in one in a series of figure 8s,

---

WHICH END is this? McCahill contends that those who know will have no trouble.

squared and cubed, on a wet Grand Prix circuit.

A lot of beer went over the bridge-work in the next quarter of a century and when GM's Ed Cole came out with the Corvair design he had the rear-engine problems pretty well licked and the car was a lot safer in the handling department than the popular VW. I was dumber and braver when the Corvair first came out, almost eight years ago, and after cinching up my safety belt I deliberately tried to wreck it—the hard way—with no driving holds barred.

CORVAIR MONZA SPORT COUPE

More Fun-Per-Dollar Than Any Other American Passenger Car

WHEN WE DECIDED to road test a Corvair, some staff members voiced their disdain, dismay, and disbelief at the wisdom of testing a car which obviously (?) is destined for imminent demise. However, after an all-too-brief test period it is our opinion that, if Chevrolet decides to let the Corvair die a lingering death through lack of advertising and further development, it will be a tragic mistake. It's too much car to kill.

The Corvair, in its present form, comes closer to being a real sports car than any of the current crop of Ponycars. True, the Corvair does not feature the lunging, neck-snapping acceleration of Ponycars equipped with monster 400-cid engines. But around town, through mountain passes and over winding secondary roadways, the Corvair is pure pleasure. Response-killing excessive understeer that plagues most domestic automobiles is absent from the Corvair. Agility and cornering power are qualities that make the Corvair worth driving. And, these are the qualities that make driving worth doing.

CAR LIFE's test car was a Monza Sport Coupe, with 140-bhp engine, 4-speed manual transmission, optional suspension package and 7.00-13 white

sidewall tires. A few other options added nothing to performance, but did supply some additional luxury, completed the $2862 list price. Note this price carefully, because a well-equipped automobile selling for less than $3000 is a rare occurrence in today's domestic market. Also, if the test Corvair was stripped of extraneous lighting packages, trim decor and non-essential nits, the list price drops to less than $2700. This price includes 4-carburetor engine, 4-speed gearbox and HD suspension. This has to be America's best bargain in sporting machinery.

Corvair styling has long been considered excellent, one of the better examples of contemporary automotive design. The test car was finished in medium metallic blue, and was pleasantly free of exterior ornamentation. The Monza interior was attractively done, adequately trimmed without being overdone in the Wurlitzer-Pullman pattern of current American cars. As one observer stated, the Corvair interior features "practical plushness." Instrumentation is legible, controls are easily reached and operated, and surfaces are shaped and finished to minimize glare. Seats in the Monza were of the pseudo-bucket type. Though lacking in side support, these seats were well designed, with acceptable seatback rake, adequate padding, and good leg and shoulder support.

Seat-to-wheel and seat-to-pedal relationships in the Corvair were excellent for average-size drivers, but lacked sufficient seat track adjustment for those of above average height. A tall owner probably would want to move the seat tracks rearward, obtaining additional leg room at some sacrifice of rear seat knee room. With the seat positioned for proper pedal and steering wheel control, another defect became apparent. The gearshift is too far away from comfortable selection of first and third gears. Obviously, present gearshift location is designed to accommodate a bench front seat (available on low-priced Corvair 500 models). Owners of bucket-seat versions could rework the shift lever to bring the knob rearward, and would then find city traffic operation much more acceptable.

For 1968, all Corvairs will feature the emission controls used in California since 1965. The test car incorporated the air pump system used on nearly all manual transmission-equipped 1968 GM models. It was expected that all sorts of driveability problems would be apparent with emission controls and four carburetors. Surprisingly, starting and driveability were good, displaying none of the symptoms frequently noticed on other cars with air pumps.

This is not to say, however, that overall engine operation of the Corvair was perfect. The throttle linkage used on 4-carburetor versions of Corvair have been cursed since its introduction in 1965, and it is no better for 1968. Idle speed fluctuated, part-throttle hangups were common, and an occasional full-throttle sticking plagued the Corvair. This is really unfortunate,

as drivers often form a poor opinion of Corvair driveability because of the miserable linkage. Surely the engineering staff of Chevrolet could solve this perpetual problem, even if a couple of dollars need to be added to the sales price. A driver has to use the throttle to drive any car, and such an oft-used control should operate flawlessly. A throttle that sticks at wide-open posi-

tion is sure to start the adrenalin flowing, if it doesn't cause an accident.

Malfunctioning throttle linkage and poor gearshift location aside, the Corvair was a delightful car to drive. Corvair handling has been the subject of analysis, legislative investigation, and ill-founded rumors. In the face of all this, it seems worthy of careful discussion. First, the old saw about "treacherous rear-end steering" or "vicious oversteer" is a lot of hot air. The Corvair was one of the best-handling automobiles tested by *CAR LIFE*. Certainly the Corvair handled in a manner different from conventional front-engine, nose-heavy domestic sedans, but different does not mean poor.

Steering response in the Corvair was excellent, despite a too-slow ratio steer-

1968 CHEVROLET
CORVAIR SPORT COUPE

DIMENSIONS

Wheelbase, in.	108.0
Track, f/r, in.	55.0/56.6
Overall length, in.	183.3
width	69.7
height	51.3
Front seat hip room, in.	2 x 21.3
shoulder room	54.7
head room	37.6
pedal-seatback, max.	35.3
Rear seat hip room, in.	54.7
shoulder room	52.6
leg room	32.2
head room	36.5
Door opening width, in.	38.3
Ground clearance, in.	6.4
Trunk liftover height, in.	28.6

PRICES

List, FOB factory	$2484
Equipped as tested	$2862

Options included: Appearance guard group, auxiliary lighting, electric clock, 140-bhp engine, 4-speed manual trans., tinted glass, AM radio, rear speaker, HD suspension, wsw tires, spare wheel lock.

CAPACITIES

No. of passengers	4-5
Luggage space, cu. ft.	7.0
Fuel tank, gal.	14.0
Crankcase, qt.	4.0
Transmission/dif., pt.	3.5/4.0
Radiator coolant, qt.	none

CHASSIS/SUSPENSION

Frame type: Unitized.
Front suspension type: Independent by s.l.a., coil springs, telescopic shock absorbers.

ride rate at wheel, lb./in.	n.a.
antiroll bar dia., in.	0.812

Rear suspension type: Independent, fixed-length axle shafts, lower control arms, telescopic shock absorbers.

ride rate at wheel, lb./in.	n.a.

Steering system: Recirculating ball-nut gear, parallelogram linkage ahead of wheels.

overall ratio	23.3:1
turns, lock to lock	4.5
turning circle, ft. curb-curb	37.0
Curb weight, lb.	2615
Test weight	2975
distribution (driver), % f/r	36.0/64.0

BRAKES

Type: Cast iron drum brakes, front and rear, duo-servo type.

Front drum, dia. x width, in.	9.5 x 2.0
Rear drum, dia. x width	9.5 x 2.5
total swept area, sq. in.	268.6
Power assist	none
line psi at 100 lb. pedal	838

WHEELS/TIRES

Wheel rim size	13 x 5.5J
optional size	none
bolt no./circle dia. in.	5/4.75

Tires: UniRoyal Laredo.

size	7.00-13
normal inflation, psi f/r	15/26
Capacity @ psi	n.a.

ENGINE

Type, no. of cyl.	opposed 6
Bore x stroke, in.	3.438 x 2.940
Displacement, cu. in.	163.757
Compression ratio	9.25:1
Fuel required	premium
Rated bhp @ rpm	140 @ 5200
equivalent mph	105
Rated torque @ rpm	160 @ 3600
equivalent mph	72

Carburetion: Rochester 4x1.

throttle dia., pri/sec.	1.25/none

Valve train: Hydraulic lifters, pushrods and overhead rocker arms.
cam timing

deg., int./exh.	70-86/98-46
duration, int./exh.	336/324

Exhaust system: Dual, reverse-flow mufflers.

pipe dia., exh./tail	1.62/1.75
Normal oil press. @ rpm	.30 @ 2000
Electrical supply, V./amp.	12/24
Battery, plates/amp. hr.	54/45

DRIVE TRAIN

Clutch type: Single dry disc, semi-centrifugal diaphragm-type pressure plate.

dia., in.	9.12

Transmission type: 4-speeds forward, fully synchronized.

Gear ratio 4th (1.00:1) overall	3.55:1
3rd (1.47:1)	5.22:1
2nd (2.20:1)	7.82:1
1st (3.11:1)	11.03:1
1st x t.c. stall ( )	

Shift lever location: Floor.
Differential type: Transaxle, hypoid final drive.

axle ratio	3.55:1

ing system. Transient oversteer could be detected, but was not vicious or uncontrollable. On the contrary, this oversteer was useful in rapid maneuvering, and was easily controlled by a competent driver.

Driving the Corvair at the limits of adhesion showed the car to understeer ultimately in slow turns, become neutral at 40–50 mph, and oversteer slightly in high-speed bends. At low speeds, transient oversteer yields to fairly strong understeer as front wheel adhesion is exceeded, although tire pressures can be juggled to alter this transition. Factory-recommended pressures specify 11–15 psi differential between front and rear tires, with the fronts carrying the lesser pressure. This obviously is done to insure understeer, but we found ourselves raising front pressure to promote response and decrease understeer at low speeds. It should be noted that the test car was equipped with optional HD springs and shock absorbers. These do not alter basic handling characteristics, but do improve response and reduce roll. At $10.55, this package is a real bargain for the sporting driver.

Straight-line acceleration is not the Corvair's forte, even with the top-output 140-bhp engine. This engine de-velops peak bhp at 5200 rpm, and peak torque of 160 lb.-ft. occurs at 3600 rpm, very high engine speed for peak torque development. Coupling these output figures with the Corvair's test weight of just under 3000 lb. results in an expected lack of initial acceleration. The excellent traction afforded by Corvair's rearward weight bias eliminates wheelspin as a means for avoiding engine "bogging down" on takeoff. Thus, the alternatives are to either accept some bogging and stumbling, with attendant slow initial acceleration, or resort to excessive clutch slipping.

Because we had no desire to return the test car with a burned clutch, we chose to accept some stumbling for the first few feet, and take the consequent lag in acceleration. Figures given in the data panel, therefore, are handicapped by a very slow takeoff, and are not really representative of the Corvair's best road performance. Although takeoff was rather slow, performance in the mid and upper speed ranges was more than adequate, and the engine remained smooth and free-running up to 5000 rpm. For some reason, the test car was reluctant to rev beyond 5000. But it is doubtful that an additional 500 rpm would have

CAR LIFE ROAD TEST

ACCELERATION & COASTING

Chart axes: MPH (vertical, 10–120) vs ELAPSED TIME IN SECONDS (horizontal, 5–45). Curves labeled 1st, 2nd, 3rd, 4th, SS¼.

CALCULATED DATA

Lb./bhp (test weight)	21.2
Cu. ft./ton mile	95.2
Mph/1000 rpm (high gear)	20.1
Engine revs/mile (60 mph)	2980
Piston travel, ft./mile	1460
CAR LIFE wear index	43.6
Frontal area, sq. ft.	19.9
NHRA-AHRA class	J/S-M/S

SPEEDOMETER ERROR

30 mph, actual	28.2
40 mph	38.1
50 mph	48.4
60 mph	58.0
70 mph	68.3
80 mph	78.5
90 mph	88.7

MAINTENANCE

Engine oil, miles/days	6000/180
oil filter, miles/days	6000/180
Chassis lubrication, miles	6000
Antismog servicing, type/miles	replace PCV valve/12,000, tune check/12,000.
Air cleaner, miles	clean, 6000
Spark plugs: AC44FF	
gap, (in.)	0.031
Basic timing, deg./rpm	4BTDC/650
max. cent. adv., deg./rpm	26/4400
max. vac. adv., deg./in. Hg	24/15
Ignition point gap, in.	0.019
cam dwell angle, deg.	31-34
arm tension, oz.	19-23
Tappet clearance, int./exh.	0/0
Fuel pressure at idle, psi	5.5
Radiator cap relief press., psi	none

PERFORMANCE

Top speed (4870), mph	98
Test shift points (rpm) @ mph	
3rd to 4th (5100)	70
2nd to 3rd (5100)	47
1st to 2nd (5100)	34

ACCELERATION

0-30 mph, sec.	5.5
0-40 mph	8.0
0-50 mph	11.2
0-60 mph	15.6
0-70 mph	22.7
0-80 mph	33.3
0-90 mph	
0-100 mph	
Standing ¼-mile, sec.	19.84
speed at end, mph	66.6
Passing, 30-70 mph, sec.	17.2

BRAKING

Max. deceleration rate from 80 mph ft./sec.² ... 26
No. of stops from 80 mph (60-sec. intervals) before 20% loss in deceleration rate ... 7, 15% loss
Control loss? None.
Overall brake performance: very good

FUEL CONSUMPTION

Test conditions, mpg	17.1
Normal cond., mpg	16-20
Cruising range, miles	200-260

GRADABILITY

4th % grade @ mph	10 @ 44
3rd	14 @ 38
2nd	20 @ 33
1st	27 @ 29

DRAG FACTOR

Total drag @ 60 mph, lb. ... 82

CORVAIR

materially altered acceleration times.

The Corvair's 4-speed transmission was excellent. Ratios were spread fairly wide, as they should be in a transmission designed to increase flexibility in a standard passenger car. First gear (3.11:1) was low enough for easy starts, and third gear provided additional passing acceleration up to 70 mph. Top gear was a satisfactory compromise between general flexibility and effortless high-speed cruising. Synchronizing was perfect in all respects, although shift linkage added excessive effort to rapid gear changes. With its relatively low torque output, the Corvair requires frequent use of the transmission for satisfactory performance, and it is fortunate the Corvair's transmission is such a pleasure to use.

A strong point in Corvair performance was the brake system. Stopping is aided by the Corvair's rearward weight bias, as weight transfer during hard braking tends to equalize tire loading. The Corvair attained a maximum sustained deceleration rate of 26 ft./sec.^{2}, a commendable figure. Along with this outstanding deceleration rate, the Corvair maintained a rate of 22 ft./sec.^{2} through seven stops from 80 mph, stops being made at one minute intervals. This is superb braking performance, and such figures are obtained from only a handful of the best-stopping cars in the world. This performance was realized from the standard Corvair braking system. No discs, power boosters or special optional linings were fitted to the test car, and none were needed. Indeed, the Corvair sets a commendable performance goal for standard-equipment brakes, a standard which is not likely to be met by other models for several years, if ever.

Tempering the pleasurable handling and braking of the test car was an overall quality level that borders on the worst seen by *CAR LIFE*. Admittedly, the Chevrolet personnel from whom the test car was obtained had almost no time for checkout and preparation. Still, there is no excuse for assembly quality of this level. Surely, Chevrolet could have spared the required two screws to hold down the

rubber gearshift lever boot, and could have installed the clutch actuating rod so that it wouldn't beat against the floorpan when the pedal was released. Then there were things like windows that missed vertical seals by several hundredths of an inch, a clock that operated only when the ignition was turned on (engine-hour meter?) and a speedometer cable that failed at 28 miles. True, a dealer would, or should, take care of most such problems. But, wouldn't it be better to build the car properly in the first place? We certainly think so. At least the customer would be spared the trouble of returning to the dealer to have deficiencies corrected, and would not get the initial feeling that his new Corvair was a basket case awaiting rebuild.

Why would anyone want a Corvair? This question was asked of testers, and the answers generally followed a standard pattern. First, to the driver of a conventional sedan, a driver who rates a car as it relates to practical, inconspicuous transportation, the Corvair would not be a wise choice. It is a small car, and although space utilization is fairly efficient, the Corvair is less utilitarian than a front-engined, square-shaped conventional sedan. Noise level, particularly engine noise, is quite high in the Corvair. Additional insulation in the engine compartment would help some, but the standard Corvair is a noisy car. Thus, the driver seeking isolation from automotive mechanical function would be displeasured with the Corvair. The seeker of sensual thrills through brute acceleration would also find the torqueless Corvair unsatisfactory, although performance is perfectly adequate for general city and highway operation.

The Corvair appeals to the driver who is a driver. That is, the Corvair is a car in which to enjoy the application of skillful handling. The Corvair is not a car for luxurious, smooth, silent transportation in the current domestic manner. The Corvair possesses qualities of agility, maneuverability and cornering power that enable a good driver to cover stretches of twisting pavement rapidly, and with a feeling of satisfaction.

With a few changes, like greater engine displacement to increase low speed torque, redesign and relocation of gearshift linkage, improved soundproofing in the engine compartment, and a few minor alteration to interior and running gear, the Corvair could move from a very good car to a great one. Unfortunately, this appears unlikely. The Corvair will be allowed to die, through lack of promotion and development—a sad commentary on today's automotive industry. This really enjoyable automobile deserves a much better fate. ∎

RE-TESTING A SLOW CORVAIR

CORVAIR RETEST

GREAT ARMIES of Corvair owners wrote in after CAR LIFE road tested a 1968 Monza (January, 1968, page 40). While most readers felt our report was equitable and well enough done (we were generally pleased with everything about the car except its lack of power, and even this, we felt, wasn't a serious objection), all writers took us to task about the acceleration figures we'd gotten.

As the first few such letters reached our desk, we thought, "Well, it's the wounded pride of the misunderstood—the wishful thinkers." But then more and more comments kept rolling in saying the same thing, some with irrefutable evidence that our test Corvair (or driver) should have gotten *much* better acceleration times.

A reader in Whittier, Calif., representatively wrote: "I compared your recent test to the one you did on the 1964 Corvair with a 110-bhp engine. . . . This car had 30 bhp less . . . but was considerably faster in acceleration, while the top speed was the same."

As this wave of letters began to crest, we became convinced that perhaps we hadn't given the 1968 Monza its proper due. We called the local Chevrolet zone office and asked whether we could have the same Monza back for retesting. We wanted to recheck our figures and re-evaluate the car's overall performance so we could report back here in *ACTION LINE*.

Unfortunately, that particular car was no longer available, apparently having suffered some form of congenital smog device breakdown that it must latently have had when we drove it. But the Chevy boys promised us an identical car with precisely the same equipment—140-bhp engine, four-speed manual transmission with the same gear ratios, same 3.55:1 differential, handling package, and exactly the same convenience options. This car was *carefully* checked out to make absolutely sure it was in peak running condition.

Engineering Editor Jon McKibben, who put our first test Corvair through its paces, applied his driving touch to this second version. (Jon drove for the Golden Commandos team when he worked at Chrysler Engineering in Detroit, so he's no novice at getting the most from a car.)

Sure enough, the second Corvair proved much faster and also more driveable generally than the original test car. Jon cut quarter-mile times by nearly two seconds, added just under 10 mph to trap times, and shaved 4.2 sec. off 0–60 mph. Clearly, big things were wrong with our first test Corvair Monza. ∎

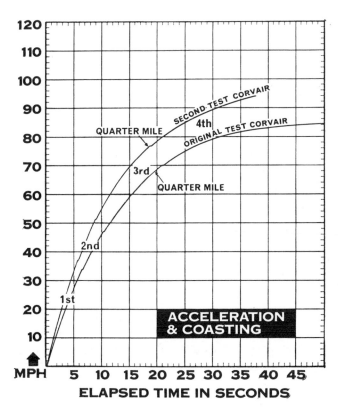

127

LIVING WITH THE WORLD'S FASTEST CORVAIR

*Not just fast, mind you—versatile. Take it to Bonneville,
the dragstrip, a slalom or sprints (or just drive it home).*

BY JON McKIBBEN

TOM KEOSABABIAN holds record from Bonneville National Speed Trials (left) with a two-way run of 156.9 mph. Intent on proving its all-round worth, he also has been taking it to slaloms (above) to develop minor suspension modifications.

AIRESEARCH TURBOCHARGER draws through small four-barrel carburetor, and discharges into converted IECO manifold. Water injection is pressure controlled, with reservoir housed in right rear fenderwell beside stock Corvair muffler.

CAR LIFE TEST PHOTOS BY SCOTT MALCOLM

STREET TURBINE section on turbocharger (center) is 30% smaller than unit Keosababian uses at Bonneville.

C AR LIFE'S ROAD TEST of a 140-bhp 1968 Corvair in January was greeted by some strange reactions:

• A few readers criticized our unbridled praise of the basic engineering of the car, claiming that the Corvair was nearing extinction because it simply isn't worth saving.

• Other readers (Corvair owners, we suspect) congratulated us on our ability to recognize a sound vehicle when we tested one.

• Still others said the test was good, but what about those low speeds on the dragstrip?

• And then there was Tom Keosababian. An *ACTION* man.

Not only did he call our editorial hand on the under-performing Cor-vair, he said rather offhandedly that he owns the "World's Fastest Corvair" if we'd like to know what one will *really* do. Better yet, why not just turn the car over to CAR LIFE for a few days? After all, that's about the only way he knew of letting the Corvair engineers in Detroit find out what a Corvair is honestly capable of.

What right has Tom Keosababian to the claim of "World's Fastest Corvair"? Just 156.9 mph at the Bonneville National Speed Trials last August.

But there's more. Much more. He did it with a *nearly* stock 164-cid Cor-vair engine. With only a change of tires it's the same car that turned 13.39 sec. quarter mile at 105 mph for CAR LIFE at Orange County Raceway. And the same car that Tom Keosababian

uses for slaloms, road course competition and half-mile sprints. And—hold on now, if you've been paying attention—it's the car that Keosababian uses daily on his commute to work.

No car should be that versatile, yet the Turbovair (our name, not Tom's) performs yeoman duty in all these areas. Total performance? It looks like the people from Detroit had better check with Tom Keosababian. He has one solution to that perennial problem—the true multi-purpose automobile.

This Corvair is deceptively simple in its modifications. A basically stock (pistons, rods, crankshaft, block) engine of the type used on the 1965-66 Turbocharged Corvairs is fitted with cylinder heads from a 1965-68 140-bhp normally aspirated engine. The induction system is a Keosababian combination, featuring a single four-barrel carburetor from a 273-cid Chrysler V-8 and an AiResearch turbocharger unit. The carburetor is mounted on an IECO adaptor casting, and all other plumbing is fabricated out of steel tubing and rubber hose. The exhaust system feeding the turbo unit is stock. An Iskenderian 505 Magnum camshaft is used, for increased high-speed breathing. Iskenderian hydraulic lifters raise the valve float point to somewhere near 7000 rpm (we didn't try to find the valve train limits).

Though simple in concept and visible alterations, Keosababian's 1965 Corvair represents an incredible amount of problem finding—and solving. That the result is relatively uncomplicated is a tribute to the direct, effective approach to the problems.

The key to the Turbovair's reliable performance and impressive power output is a water injection system built by Tom and a friend, Gary Bailey. The water storage tank is a home-type beer tapper barrel. A cap is added, complete with rubber O-ring pressure seal. The top of the tapper (in car position) has an aluminum tube weld-

AUXILIARY GAUGES record cylinder head temperature, manifold boost pressure.

TREMENDOUS cornering power and easily correctable oversteer spell pure fun.

DESPITE EXTREME rearward weight bias, Corvair smoked 10-in.-wide tires with ease. Gentle shifting still put car into low 13-sec. quarter-mile bracket.

FASTEST CORVAIR

ed in, feeding into a tubing manifold that carries water to each bank of cylinders. Water is metered through a fixed orifice, by tank pressure obtained through a tire valve welded into the side of the tank. The present tank is good for about 100 miles, after filling about half full and pressurizing to approximately 40 psi. Tom says that curing some carburetion distribution problems he now has will permit a smaller orifice, thereby reducing water consumption. The present system has high water flow to eliminate positively any full-power detonation, a critical factor in running an engine with high boost pressures.

The Turbovair's water injection system may require frequent visits to the corner service station for water and air pressure, but it *does* work. We encountered audible detonation only on 2-3 gear changes, and then the detonation lasted for less than a second. At the dragstrip, running full power acceleration runs on a warm afternoon, the engine never made a single ping.

Water flow is controlled by a very

sensitive pressure switch, which in turn is controlled by boost pressure. Thus, water is injected only when the engine speed and throttle position cause positive manifold pressure. When the turbocharger unit is simply idling along, as when cruising at 65 mph down the freeway, the pressure valve shuts off all water flow. As soon as boost pressure is developed, water is injected through nozzles tapped into the cylinder head intake plenum chambers.

A waste-gate system, built by Keosababian, using a 427-cid Chevrolet engine exhaust valve as the actual moving component, is adjustable to bleed off turbocharger boost above a predetermined pressure. For CAR LIFE's test, this waste gate was set at 15 psi. This is thought to be a good compromise setting between performance and engine longevity. More boost would naturally mean more power, but the engine's internals may protest prolonged running at such extreme pressures. Also, higher boost pressures would aggravate the detonation problem.

The AiResearch turbocharger unit is rather like an Erector Set, in that each component can be changed to provide the exact characteristics of boost and response desired for a given engine installation. As used at Bonneville, Keo-

sababian selected a high flow capacity turbine section (that part driven by the exhaust gases). This combination is great for maximum boost, but suffers from rather poor throttle response and low-speed boost. CAR LIFE's test was carried out with a turbine section approximately 30% smaller, still affording the limited 15 psi boost, but having better response. The impeller section can also be changed, but we tested the same section that ran at Bonneville. Turbocharger gearing lubrication is provided by an external oil line tapped into the Corvair's lubrication system. The AiResearch unit has given absolutely no trouble, and has performed flawlessly.

How does all this hardware work? To begin with, driving around town at slow speeds, at small throttle openings, is amazingly easy. Despite the wild camshaft (300° duration, 80° overlap, 0.505-in. lift), low-speed torque is satisfactory down to about 1500 rpm. As long as the throttle is not floored at such low speeds, the car pulls smoothly and responsively. If strong acceleration is needed, a quick downshift to raise engine speed and a brief period of gradual throttle opening to speed up the turbocharger are necessary. Because of the relatively large size (and consequent high inertia) of the turbo-

BONNEVILLE RECORD
CAR AT THE DRAGSTRIP

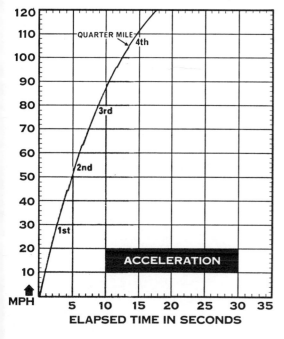

ELAPSED TIME IN SECONDS

PERFORMANCE

Top speed (6500), mph.........140
Test shift points (rpm) @ mph
  3rd to 4th (6500).............96
  2nd to 3rd (6500).............64
  1st to 2nd (6500).............45

ACCELERATION

0-30 mph, sec...................2.6
0-40 mph......................3.6
0-50 mph......................4.6
0-60 mph......................5.9
0-70 mph......................7.4
0-80 mph......................9.0
0-90 mph.....................10.6
0-100 mph....................12.6
Standing ¼-mile, sec.........13.39
  speed at end, mph.........105.26
Passing, 30–70 mph, sec.........4.8

BRAKING

Max. deceleration rate from 80 mph
  ft./sec.² 24
No. of stops from 80 mph (60-sec.
  intervals) before 20% loss in deceleration rate...........8-no loss
Control loss? Moderate.
Overall brake performance.....good

FUEL CONSUMPTION

Test conditions, mpg...........10.3
Normal cond., mpg...........10-15

GENERAL DATA

Test weight...................2980
distribution (driver)
  % f/r 35.8/64.2
Estimated bhp @ rpm...330 @ 6500
Mph/1000 rpm (high gear) 21.6

---

charger's rotating members, full boost is not obtained instantly. But once the engine is "up on boost," it pulls through the gears like it has 500 cid.

Strong starts are difficult with the Turbovair. The required procedure involves blipping the throttle several times to get the turbocharger unit spinning. Then, keeping engine speed up, the clutch is engaged abruptly. With this manipulation, the Turbovair spins its huge rear tires like a dragster, and initial acceleration is neck-snapping. If the car is simply driven away from a stoplight, it takes almost all of first gear to get churning. Then, in the next three gears, the car accelerates violently.

Sagging on takeoff is the biggest drivability problem with the car. Street racers won't like the initial lag, but overall road performance suffers very little. At higher engine speeds, boost is quickly available. The Turbovair is not unlike driving a highly tuned sports car. Most truly high-output engines have to be kept up in speed to perform properly, and the Turbovair is of the same pattern.

The Turbovair does require a knowledgeable driver; for instance, the Bonneville two-way record of 156.97 mph was set at *part throttle*, because both engine speed and boost pressure

required pedal modulation to prevent possible engine damage. If Tom can obtain a set of final drive gears with a lower numerical ratio than 3.27:1, he can run considerably faster.

Quarter-mile times were set without all-out driving techniques. CAR LIFE's testers were skeptical of the Corvair transmission's ability to handle an estimated 350 bhp under the shock loadings of power shifts, so all runs were made using relatively slow, gentle shifting and reasonably easy takeoffs. Undoubtedly, removing the muffler (a big handicap to turbocharged engines) and shifting in a more brutal fashion would have dropped the car into the 12-sec. bracket, and speed would likely have been in the 107-110 mph range. And, of course, gears suitable for Bonneville's three-mile straightaway are far from the optimum for quarter-mile competition.

Keosababian chopped the front coil springs, and the rear springs are clamped to lower the car. Goodyear sports car racing tires are fitted at each end. The result is a car with fantastic cornering power. Final oversteer is the dominant characteristic, but it is easily correctable assuming a corner has been entered at a speed somewhere near the ultimate capability of the car.

Metallic brake linings (Velve-

Touch) have eliminated fade, even under severe road course use. Prolonged racing has apparently warped the rear drums on the Turbovair, though, and rear-wheel lockup limited maximum deceleration to 24 ft./sec.² in CAR LIFE's standard 80-0 mph test. However, control of lockup was easy, and no fade or inconsistency was noted throughout the test period.

There have been other modified Corvairs, both turbocharged and normally aspirated. Some of these have distinguished themselves in drag racing. Doug Roe, an engineer at the GM Proving Grounds at Mesa, Ariz., has an early Corvair that he uses to humble Group 7 sports/racing cars at fast road races, hillclimbs and slaloms. Roe's turbocharged Corvair is extensively lightened, and is extremely quick. Dick Griffin of Lansing, Mich., has been a Corvair fan since the first models were introduced. Griffin has campaigned turbocharged and supercharged Corvairs, both stock and modified, in drag racing. His successes are almost countless.

Although other Corvairs have been impressive in specific fields of competition, none have demonstrated the versatility of Tom Keosababian's. The major accomplishment of the Turbovair, in terms of national prestige, have come at Bonneville. However, because of the low interest associated with Bonneville activities (except for Unlimited records), Keosababian tries to create a name in road racing, with side activities on the dragstrip. He feels that road racing offers a greater challenge, since not only the engine but the entire chassis of the car must be reworked for maximum performance. Also, road racing offers an excellent showcase for the outstanding roadability and maneuverability of the Corvair chassis.

Tom's future plans call for the installation of a pair of smaller turbocharger units, with a separate induction system for each bank. This should eliminate most of the low-speed lag which is the only legitimate criticism of the present car. With improved response and better distribution, the car should perform better, and be even more drivable around town.

A further development of the Turbovair theme is a lightweight two-seater sports/racing car, with Corvair engine and suspension. And seeing the way Tom's engine propels a 2600-lb. stock Corvair coupe, we can't wait to see the racing roadster.

Life with the "World's Fastest Corvair?" Sweet. ∎

MARTYR

by Michael Lamm, *Editor*

No one has ever given an unemotional appraisal of the Corvair as simply a motorcar, but here's trying. We drive two turbocharged convertibles—1962 Spyder and 1965 Corsa—and we delve into Corvair's developmental history.

NO AMERICAN CAR has ever been so severely raked over the coals as the Corvair. One thing I don't want to get into here is this car's safety controversy. It's beyond the scope of this driveReport. Books *have* been written both pro and con. (As an aside, it was interesting to me to find out that only the first chapter of *Unsafe at Any Speed* deals with the Corvair. The other seven chapters hardly mention it again. I hadn't realized until now that Nader's attack wasn't so much against the Corvair as against the auto industry in general.)

People around General Motors have become understandably gun-shy about the Corvair. They don't like to talk about it, having pretty much exhausted the subject in front of congressional committees, lawyers, judges, and news-

men, some of whom didn't treat their words very kindly.

One of the few people still willing to discuss the Corvair freely, I found, was Ed Cole, who's now president of GM and who, more than any other person, fathered the Corvair. Mr. Cole has always been one of Detroit's more approachable auto executives.

Interestingly, too, Chevrolet Div. had written the Corvair out of its official history book for a number of years, but I'm pleased to see it's back in the 1974 revision of *The Chevrolet Story Since 1911*. This fine book, prepared and updated each year by Chevrolet public relations, now includes one picture of a 1960 Corvair along with this text (quoted in its entirety): "Also in 1959, Chevrolet unveiled the 1960

Corvair economy car in advance of the other cars for the 1960 model year. The Corvair's rear-mounted engine was the first air-cooled Chevrolet power plant in 37 years."

That statement seems a little modest considering that here we have one of the most interesting, innovative, advanced, and in many ways the most daring production automobiles of recent times. The Corvair marks, among other things, the first unit-bodied car ever produced in the U.S. by GM, the first rear-engined car ever mass-produced by any major U.S. automaker, the first American production car in decades with all-independent suspension, the second turbocharged U.S. production car (after the Olds F-85) and, perhaps most important of all, the first major break with traditional engi-

Cobbled "Holden" mechanical mule wore fake grille, ran from Arizona heat to Pikes Peak snow in '58. GM president Ed Cole (center) fathered Corvair.

neering practices by any big domestic automaker.

Until the Corvair, all mass-produced American cars had been conceived on one basic plan: four wheels, engine up front, rear drive. Except for a few innovators like E.L. Cord, Gary Davis, and Preston Tucker, no one in modern times had even tried to deviate from that formula. The sameness of American cars had become almost a joke. Anyone who tried to break with tradition, like Bill Stout, got branded as slightly dotty.

Yet in Europe, there was great diversity—amazing success with what Detroit engineers considered so odd as to be almost experimental: front-wheel drive from Citroen, Saab, DKW, and Panhard; rear engine placement in the Volkswagen, Renault, Tatraplan, etc. Postwar European buyers were open-minded enough to accept such cars; in fact, they seemed to relish their unconventionality.

Here in this country, a few minds began to open, too, leading to the very surprising success of the Volkswagen. No one in Detroit could have predicted the VW's tripling and retripling sales each year after about 1954. The market was changing, because in addition to the success of certain imports, small cars from Rambler and Studebaker (the Lark) were also catching on. After the big-car debacle of 1958, the swing toward compacts became unmistakable, and in 1960 and '61, Rambler held third place in nameplate sales—another unpredictable and almost unbelievable performance.

"**t**he Corvair actually started," says Ed [Edward Nicholas] Cole, who not only sparked this car but who was instrumental in developing the first ohv Cadillac V-8 of 1949 and who engineered the first lightweight Chevrolet V-8 of 1955, "back in about 1955, with the idea of a need for a smaller...car, and we looked at many, many configurations. Maurice Olley headed up our [Chevrolet's] research and development, and we asked him to sort out all the suspensions, all the powerplant locations and so on from the standpoint of looking at the overall economics to see what would give the consumer the best total transportation value. We looked at the conventional front-engine/rear drive; at, of course, the rear-engine/rear drive; we looked at air cooling in both configurations, and we examined very thoroughly the Volkswagen, which was doing very well at that time—still is, for that matter.

"What we concluded was that we needed a vehicle that could have some of the features of the big cars without the expense. For instance, a rear-engine/rear drive tended to remove some of the load from the front wheels, which made the car easier to steer without power steering. And by having consistent loading front and rear, fully loaded you had a better

balance and utilization of tires and brakes. Further, because the driveshaft was gone, you had no tunnel. Three adults could sit on each bench, making this a true 6-passenger automobile. The lack of a transmission hump and driveshaft tunnel also allowed the body designers to get the very low silhouette we wanted.

"Another thing we wanted was to get the center of gravity as low as we could for greater cornering stability. And by not having the engine up front, with its hot air-flow pattern underneath the car, you didn't require so much air conditioning for comfort. All of these things tended to add up to the rear-engine/rear drive configuration."

Cole was by no means alone in developing the Corvair, nor has he ever claimed to be. Kai H. Hansen was assistant director of research for Chevrolet and had worked with Cole at Cadillac. Maurice Olley had charge of testing and evaluating all possible engine/drive arrangements. Harry Barr, who'd also moved from Cadillac to Chevrolet in the early 1950s, became Chevy's chief engineer after Mr. Cole took over the division's general managership in 1956. Barr and Hansen were both instrumental in the Corvair's engineering.

Robert P. Benzinger, now a professor of engineering at Arizona State in Tempe, had charge of the Corvair's engine development, at first under A.E. Kolbe and later on his own. Benzinger took over from Kolbe in late 1957 and continued with the Corvair until the end of production in 1969. Frank J. Winchell directed the Corvair's automatic transmission development. Robert Schilling handled the first-series Corvair's suspension, and Frank Winchell developed the second. James Wernig, Fisher Body's engineering director, oversaw development of the Corvair's unitized body.

Early styling was directed by Harley Earl before his retirement in Nov. 1958 and by William L. (Bill) Mitchell afterward. Ned Nickles had charge of the experimental design studio from which the first series (1960-64) Corvairs grew, and Ron Hill directed the second series' (1965-69) exterior styling. (*See the following*

article for a more complete account of the Corvair's styling evolution.)

One of the main concerns of this overall group, even before Ed Cole presented the Corvair idea to GM management, was to make the car as different as possible from larger Chevys. He didn't want it stealing sales away from the Biscayne (nor later from the Chevy II, which soon came in response to the conventional Falcon and Valiant). Cole's plan was to augment Chevrolet's line with a lighter, smaller, thriftier, inexpensive, slightly exotic compact that could capture sales from VW and the other imports—plus, initially, Rambler and Lark.

Cole felt that young buyers, especially, would go for the Corvair's low profile, its rear-mounted aluminum alloy engine, the all-independent springing, and the clean boldness of the design. In all this he was right, and it became these younger buyers who promptly turned the Corvair from a pure economy sedan into something of a vest-pocket Corvette—a GT car that was sporty, fun to drive, and fun to tinker with.

But during the production engineering stage, the sporty versions were still a long way off. The initial trick was to design an *inexpensive* car—inexpensive to manufacture and inexpensive to buy. Cole and his colleagues ended up finding their main challenge not so much in the realm of pure engineering but in the realm of engineering for cost feasibility. It often turns out that way. As the Corvair progressed, it became more and more complicated, heavier, and thus more expensive. To bring its costs back down, the engineers had to make certain compromises. It's interesting to see what they did and didn't compromise in the Corvair.

"**W**hen Ed Cole managed Cadillac's tank manufacturing plant in Cleveland back during the Korean War, he and Kai Hansen and Harry Barr used to get together at the Lakeshore Hotel during their off-hours and lay out cars, some rear-engined, some not. The M-42 tank that Cole's plant was turning out at that time used a flat, air-cooled Continental 6, as did Cole's own Beechcraft Bonanza. So those might have helped inspire the Corvair's opposed 6.

The Corvair grew around its engine more than any other single component. Prof. Robert Benzinger, one of the men charged with developing the lightweight, flat 6, had been with Chevrolet since 1952, but he'd never worked on anything so different before. He calls the startup of the Corvair engine project, "... probably about the blankest piece of paper that we'd had in a long time."

In its earliest form, the Corvair 6 was to be made up of two mirror-image halves. Each half would have been a single aluminum casting that incorporated the three finned cylinder barrels

Gas tanks and wheel wells intrude on Corvairs' trunks, but rear seats fold in most body types.

1962 Spyder (top) and 1965 Corsa use complete instrumentation in good-looking, legible panels.

Corsa's top lowers electrically, but Spyder's goes down by hand. One man can easily drop it.

Martyr driveReport

with non-detachable heads and half the crankcase. If this far-out idea had worked, it would have saved considerable weight and money.

"Mr. Cole and Mr. Kolbe wanted rather importantly to have aluminum in the cylinders," recalls Prof. Benzinger. "The only ones around at that time in any volume were the Porsche's. Porsche used heavy chrome plating over the aluminum bores so that the rings actually rode on the chromed surfaces. But this loomed up as so expensive and difficult from manufacturing and quality standpoints that we were quickly discouraged. It worked at Porsche's price and volume but not at Chevrolet's."

After extensive studies and trying to run on bare aluminum, Kolbe and Benzinger, with the help of metallurgists from Reynolds Metals Co., tried to adapt an aluminum-silicon alloy —the material Chevy's Vega block uses today. But in '1957-58, the state of the art hadn't progressed far enough to allow it. Machining a 17%-18% aluminum-silicon alloy couldn't be done by conventional methods. So the Corvair engine ended up with cast-iron cylinder barrels sandwiched between an aluminum crankcase, with detachable aluminum heads—same as the VW. The breakthrough that made the sleeveless Vega aluminum engine possible is bore honing by acid etch. Acid eats away a tiny bite of aluminum inside the bores and lets the piston rings ride on metallic silicon crystals. There were other problems, too, with the projected all-aluminum, 2-piece Corvair engine, notably in casting it.

So instead, the aluminum/cast-iron Corvair engine was cast in 10 basic parts, not two as originally envisioned. I'm including the 2-piece crankcase, six cylinder barrels, and two heads. I'm *excluding* cover plates and housings.

"Quite early in the game," continues Benzinger, "before I was assigned to the project, there was some thought given to other engines. They considered 2-cycles briefly. And four cylinders very briefly. But being a rear-engined car, there wasn't any serious consideration of

CORVAIR CHRONOLOGY

May 1952—Edward N. Cole moves from Cadillac to Chevrolet's top engineering spot, brings key men with him. Their assignment: "Enliven Chevrolet's staid product line." Cole has already put considerable thought and work into rear-engined experimentals.

1955—Chevy R&D chief Maurice Olley reports to Cole on various engine placements and drive configurations in terms of economics and manufacturing feasibility. Preliminary research begins on 2-piece aluminum flat 6, but idea is soon shelved due to lack of technology.

July 1956—Cole becomes Chevrolet's general manager, moves ahead with Corvair (called Holden La Salle II) phototypes.

Aug. 1957—Ned Nickles begins styling studies for Corvair under watchful eyes of Cole and Harley Earl.

Sept. 1957—GM president Harlow Curtice sees styling clays, hears Cole's presentation, gives his blessing. Soon afterward, GM's engineering policy committee and board of directors also approve Corvair. For the first time, it's officially on its way to production.

Winter 1957 thru summer 1958—Corvair evolves mechanically, its engine and drivetrain tested in cobbled Porsches, a Vauxhall, and one full mechanical prototype. Cole pleased.

Spring 1958—Second and third "Holden" mechanical prototypes built and tested. Detail engineering and planning for new Willow Run Corvair plant now at full tilt.

July 1958—Conversion of GM plant at Willow Run started: Corvair's official home.

Sept. 1958—**Motor Life** predicts the Corvair in amazingly accurate detail, based on tooling orders.

May 22, 1959—GM announces it will introduce a compact for 1960. Name Corvair becomes official. (Chrysler had made a similar announcement on the Valiant on Mar. 10, and so had Ford on the Falcon, Feb. 19.)

Oct. 2, 1959—First Corvair bows. Falcon debuts six days later, and Valiant arrives Oct. 29. Falcon outsells Corvair immediately.

Apr. 1960—**Motor Trend** names Corvair *Car of the Year*.

May 1960—First Corvair coupe arrives, as does Monza 900 series, with 95-bhp engine and 4-speed gearbox optional. A Paxton-supercharged Corvair sedan hits 0-60 in 15.8 sec. as compared with 21.2 sec. stock; top speed increases from 88 to 95 mph. Corvair is turning into a performance machine.

Sept. 1960—Lakewood wagon introduced for 1961; also Greenbrier, Corvan, Rampside, and Loadside vans and pickups. Bore increased from 3 3/8 to 3 7/16 inches to up displacement from 140 to 145 cid.

Mar. 1961—First Monza sedan debuts. Ed Cole leaves Chevrolet to become GM car and truck v.p. His place is taken by Semon E. Knudsen.

Map pocket adds to Corsa's European flavor.

The turbocharged flat 6s put out 150 and 180 horses respectively.

Heater has rear vent (top). Oil-and-weight-filled vibration damper (lower left) counters Corsa convertible's body drumming.

Sept. 1961—Chevy II introduced, competes directly with Falcon and Valiant but also with Corvair, particularly wagons.

Apr. 1962—Corvair wagon dropped; 32,120 produced. Monza convertible introduced. Spyder package released, has 150-bhp turbocharged engine. Two-passenger Sebring Spyder makes New York show.

May 1962—Design begins on 1965 Corvair under Ron Hill. It's based largely on Monza GT showcar.

June 1962—Monza GT coupe bows at Elkhart Lake.

Mar. 1963—Corvair Bertone Testudo at Geneva salon.

Apr. 1963—Monza SS showcar at New York auto show.

Oct. 1963—Spyder becomes a standard 1964 model instead of an option package. Stroke increased from 2.60 to 2.94 inches to up displacement to 164 cid. Swing axle suspension bolstered by addition of factory leaf spring. Further 1964 suspension improvements include standard front stabilizer bar plus recalibrated coil springs and shocks.

Apr. 15, 1964—Ford releases Mustang, which was conceived as response to Corvair, and Mustang becomes a prime contributor to Corvair's demise.

Sept. 1964—1965 Corvairs bow with new styling and fully independent rear suspension. Car remains basically the same as this through the end of production.

Dec. 1964—Greenbrier dropped; only 1528 built this model year.

Apr. 1965—Management instructs Chevrolet engineers not to further develop future Corvairs—to freeze design and merely meet safety and smog standards.

Nov. 1965—Ralph Nader publishes *The Corvair Story*, an article in *The Nation*, which formed the basis for the first chapter (only) of his book, *Unsafe at Any Speed*, also published the same month.

1965—This becomes peak year for the restyled Corvair, but it can't stem the Mustang's tide. With greater performance demands, turbocharged engine delivers 180 bhp. Nader's book plus the Mustang spell a downhill run for the Corvair.

Oct. 1966—1967 Corvairs introduced, Corsa models and 140-bhp engine dropped but later re-instated due to popular demand.

Mar. 1967—Astro I showcar at New York show.

Oct. 1967—Four-doors dropped with 1968 introductions.

May 14, 1969—The last Corvair, a golden coupe, rolls off assembly line. By this time Corvair quality has reached a very low ebb. The factory offers a $150 certificate with each 1969 Corvair, good on the purchase of a new Chevrolet anytime before 1974. Total production: 1,710,018.

liquid cooling. The car demanded air cooling because of space and weight distribution."

Asked whether Chevrolet researchers went to aircraft flat 6s for background, Benzinger answered that they surveyed the literature in terms of operating temperatures but that otherwise aircraft practices, "...were just worlds different from what we were doing. Typically, they machine their cooling fins to get them very closely spaced and with a fine pitch. They usually cast a big slug of solid metal and then go into it to machine out the fins. That, of course, is just unreasonable for a high-volume auto engine.

"There was nothing really to follow, in spite of the VW and Porsche. The differences between a flat 4 and a flat 6 are just enormous. It's as good as starting over, because all the things that are applicable to the 4 don't apply to the 6. The center cylinder in a bank of three turns out to be the real troublemaker.

"On a 4, you can dump the exhaust out the outboard end of each head. On a 6, though, you have to figure a way to get the exhaust out of the middle cylinders without overheating everything.

"And carburetion becomes a problem. We tried single carburetion but found it totally unworkable. The long distance between where you'd have to locate a single carburetor and the intake valves just destroyed any possibility of reasonable fuel distribution among the six cylinders. We had to go with the two carburetors sitting down as close to the heads as possible."

Actually there were severe limitations built into the Corvair, and these limitations alone dictated compromises. They were purely practical considerations like size, weight, ground clearance, etc. To let Prof. Benzinger explain: "The biggest limitation...was the camshaft. Clearance for the crank. Perhaps you've noticed ...that there were corners on the cam lobes bobbed off in the late-series engine. Those were to clear the crankshaft which, by the way, needs no counterweights. Both a flat 6 and an in-line 6 crank can be perfectly balanced without counterweights. Anyway, the camshaft location was also determined by ground clearance. We couldn't put the cam up top, because we were committed to hydraulic lifters. Hydraulic lifters would drain dry if they weren't down low in the oil.

"Then, too, we were locked in by the driveline centerline. The output centerline into the axle was pretty much fixed by tire and wheel sizes. These determined ground clearance, thus clearance for the oil sump and thus clearance for the camshaft. So cam location was all important."

The Corvair's cam has only nine lobes, since the exhaust lobes double for both banks. Air-

Spyder's H-D suspension and Corsa's double-jointed axles feel similar in hard cornering, show no tuck-under, flat stance, light and neutral steering.

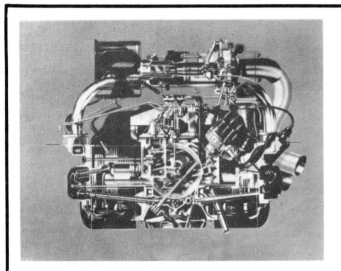
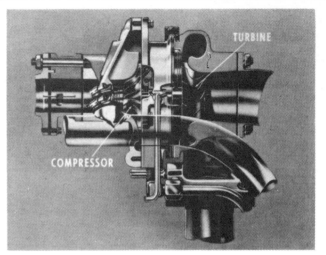

TURBINE

COMPRESSOR

Spyder Packages, the Corsa, and Turbochargers

Chevrolet announced the Spyder package on Mar. 25, 1962 and began offering it in April. Designated RPO 690, it added $317.45 and 48 bhp to the basic 1962 Monza coupe or convertible.

The Spyder package itself included the 150-bhp turbocharged engine, a neat and complete instrument panel, plus special insignia. But to get RPO 690, you initially also had to buy RPO 651 (the 4-speed transmission at $64.60), RPO 696 (heavy-duty suspension, $10.80), and RPO 686 (sintered metallic brake linings, $37.70). A 3.55:1 rear axle (RPO 693) came at no charge, and Positraction plus seatbelts were recommended but not mandatory.

After about three months, the above options were no longer mandatory, and the 3-speed transmission became standard with the Spyder package. The manual 4-speed, though, which had been created by simply modifying the 3-speed and adding an extra ratio, enjoyed great popularity throughout the life of the Corvair. The Monza became, in fact, one of the first domestic sporty cars with four on the floor.

At least three aftermarket superchargers had been offered for Corvairs before the Spyder package came along. These were the Paxton centrifugal, the Judson sliding vane, and the Latham axial (priced at $365, $232, and $625 respectively.).

The turbocharger had been invented by Alfred J. Buchi in Switzerland in 1905 and had first been successfully applied to high-altitude, prop-driven aircraft. Turbochargers were later used on big diesel trucks and industrial powerplants.

Corvair wanted to be first out with a turbocharger, but the Olds F-85 beat Corvair by several months. The men responsible for the Corvair's turbo were Chevy engineers James O. Brafford and Robert E. Thoreson, under Robert Benzinger. They looked into mechanical supercharging but discarded it on these counts: power and fuel drain, limited under-hood space, addition of another belt to an already tenuous belt situation, and the heavy impeller might cause noise and vibration.

On the other hand, the turbocharger presented these advantages: No loss of part-throttle fuel economy, because the turbine merely freewheeled in the exhaust stream when not in use. Corvair could also finally use one carburetor instead of the two or four used otherwise. Tooling costs for the turbo were low. No need for belts or gears to drive it. Easy mounting and

good space utilization; compactness. No noise or vibration. So the turbocharger was on.

It's basically a very simple device. Driven by exhaust gases rushing by it, a 3-inch turbine turns a 3-inch impeller that, in effect, stuffs fuel/air mix into the cylinders at a maximum 10-psi boost. Both the turbine and impeller turn on a common shaft at speeds up to 70,000 rpm. This 3.5-inch-long shaft rides in a single, floating aluminum bearing that's lubricated under pressure by the engine's oil supply. The entire turbocharger weighs only 13.5 pounds. A chromed shield covers the turbine housing to keep exhaust heat from scorching the Corvair's rear-mounted spare tire.

The Spyder engine was basically the 102-bhp unit but got an 8:1 compression ratio (down from 9:1) plus extensive internal mods—a harder crankshaft, stronger rods, a crankcase oil separator, higher temp valves, and different guides. Ignition timing was also radically changed with the turbocharger (it used a pressure retard system), and the engine *would* ping on regular-grade fuel.

The turbo unit itself was built and supplied to Chevrolet by TRW (Thompson-Ramo-Wooldridge, Inc.). For 1964, the Spyder became a full-fledged Corvair model instead of just an option package. And for 1965, the name Spyder gave way to Corsa. The Corsa's horsepower rose to 180 (gross), still from 164 cid.

The one serious flaw enthusiasts find in the turbocharger is its lag upon floorboarding below 2800-3000 rpm. Since rpm feeds the turbine, and since the turbine drives the impeller, the impeller doesn't get going until there's substantial exhaust flow. And there can't be much of that until revs rise, so it's a viscious cycle. It means a one- or 2-second wait until the engine takes hold. Once it does, though, look out!

According to **Popular Science,** here are some Corvair comparisons for 1962 (in seconds):

	80 bhp*	102 bhp	150 bhp
0-60 mph	23.2	16.8	9.7
0-80 mph	64.1	31.6	18.5
40-80 mph	53.8	21.6	10.0

Top speed rose from 88 mph to over 110.

* Powerglide.

specifications

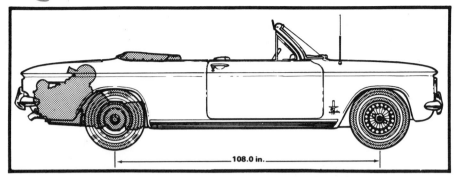

RUSS VON SAUERS, THE GRAPHIC AUTOMOBILE STUDIO

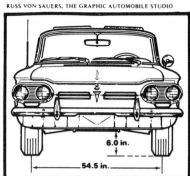

108.0 in.

6.0 in.

54.5 in.

1962 Corvair Spyder (1965 Corsa) convertible(s)

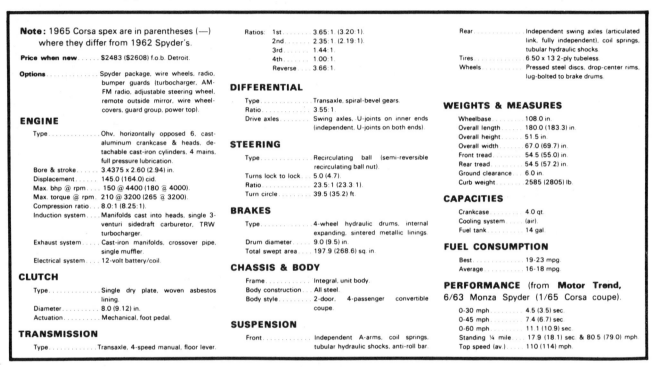

Note: 1965 Corsa spex are in parentheses (—) where they differ from 1962 Spyder's.

Price when new . . . . . $2483 ($2608) f.o.b. Detroit.

Options . . . . Spyder package, wire wheels, radio, bumper guards (turbocharger, AM-FM radio, adjustable steering wheel, remote outside mirror, wire wheel-covers, guard group, power top).

ENGINE

Type . . . . Ohv, horizontally opposed 6, cast-aluminum crankcase & heads, detachable cast-iron cylinders, 4 mains, full pressure lubrication.
Bore & stroke . . . . . . 3.4375 x 2.60 (2.94) in.
Displacement . . . . . 145.0 (164.0) cid.
Max. bhp @ rpm . . . 150 @ 4400 (180 @ 4000).
Max. torque @ rpm . . 210 @ 3200 (265 @ 3200).
Compression ratio . . . 8.0:1 (8.25:1).
Induction system . . . . Manifolds cast into heads, single 3-venturi sidedraft carburetor, TRW turbocharger.
Exhaust system . . . . . Cast-iron manifolds, crossover pipe, single muffler.
Electrical system . . . . 12-volt battery/coil.

CLUTCH

Type . . . . Single dry plate, woven asbestos lining.
Diameter . . . . 8.0 (9.12) in.
Actuation . . . . Mechanical, foot pedal.

TRANSMISSION

Type . . . . Transaxle, 4-speed manual, floor lever.

Ratios: 1st . . . . 3.65:1 (3.20:1).
2nd . . . . 2.35:1 (2.19:1).
3rd . . . . 1.44:1.
4th . . . . 1.00:1.
Reverse . . . 3.66:1.

DIFFERENTIAL

Type . . . . Transaxle, spiral-bevel gears.
Ratio . . . . 3.55:1.
Drive axles . . . . Swing axles, U-joints on inner ends (independent, U-joints on both ends).

STEERING

Type . . . . Recirculating ball (semi-reversible recirculating ball nut).
Turns lock to lock . . . 5.0 (4.7).
Ratio . . . . 23.5:1 (23.3:1).
Turn circle . . . . 39.5 (35.2) ft.

BRAKES

Type . . . . 4-wheel hydraulic drums, internal expanding, sintered metallic linings.
Drum diameter . . . . . 9.0 (9.5) in.
Total swept area . . . . 197.9 (268.6) sq. in.

CHASSIS & BODY

Frame . . . . Integral, unit body.
Body construction . . . All steel.
Body style . . . . 2-door, 4-passenger convertible coupe.

SUSPENSION

Front . . . . Independent A-arms, coil springs, tubular hydraulic shocks, anti-roll bar.
Rear . . . . Independent swing axles (articulated link, fully independent), coil springs, tubular hydraulic shocks.
Tires . . . . 6.50 x 13 2-ply tubeless.
Wheels . . . . Pressed steel discs, drop-center rims, lug-bolted to brake drums.

WEIGHTS & MEASURES

Wheelbase . . . . 108.0 in.
Overall length . . . . . . 180.0 (183.3) in.
Overall height . . . . . . 51.5 in.
Overall width . . . . . . 67.0 (69.7) in.
Front tread . . . . 54.5 (55.0) in.
Rear tread . . . . 54.5 (57.2) in.
Ground clearance . . . 6.0 in.
Curb weight . . . . 2585 (2805) lb.

CAPACITIES

Crankcase . . . . 4.0 qt.
Cooling system . . . . . (air).
Fuel tank . . . . 14 gal.

FUEL CONSUMPTION

Best . . . . 19-23 mpg.
Average . . . . 16-18 mpg.

PERFORMANCE (from **Motor Trend,** 6/63 Monza Spyder (1/65 Corsa coupe).

0-30 mph . . . . 4.5 (3.5) sec.
0-45 mph . . . . 7.4 (6.7) sec.
0-60 mph . . . . 11.1 (10.9) sec.
Standing ¼ mile . . . 17.9 (18.1) sec. & 80.5 (79.0) mph.
Top speed (av.) . . . . 110 (114) mph.

Martyr driveReport

craft engineers and VW had used that trick for years. The cam drive itself proved much more of a challenge, and Benzinger came up with an interesting solution. In conventional engines, the cam is driven by a chain or gear at the front —the end of the engine away from the flywheel. But if this were done in the Corvair, the rear of the oil sump would have had to be so deep and so low to the ground that it would scrape bottom going over driveways or shallow ditches. So Benzinger put the cam drive onto the front of the Corvair engine, right behind the flywheel.

And on the rear end of the crank—the end facing out behind the car—he placed a pulley to run the generator and blower fan. A long V-belt, which lapped over on itself four times and ran through 540° (instead of the normal 360°), soon got a reputation for leaping off its pulleys, but this was more rumor than fact. Deeper pulleys were used in early 1960.

Says Benzinger, "This round-about belt drive surely wasn't original with us. It was used in a lot of farm machinery and industrial situations and is usually called 'mule drive.' From the earliest inception of this idea on the Cor-

vair, we at least tripled its durability before the car came on the market. We worked principally with Goodyear and some with U.S. Royal and Dayco on groove configuration, belt construction, location of pulleys, etc."

Another long-fought battle with this engine was intake and exhaust manifolding. One single carburetor, as explained, would have been less expensive but simply didn't work. The solution called for intake manifolds cast directly into the tops of the heads, with a separate one-barrel carburetor bolted to each head. Despite complicated linkage, vacuum connector tubes, two fuel lines, and new adjustment procedures, this worked. Not until the turbocharger came along in 1962 did the Corvair get by with a single carburetor (and the turbo proved an expensive way to get it). In fact, induction engineers went the other way and adapted four single-barrel carbs to the 140-bhp 1965 engine—the first and perhaps only 4-carb factory setup ever to grace an American passenger-car engine.

Exhaust manifolding also proved a challenge, because a conventional manifold would collect heat and take up space needed for cool-

ing fins. So they shrunk a short steel tube into each exhaust port in the bottom of each head. These three tubes became, in effect, exhaust stacks on each side. Then the cast-iron manifolds were attached to the outer ends of these stacks via pressed steel clamps.

"Cooling, too, is considerably different in a flat 6 than in a 4. Due to styling considerations," continues Prof. Benzinger, "we had to keep the engine low. In order to do that, the blower cooling fan had to be horizontal. Joe [Joseph F.] Bertsch was the fellow who did most of the work on the Corvair's cooling system. He couldn't use a big upright blower like the VW and Porsche, because height would have been excessive, and you'd get into some serious mounting and support problems." The low-pressure horizontal blower worked fine, and Chevy production engineers, along with the Karl Schmidt foundry in Germany, worked out the problem of casting fins into the aluminum engine parts.

"Another problem was sealing and gasketing," muses Prof. Benzinger. "This engine was running at higher temperatures than others, so these wiped out all the gasket materials we were used to. They were inadequate at those temperatures." Eventually Chevrolet worked with gasketmakers on special materials.

In all, the 1960 Corvair engine was targeted for a total weight of 288 pounds. With aluminum cylinder barrels and non-detachable heads, it might have hit that goal. But as it turned out, the production engine weighed in at 366 pounds with clutch and transmission. Pounds, of course, cost money, and with the cost of the engine up above projection, something else in the car would have to be reduced to compensate. To the buyer of that new 1960 Corvair, it showed up in terms of rubber floormats, a rather stark and pleatless set of seats, thin bumpers, and an extensive cost-reduction program through more efficient manufacture.

When the first couple of prototypal flat 6s had been dynoed in early spring 1958, Ed Cole had one put into a nearly stock Porsche coupe. It was shoe-horned in along with Chevy's experimental drivetrain. One of the first to drive this Porsche was, of course, Mr. Cole himself. He hot-footed it around Warren, Mich. and returned an hour or so later with a big smile on his face. "This is it!" he grinned.

Even at that time, though, there was no

assurance that a rear-engined car would ever be produced. It was still just R&D pie in the sky and several engineers' pet. The Corvair's status had changed drastically, though, in July 1956 when Cole found himself lofted into Chevrolet's general managership. Suddenly he'd become Management, with a capital M, and that made a difference in the Corvair's status. It didn't

automatically assure the car's acceptance by a long shot, but it surely helped.

Soon after he became general manager, Cole arranged with Harley Earl, GM's v.p. of design, to get someone working on the Corvair's styling right away. Earl chose Ned Nickles, head of Experimental Studio One. Nickles

Acceleration from standstill is okay but not neck-snapping. Keeping revs above 3000 prevents turbocharger lag. These Corvairs get in the neighborhood of 20 mpg even when driven vigorously.

How Many Corvairs?

1960 - Total Production 250,007

Corvair coupe, model 527	14,628
Corvair sedan, model 569	47,683
Corvair 700 coupe, model 727	36,562
Corvair 700 sedan, model 769	139,208
Monza 900 coupe, model 927	11,926

1961 - Total Production 329,632

500 coupe, model 527	16,857
500 sedan, model 569	18,752
Lakewood 500 wagon, model 535	5,591
700 coupe, model 727	24,786
700 sedan, model 769	51,948
Lakewood 700 wagon, model 735	20,451
Monza coupe, model 927	109,945
Monza sedan, model 969	33,745
Greenbrier, model R1206	18,489
95 Corvan, model R1205	15,806
95 Rampside, model R1254	10,787
95 Loadside, model R1244	2,475

1962 - Total Production 328,500

500 coupe, model 527	16,245
700 coupe, model 727	18,474
700 sedan, model 769	35,368
700 wagon, model 735	3,716
Monza coupe, model 927	151,738
Monza sedan, model 969	48,059
Monza wagon, model 935	2,362
Monza convertible, model 967	16,569
Greenbrier, model R1206	18,007
95 Corvan, model R1205	13,491
95 Rampside, model R1254	4,102
95 Loadside, model R1244	369

1963 - Total Production 281,539

500 coupe, model 527	16,680
700 coupe, model 727	12,378
700 sedan, model 769	20,684
Monza coupe, model 927	129,544
Monza sedan, model 969	31,120
Monza convertible, model 967	44,165
Greenbrier, model R 1206	13,761
95 Corvan, model R1205	11,161
95 Rampside, model R1254	2,046

1964 - Total Production 207,114

500 coupe, model 527	22,968
700 sedan, model 769	16,295
Monza coupe, model 927	88,440
Monza sedan, model 969	21,926
Monza convertible, model 967	31,045

Spyder coupe, model 627	6,480
Spyder convertible, model 667	4,761
Greenbrier, model R1206	6,201
95 Corvan, model R1205	8,147
95 Rampside, model R1254	851

1965 - Total Production 237,056

500 coupe, model 10137	36,747
500 sedan, model 10139	17,560
Monza coupe, model 10537	88,954
Monza sedan, model 10539	37,157
Monza convertible, model 10567	26,466
Corsa coupe, model 10737	20,291
Corsa convertible, model 10767	8,353
Greenbrier, model R1206	1,528

1966 - Total Production 103,745

500 coupe, model 10137	24,045
500 sedan, model 10139	8,779
Monza coupe, model 10537	37,605
Monza sedan, model 10539	12,497
Monza convertible, model 10567	10,345
Corsa coupe, model 10737	7,330
Corsa convertible, model 10767	3,142

1967 - Total Production 27,253

500 coupe, model 10137	9,257
500 sedan, model 10139	2,959
Monza coupe, model 10537	9,771
Monza sedan, model 10539	3,157
Monza convertible, model 10567	2,109

1968 - Total Production 15,399

500 coupe, model 10137	7,206
Monza coupe, model 10537	6,807
Monza convertible, model 10567	1,386

1969 - Total Production 6,000

500 coupe, model 10137	2,762
Monza coupe, model 10537	2,717
Monza convertible, model 10567	521

1962 - 1963 Spyder Option

1962 Spyder coupe	6,894
1962 Spyder convertible	2,574
1963 Spyder coupe	11,627
1963 Spyder convertible	7,472

Corsa 180 hp Turbocharged Engine Option

1965	7,206	1966	1,951

Total 1960 - 1969 Production 1,786,243

Source: Chevrolet Motor Div. via Corvair Society of America.

became a logical choice, because he'd worked with Earl and GM president Harlow Curtice when Curtice still had Buick. Curtice would have to be the first man Cole would have to convince of the Corvair's practicality.

Meanwhile Cole, Barr, Hansen, and others had put together several mechanical prototypes. Two of these used Porsche bodies, one was a cobbled Vauxhaull, and one was simply a scratch-built workhorse put together for road-testing purposes. Since the workhorse would appear on public roads, it got the usual disguises: a fake grille (with bug screen yet), rounded lines, and the name *Holden Special* front and rear. Holden was (and is) GM's Australian car. The Holden ruse went so far as ordering tooling and parts on Holden requisition forms and using genuine Holden drafting paper, shipped over especially, for most of the layouts.

Development of the Corvair's transaxle fell to Frank J. Winchell. Ed Cole had originally wanted to make an automatic transmission standard, but costs ruled this out. The Corvair 2-speed automatic was built mostly from existing big-Chevy Powerglide parts, and later the 1961 Tempest used basically this same transaxle, supplied by Chevrolet. A 3-speed manual gearbox was also engineered, again mostly using existing Chevrolet parts. The 3-speed's floor shifter seemed radical in 1960, but it had been part of the VW's appeal and proved a lot more practical in the Corvair than a column lever. From this 3-speed came the Monza 4-speed, which by clever engineering fit fourth gear in place of a previous idler.

Suspension design grew out of work by Robert Schilling. Karl Ludvigsen says in AUTOMOBILE QUARTERLY that Schilling could have done a lot better. As originally introduced in Oct. 1959, the Corvair's conventional SLA front setup and swing-axle rear showed very definite compromise. Expenses again forced a decision against a front anti-roll bar. This bar had been included right up to the last minute. Corvair critics said later that it would have cost the company $4 a car extra. The bar became optional in RPO 696, a heavy-duty suspension package offered for 1962.

For 1964, Corvair engineers added a single-leaf spring across the rear suspension. This spring carried some of the car's weight, thus the coil springs could be softened for a gentler ride. The leaf spring prevented rear-tire tuck-under on hard cornering, and a front anti-roll bar was added to this package (we're talking now about 1964 models only) to help neutralize steering characteristics. (The 1964 Corvair's rear leaf spring shouldn't be confused with so-called camber compensators offered by Empi and other aftermarket retailers. Camber compensators carried no car weight and only prevented tuck-under.)

For the 1965 and later Corvairs, Frank Winchell and Zora Arkus-Duntov completely modified the rear suspension to give double-jointed axles instead of the previous single-jointed ones. This later suspension was an adaptation of the Corvette's rear system, which Duntov had developed.

Fisher Body Div. did the unit body engineering, much of the work being done by Fisher's engineering director, James Wernig. The Corvair marked a first for GM in this country, yet General Motors had plenty of unit-body exper-

ience to draw upon through its overseas adjuncts. Opel of Germany and Vauxhall of England had pioneered unit construction in 1937, and most of GM's overseas-made cars have used unit bodies ever since. Says Mr. Wernig: "We'd done a lot of feasibility studies for all five General Motors divisions prior to the Corvair to determine the practicality of frame-integral [unit] construction. It always appeared to the cost boys that frame-integral must be the answer, because otherwise why would so many European cars be that way? The thing that always upset the applecart up until the Corvair was that GM was dealing with five lines of cars whose bodies were, to a great extent, interchangeable. A frame-integral car just about requires that it be an individual car for an individual division, as the Corvair was."

The Corvair evolved with a heavily ribbed underbody and almost no floor tunnel at all. With the engine at the rear and no driveshaft to worry about, it would have been criminal to consider frame/body construction. The lack of a frame and tunnel gave wide footwells, a low floor, and thus a low roof height. Besides, frameless construction was less expensive in this case since it used quite a bit of automatic welding and not so much hand labor. Vestigal box-section siderail extensions were kept front and rear, and the roof and pillars all had box sections, too. As it evolved, the first series Corvair body was very strong for its weight, even in the convertible. The second series was less so.

but Ed Cole still had a selling job on his hands. In Aug. 1957, he and his staff were strongly convinced of the Corvair's necessity. Cole now saw his compact as a market wedge against the imports and a hedge against any reduction in sales of big cars. The year 1958 would become one of the worst for behemoths and another recordbreaker for imports, so Cole picked the right time for his presentation.

He met GM president Harlow Curtice inside Ned Nickles' experimental design studio, where an early clay of the "La Salle II by Holden" had been finished. Curtice was no easy man to convince, being prejudiced in favor of large cars of the earlier Buick persuasion—hoods higher than fenders, rounded shapes, etc. But Cole and Nickles had sold cars to Curtice before. Besides, Cole's stature within the corporation stood him in good stead. He fielded questions about costs and manufacturing problems, and Cole did manage to get a tentative go-ahead.

He still had to present his case to GM's powerful engineering policy committee and to the corporate board of directors. But with Curtice behind him now, these presentations in December and January went smoothly and also received approval.

Everything was finally set, then, except ironing out the Corvair's details and figuring out where and how to build the car. *Where* became one critical question, because with so radically different a job, it wasn't something you'd simply slip onto existing assembly lines. It used a great deal of aluminum, and since its body was to be unitized, the Corvair would properly need a plant all its own. This, too, got approval and was actually part of the package Cole sold to Curtice to begin with. It was decided, then, to add a section to the existing truck plant at Willow Run, Mich., with supplementary assembly in Oakland, Calif. and St. Louis, Mo. Ground for the addition to Willow Run was broken in July 1958, and since finished cars were rolling off those lines 13 months later,

you can imagine what a quick piece of conversion that had to be.

Nor were the Corvair's manufacturing considerations easy by any means. The aluminum engine and early transmission castings used a new low-pressure, permanent mold process that hadn't been tried before in this country. In Europe, VW *had* used it, so Corvair production worked with the Karl Schmidt foundry in Germany on manufacturing techniques, setting up GM's Messina, N.Y. aluminum foundry, and developing the molds, fixtures, machine tools, etc. The complete engine was manufactured at Chevrolet's Tonawanda, N.Y., engine plant, with the assemblies shipped to Willow Run. The manufacture of unitized bodies in Willow Run, next door in the Fisher Body plant, also gave some preliminary headaches, but those were ironed out without too much trouble.

Chevrolet launched the Corvair on Oct. 2, 1959. It became the first of that year's crop of new Big 3 compacts (the Rambler and Lark were old hat by then). The Falcon followed on Oct. 8, and Plymouth's Valiant came along on the 29th. For a week, at least, the Corvair held center stage, and it was met with mixed reaction.

I well remember the first day of Corvair showings. A friend and I went down to the mid-town Manhattan Chevy agency and scrutinzed a metallic green sedan. I was driving a Volks at the time and was anxious to compare the two cars. The Corvair initially struck me as remarkably stark, but I really liked the car's styling and the fact that the rear seat folded down for extra cargo space 29 cubic feet, said the salesman, if you include usable trunk space under the hood). I also admired the gas-fired heater, and it reminded me of my old South Wind.

About a week later I did a driving impressions report on the Corvair for FOREIGN CAR GUIDE. The car had Powerglide, which gave sluggish acceleration; the steering was terribly slow; and the rear did a lot of bouncing up and down. I've driven a number of Corvairs since then, including a Monza sedan my mother bought in 1963 plus the '62 Spyder and '65 Corsa convertibles you see pictured here, so this driveReport will turn out to be something of a composite. I really got very little time behind the wheels of the two turbocharged convertibles.

The 1962 Spyder belongs to Ron Myers of San Mateo, Calif. Ron bought this car from a friend last year—it had 37,000 miles on it when he got it and the odometer shows 47,000 now. He sold a 1951 Ford wagon to buy the Spyder. The Corsa's owner is Tony Richards from Mill Valley, Calif., who originally drove an MGB but then decided Corvairs handled and looked so much better. He became so enthused that he now owns four Corvairs in all (and on that topic, I discovered that Ed Cole still owns two Corvairs and so does Kai Hansen).

When I compare the '62 Spyder's handling with the '65 Corsa's, I can't feel any difference. They're both very stable, good-handling, quick, responsive, forgiving cars. They feel nothing like the 1960 sedan I remember, nor like my mother's 1963. These two turbocharged cars, with their heavy-duty suspension (and, of course, the 1965 Corsa has doubled-jointed axle shafts instead of the previous single-joint swing system), showed me, at least, no signs of oversteer nor even blatant tail heaviness.

Continued on page 140

Continued from page 139

Chevrolet engineers had originally wanted to hold the Corvair's weight distribution to 40/60 empty, but even the 1960 models turned out 38.5/61.5. Then when they moved the spare tire to the rear, and since the battery was already back there, weight distribution jumped to 37/63. My mother's car, which also had air conditioning, must have been more like 36/64, and you could really feel this in high crosswinds.

Tire pressures are generally considered pretty critical in Corvairs, and there's been a lot written about this. The factory recommended 15 psi in the front (cold) and 26 psi in the rear. Not too many owners respected those figures, and some probably got in trouble for that reason. To me, a Corvair's handling depends an awful lot on which Corvair you're talking about, which suspension you're running, and what tire pressures you carry. H-D suspension and proper tire inflation can make a big difference.

One engineer told me that right after the 1965 models came out, a memo came down to stop further development work on the Corvair. Just do enough to satisfy federal smog and safety requirements. By that time, the Mustang had hit, and the Corvair found itself boxed in by an engine that couldn't grow much. Bore and stroke had gone almost to the limit at 164 cid (prototypes went as far as 176 cid in the Astro I), while Ford could and did stuff everything up to the 390 V-8 into the Mustang. To make the Corvair engine bigger would have meant starting over from scratch, and that wasn't very likely, especially with the Camaro on the horizon for 1967. Prof. Benzinger says, "Yes, we even had some 283 V-8s stuffed into the back ends of Corvairs, but they all quickly turned grotesque."

I asked several people at Chevrolet about a long-standing rumor: Would the Corvair have been dropped sooner if Nader's book hadn't come out? In other words, was the Corvair kept in production until May 14, 1969 to spite Nader —so Chevy wouldn't be admitting defeat? Everyone I asked said no—the Corvair's life ran its natural course. Death was caused by falling sales, and these were caused by a combination of Nader-generated criticism plus the rise of the Mustang and attendant ponycars. And another factor was simply that Chevrolet management, which now no longer included Ed Cole, had lost interest in the Corvair.

The Corvair, though, actually led to the Mustang. The Corvair evolved from a very austere economy compact to an economical GT. That gave Ford the courage and perhaps even the inspiration to bring out the Mustang which, after all, was intially based on Falcon components. It's ironic that we always talk about the demise of the Corvair and never give much thought to the demise of the Falcon. The Falcon was discontinued only 19 months after the Corvair (Dec. 1970), and it seems to have died of plain old natural causes—no Nader, no lawsuits, no bad press, just no interest. Ed Cole says he could have sold a million Corvairs this year if he'd had them to sell, and I, for one, don't doubt it. 👓

Our thanks to Edward N. Cole, Kai H. Hansen, Carl Hedeen, Joe Karshner, Art Baske, Jim Williams, Jim Sponseller, and Gloria Jezewski of General Motors Corp.; Harry Barr, Franklin, Mich.; James Wernig, Kennebunkport, Me., Dave Newell, Mark Ellis, Ron Myers, and Tony Richards of The Corvair Society of America, 145 Ivywood, Radnor, Pa. 19087; Prof. Robert P. Benzinger, Tempe, Ariz.; and Karl Ludvigsen, Pelham Manor, N.Y.

Chevrolet Corvair Monza

Like Nikita Khrushchev, the Corvair has become an un-persön. Chevrolet policy is to keep chipping away at it (by removing the Corsa models for '67 and the 4-door models for '68), in the hope that it will go away. Happily it refuses to do so, and Corvair lovers get more passionate with each passing year.

Despite this, and despite the fact that its predecessor (the '60-64 model) is probably the most maligned car in the history of the automobile, the Corvair is one of the best handling cars—in stock trim—ever built. The steering is light and precise and, although its rear-mounted air-cooled engine gives it a slight rearward weight bias, its all-independent suspension gives the Corvair road-holding qualities second only to the best GT cars.

The Corvair Monza touched off the current wave of American sporty cars, but it has lost some favor with the enthusiasts market because of its limited horsepower— the top engine option, 140-horsepower, is a far cry from the 300-plus Super Cars. Nevertheless, the Corvair is light enough that 140 horsepower is sufficient to keep pace with many higher-powered cars.

Trunk space is somewhat limited, and the rear seat accommodations are not what we would like, but those are our only major objections.

CHEVROLET CORVAIR MONZA

Manufacturer:	Chevrolet Division General Motors Corporation Detroit, Michigan

Engine	140-hp, 164 cu. in. Flat-six
Transmission	4-speed manual
Steering	Standard
Suspension	Standard
Brakes	Drum F, Drum R

CHECK LIST

ENGINE
Throttle Response	Good
Noise Insulation	Fair

DRIVE TRAIN
Shift Linkage	Fair
Synchro Action	Very Good

STEERING
Effort	Good
Response	Excellent

HANDLING
Predictability	Excellent
Evasive Maneuverability	Very Good

BRAKES
Directional Stability	Excellent
Fade Resistance	Very Good

INTERIOR
Ease of Entry/Exit	Fair
Driving Position	Good
Front Seating Comfort	Good
Rear Seating Comfort	Poor

GENERAL
Vision	Excellent
Heater/Defroster	Fair
Weather Sealing	Very Good
Trunk Space	Poor

Is The Corvair Unsafe?

[Continued from page 121]

seconds, 0 to 70 was 19.1. It was quite quick in the 0 to 30 range, averaging 3.6 seconds. Around the hard sports-car course the Corvair handled extremely well but you have to remind yourself in some bends that the principal weight is on the rear axle, which makes it more susceptible to a tail slide-out.

The front legroom is ample for most citizens, up to those of 6-ft.-2, and the rear legroom is dandy if you happen to be a worm. The instruments are on the sparse side and the front bucket seats are a little skimpy and not too comfortable if you have an oversize bucket-filler. The ease of getting in and out is not bad. The gas pedal could have stood a little extra thought because it's almost straight up and down and there's no easy place to rest your foot.

In summing up, the Corvair has been maligned badly, in my opinion. Thousands of people have a lot of comparatively inexpensive fun with this car. The Corvair has a tendency to get a little squirrely at turnpike speeds in a heavy crosswind but I consider it a thoroughly safe road car when driven with intelligence. This means knowing it is different in the balance department from Uncle Herman's Deusenberg. •